Exploring Cambridgeshire
Churches

Exploring Cambridgeshire Churches

Carolyn Wright

illustrated by Anthony Sursham

Paul Watkins

for

Cambridgeshire Historic Chuches Trust

Stamford 1991

©1991 Text, Carolyn Wright

©1991 Illustrations, Anthony Sursham

©1991 Map and glossary illustrations, Martin Smith

Published by

Paul Watkins

18, Adelaide Street, Stamford, Lincolnshire, PE9 2EN.

ISBN *hardback* 1 871615 91 7

ISBN *softback* 1 871615 92 5

Photoset from the discs of Carolyn Wright in Times Roman (text) and Garamond (headings)

Designed by Martin Smith for Paul Watkins (Publishing)

Printed and bound in Great Britain by Woolnough Bookbinding, Irthlingborough

CONTENTS

PREFACE
and Acknowledgements

Happiness is finding a church open; but then if I had not had the opportunity to meet the keyholders, I would have missed meeting some wonderful people. There was always a little extra information about their church which had escaped the church leaflet and even Pevsner's Guide too. It has been a happy experience gathering the information for this book and I hope it may encourage others to visit our county churches. You will find something special in each and every one.

It began in 1988 when Pamela Tudor-Craig and Robert Van de Weyer introduced me to the delights of Church Tours and to the other activities of the Cambridgeshire Historic Churches Trust. Then, somewhat to my surprise, I found myself on the roads of Cambridgeshire visiting obscure churches in isolated hamlets, rather grand churches in rather small villages, and getting hopelessly lost looking for a friendly spire in city streets. I soon became quite fascinated with churches in general and our county's churches in particular. My family and friends have had much to put up with since I first set out with Pevsner's excellent but somewhat daunting Guide.

My first thanks go to the Trust which gave me this opportunity to see and learn about these churches; and then to Tony Sursham who so generously gave so much of his time and talents to provide the illustrations.

Then sincere thanks to Simon Cotton who supervised many of my early Cambridgeshire explorations, answered endless questions and read through the ever-growing typescript with red pen in hand.

Lynne Broughton and Robert Walker answered still more questions and Pat Saunders encouraged me through difficult times, especially when the Word Processor was getting the upper hand.

Also a very grateful thank you to the many clergy, church wardens and key-holders, who took the time to tell me about *their* church; the plainest church comes to life when you are shown round by someone who cares.

I am also grateful to Philip Riley for his careful proof-reading, John Smith of the Stamford Museum for his helpful comments and especially to publisher Shaun Tyas for his patience and encouragement.

Thank you to Lucy for those hours spent in the library and to Tom who encouraged me on my way. Last but not least I thank Valerie Gravatt who has taken part in so many of these expeditions and whose friendship never wavered during the endless quest for gargoyles, graffiti and Green Men.

Cambridge. January 1991.

Cambridge, St. Mary Magdalene (leper Chapel)

FOREWORD

by the Revd. Robert Van de Weyer

Chairman, Cambridgeshire Historic Churches Trust

At a glance, all churches seem much the same. Outside you see lots of gothic windows, and a tower and a steeple at one end. And inside lots of pointed arches and pews, with some memorials scattered round the walls.

But look closer, and you'll find every church, even the most humble, has unique treasures. In fact each church is a living building, containing priceless artifacts accumulated over hundreds of years. Some of the treasures may be in dark corners, or high up in the roof. Yet if you explore carefully, you shall find exquisite carvings in stone and wood, some of the finest furniture in the country and enchanting relics of bygone ages.

And each church has its own unique story to tell, embodied in its architecture. With only a little rudimentary knowledge of the history of church building you can be as expert as the experts in working out the evolution of the church. You can tell from the shapes of the arches, and the style of the carvings when each bit was added.

In short, you should visit churches with the eyes of a child, hunting for hidden treasure and uncovering the mysteries of the past. There is no happier way of spending a summer's day than driving or cycling to a part of the countryside, and exploring three or four churches in the vicinity. And, remember, no church is boring - every one has its own special story.

This book is a guide for the amateur church explorer in the county of Cambridgeshire - which now includes the four old counties of Cambridgeshire, Huntingdonshire, the Isle of Ely, and the Soke of Peterborough. It doesn't offer detailed descriptions of each church, which are usually rather hard to digest - and anyway are available in more scholarly guides. Rather it points you to the special treasures and features of each church - and so it shows why each church is worth visiting.

It is written by an "amateur" in the proper sense of that word: someone who has got to know the county's churches because she loves them. And it is illustrated by a retired architect who over the years has advised on the care of many of these buildings. Both writer and illustrator are simply inviting you to share their child-like pleasure.

Of course, above all things, churches are places of worship. Today - as in past ages - there are many people who cannot accept every aspect of the Christian creed. But all people, whatever their personal faith, can respond to places of beauty which point beyond themselves to an eternal spiritual beauty. The ancient churches of Cambridgeshire are such places.

Robert Van de Weyer,

Leighton Bromswold. January, 1991.

The Cambridgeshire Historic Churches Trust

The Trust was formed in 1983 to give financial help for the repair of church fabric and to encourage interest in the county's churches.

Cambridgeshire has over 300 excellent churches, many in villages whose population is now so small that they cannot afford to maintain them. The Trust raises money throughout the county, to assist churches in need. It also organises tours of churches and conferences on church architecture. The Trust is a registered charity, and non-denominational.

Please join! Write for information to Robert Walker, 14 Clay Street, Histon, Cambridge. CB4 4EY.

GAZETTEER: CATHEDRALS

ELY CATHEDRAL [F5]

The amazing skyline of Ely Cathedral is visible for miles across the flat fenland, standing on the highest and largest of the old fenland islands. This was the site chosen by Etheldreda to found her monastery in 673, in memory of her father King Anna of East Anglia who was killed by the Mercians. The cathedral is a monument to this event and is one of the most remarkable buildings in Europe. Not only does it contain outstanding work in all the main medieval styles, except Perpendicular, it also manages to combine them in a wholly unique way, to make Ely a dynamic and exciting experience. Viewed from the E by the River Ouse, the building rises in tiers from the Early English E end, via the wide, squat octagon with its beautiful lantern, to a crescendo at the W end. Few buildings can match this complexity and refinement.

The earliest visible building work began with the Normans and exists in the transepts. Following its new status as a cathedral in 1109, the building was extended westwards to the monumental W front. This is what first greets the visitor on arrival and it is an awesome and unusual experience. Instead of twin W towers there is a huge central tower, now topped with a 14th century octagon, and a magnificent SW transept - its N partner fell down in the 15th century and was never rebuilt. This transept has tiers of Romanesque arcading gradually evolving into Gothic as it goes up. The polygonal turrets to the S are absolutely stunning and like nothing else in the country now that the similar W front at Bury St Edmunds no longer survives.

Entering the cathedral through the elegant 13th century Galilee Porch, with its tiers of blind arcading, one enters into the immense cavern of the three storey Norman nave, which marches relentlessly up to the crossing Octagon. It is powerful and stark, and devoid of any ornament, except for the wonderful timber ceiling which was painted by Gambier Parry in 1878. This takes its inspiration from Peterborough, and both cathedral naves create a similar impression, but Peterborough is more ornate and ends in a superb 12th century apsed chancel. There are two doorways in the south aisle which are reminders of the original monastic function of the building. Of these the Prior's Door is the most important and contains some of the best Romanesque carving in the country (also worth seeing is the marble monument to a bishop of c.1150). Go to the E end to view the cathedral's next stage of development. The majestic Early English retro-choir was added under Bishop Northwold, and was copied from Lincoln, with a splendid E wall full of lancet windows.

Then on 22 February 1322, the Norman crossing tower collapsed into the choir. This disaster was transformed into a triumph by the inspiration of John Crauden, prior, and Alan Walsingham, sacrist. They devised what was to be the most innovative and daring architectural feat of the Middle Ages; they rebuilt the crossing in the form of an octagon and then in a moment of architectural virtuosity, they extended it up to a timber lantern resting on eight huge oak supports. These were covered

After the Lady Chapel was finished in the 1350's, there were no more major building programmes. The only Perpendicular work is the elaborate and rather excessive chapel to Bishop Alcock of *c.*1488 and the later 16th century chapel to Bishop West, with Renaissance detailing and sculpture. The cathedral was restored by Sir George Gilbert Scott who put in the choir screen, altered the stalls and reconstructed the lantern of the Octagon. The best fittings are still the Decorated stalls, which originally stood in the Octagon and are embellished with 47 misericords. Ely has the best collection of monuments in the county, including two 13th century Purbeck marble slabs to Bishops Northwold and Kilkenny, the Decorated monument to Bishop Hotham and the unusual memorial to two men who died in a railway accident in 1845.

PETERBOROUGH CATHEDRAL [B3]

At the same time as Etheldreda was establishing her monastery at Ely, thirty five miles north west across the fens, Peada, King of Mercia, was also founding a monastery. This grew to be one of

inside by a complex skin of ribs and stars out of which the lantern explodes. It was a technical and artistic masterpiece and the sense of architectural space is breathtaking. Also of this date is the choir, which also had to be rebuilt, and the equally revolutionary Lady Chapel. The span of the chapel is remarkable and the rich Decorated carving of the canopies undulates in a wave around the room. This and the sumptuous Prior Crauden's Chapel were to be highly influential on Cambridgeshire churches.

the great Benedictine monasteries of Britain, with a famed collection of relics, housed in a magnificent Romanesque building. Whilst Ely, visible on a clear day from Peterborough, gained cathedral status early on, it was only after the Reformation that Peterborough was raised to cathedral rank. Although it has none of the later medieval architectural virtuosity of Ely, it is important because of the almost complete survival of the Romanesque building. The only major alteration has been the addition of the distinctive and idiosyncratic W front which dominates the market square. In the same way as Ely was an administrative centre, so also was Peterborough, and it controlled its own affairs in its Soke in the NE corner of Northamptonshire.

The present building was begun after a fire in the early 12th century, and as with all Norman churches, work started at the E end and developed through to the W. On entering at the W one is presented with an exceptional vista; the strong, robust three storey Norman nave leads without interruption into the Norman chancel finishing in the spectacular apsed E end. This unity allows one to gain an excellent impression of a complete Norman building constructed in about sixty years without stylistic change. There is more decoration than at Ely: zigzag mouldings, decorated tympani, interlacing blind arcading and early rib vaulting in the aisles. The transepts are also Norman and are aisled to the E, containing little chapels, and at the W two smaller transepts were built.

The exterior, though, is less intact, for the tall Norman crossing tower was replaced in the early 14th century by a squat tower (rebuilt in 1882-6 by J. L. Pearson) originally topped by a timber octagon as at Ely, and most of the windows are later medieval replacements. The W front is the main alteration and was added to the Norman nave in the early years of the 13th century. It is entirely in the Early English Gothic style, but is an unusual interpretation of it. It seems the original intention was to have two W towers with a front containing three portals, as at Lincoln, with the central portal being the largest. The whole front was to be one bay deep. After the N tower was built, which has tall blind arcading, it appears the architect changed his mind. The front was extended out further than the transepts to allow for two flanking pinnacled turrets and the two outer portals or niches were made larger than the central one. This means they bear no relation to the W wall behind and the side portals are off centre. The whole thing is topped with pinnacles and gables. Pevsner is very dismissive of this design, but it has an unusual beauty and a monumental grandeur that is like nothing else in the country.

Right in the centre of all this Early English grandeur is a modest two-storey Perpendicular porch built in the late 14th century and now housing the treasury. Also of the Perpendicular period is the bold panelled chancel ceiling, enhanced by a multitude of bosses, which leads us up to the highlight of the later medieval work - the surprising and extravagant retrochoir which surrounds the great Norman apse on the ground floor. It was erected by Abbot Robert Kirkdon between c.1496 and 1508 and is similar in detail and quality to King's College Chapel in Cambridge, with its open work parapet and luscious fan vaulting. It has been suggested that John Wastell, who built the fan-vault at King's from 1508, was the designer.

In the retrochoir is the county's most important piece of Anglo-Saxon sculpture, the 8th century Hedda stone. It has standing figures of the apostles set in arcading with a pitched roof above. In the S chancel aisle are the remains of four monuments to Abbots, all carved in Alwalton marble and dating from the early 13th century. The imposing baldacchino over the high altar is of 1894 and probably by J. L. Pearson, who rebuilt the tower. In the S transept S wall is a very early and very fine William Morris window of 1862.

GAZETTEER: PARISH CHURCHES

ABBOTSLEY *St. Margaret* [C7]
A church quite frequently has pinnacles embellishing the tower but here there are four large kingly figures - William the Conqueror, Harold, Macbeth and Malcolm. The link with Scotland goes back to the early 12th century when King David I of Scotland, also Earl of Huntingdon, gave the manor here to Gervase Ridel. It would be good to think one of them was King David, but you must go to the fine church at Conington near the A1 to find a memorial to him. The chancel arch is perhaps all that remains of the earliest 13th century building; the arcades and aisles are from the Decorated period, as is the lovely, though damaged, tomb recess in the S aisle. Major restoration by Butterfield in 1861 and most of the stained glass from this period too. Outside, to the SW, stands the large table-tomb of a generous parishioner (d.1688) who left £5 a year to the village, "for ever". The nave and tower are now in the care of the Redundant Churches Fund but the chancel is looked after by the parish and is used regularly for services.

ABBOTS RIPTON *St. Andrew* [C5]
Land for the first church was granted to the Abbot of Ramsey c.974. What you see now is much later - mainly in the Perpendicular style of the 15th century. But look at the S doorway: it has the pointed arch of the Early English period and the S arcade is of the same era. Large Jacobean figures dominate the chancel roof and the altar is late 16th or early 17th century. A tablet (1775) remembers a Sergeant of Arms at the House of Commons. 19th century stained glass and handsome Victorian pulpit.

ABINGTON PIGOTTS *St. Michael* [D8]
A tree-lined path leads to this mainly 15th century church, situated away from the village. A Mass Dial on S buttress and battlements on nave and tower. Tall Perpendicular windows make for a light interior. Two odd little niches either side of tower arch. Good 17th and 18th century monuments to the Pigott family. A two-decker pulpit remains in fragile condition; a clerk once sat at the lower desk leading the responses. In the chancel floor a large brass, 1460, shows a plainly dressed gentleman with 16 of his children - his poor wife is not to be seen. Look up and see the medieval angels clinging to the nave roof.

Alconbury

ALCONBURY *St. Peter and St. Paul* [B5]
If you enjoy the elegant simplicity of the Early English period, then you must visit this church, and later perhaps go on to Etton in the north of the county. The chancel, arcades, clerestory and tower, with typical broach spire, were built between 1200 and 1290. The chancel gives the greatest delight with blind arcading outlining the lancet windows. However, it is not all Early English, there is one Perpendicular and one Decorated window to the E of the porch. The 15th century roof is supported by eight large angels - no two alike. This is a very lovely place.

ALWALTON *St. Andrew* [B3]

An Early English church with large transepts. Particularly handsome tower; notice the lancet windows and blank arcading on the upper stage; the decorative corbel frieze terminates in battlements, which are also continued on the N stair-turrret. Interesting windows, a double low-side to the S and outside you can see a blocked N low-side. The S aisle was added in 13th century but the late 12th century Norman doorway was retained. Notice also the difference between the C12 N aisle, where four arches were needed, and the finer piers in the three-arched S arcade, built perhaps 100 years later.

ARRINGTON *St. Nicholas* [D7]

Quite a simple country church now, but it was much more imposing in the 13th century, with substantial aisles on both sides of the nave - you can still see the blocked arches in the nave walls. There is a lovely piscina in Jesus College which was copied by several churches in the county, and here is one of them: its size and extravagance well suited to that early building. The simple font is from the earlier Norman church. The tower was partly rebuilt with brick after the Reformation, perhaps at the same time as the aisles were taken down.

ASHLEY-CUM-SILVERLEY *St. Mary* [H6]

Neo-Norman, built in 1845 by the Marquis of Bute whose wife had been patron of the living here. First dedicated to the Holy Trinity, but in 1873 transepts and chancel were added and the church re-dedicated to St. Mary. The previous church of St. Mary, nearby on the Dalham Road, had already fallen into disrepair by 1800 and now only a few gravestones remain. Silverley had its own church too, but all that remains now is the ruined tower which can still be found, hidden away in a dense little wood at the road junction.

BABRAHAM *St. Peter* [F7]

Light and spacious 15th century nave. Splendid lifesize memorial to the Bennet brothers - both baronets who married two sisters. The E window, by Patrick Reyntiens and John Piper, was given in 1966 by Sir Robert Adeane in memory of his father; many other memorials to the Adeane family. A tablet near the S door remembers John Hullier "who burnt at Cambridge during the Marian persecution for his adherence to the Reformed Faith, 1556". A fine pulpit on wineglass stem faces the two-tiered desks for Reader and Clerk. The organ and loft at W end are a 20th century addition and the ghost of an organist's widow is said to visit on occasion.

BAINTON *St. Mary* [A2]

Fine 13th century tower and on its eastern face you can see the outline of the earlier, steeper nave roof. Windows either side of the porch, and the S doorway are Decorated. Our forebears were also interested in recycling materials as is shown by the rather haphazard arch over the outer porch door. During a 15th century rebuilding stones from an earlier, more curved archway were reused. Inside, rounded Norman arcades are the earliest part of the church. Two ornate piscinas grace the chancel with the natural leaf decoration of the 13th century. Monument to Robert Henson, 1755, who received "the applause of all... bribes not being able to corrupt, promises seduce, nor threats deter him from doing his duty".

Balsham

BALSHAM *Holy Trinity* [F7]

A spacious church with much to see. 13th century tower with more buttresses added in C16 making a grand total of nine. Decorated chancel; early Perpendicular nave. The font is topped by a dramatic 30ft cover, carved in the 1930s by Canon Burrel. This indefatigable rector and wood-carver, together with the

14

villagers he trained, was responsible for much of the craftsmanship here. Two elaborate brasses to earlier rectors in the chancel. John Sleford, 1401, holder of several offices including Archdeacon of Wells and Keeper of the Wardrobe to Edward III, was responsible for building the nave and also the marvellous chancel stalls, with their highly carved double armrests and equally splendid misericords - make sure you see each and every one. The rood screen may date to Sleford's incumbency, but the loft was probably added later. The other fine brass is of John Blodwell, 1462. A modern curiosity is the huge shell case used as a counter-weight for the font cover!

BARHAM *St. Giles* [B5]
A tranquil churchyard surrounds this ancient little building, topped with a sprightly 19th century bellcote. S doorway with zigzag decoration and slightly pointed arch may be late 12th century - the Transitional period between the Norman and Early English styles. Lancet windows with Y-tracery, a sure sign of an Early English building. The bell in the N aisle once hung in the church of St. Mary's in Woolley (demolished in 1961). The bell was given to St. Mary's by the Revd. Mikepher Alphery, a descendant of the Russian Czars, who was given the living here in 1618. He was deprived of the living during the Civil War, but returned after the Restoration and remained here until he retired. He died in 1668. His wife's grave, 1655, is in the churchyard.

BARNACK *St. John the Baptist* [A2]
It really is "one of the most rewarding churches in the county" (Pevsner). Magnificent early 11th century tower with all the details of the Saxon period: long-and-short work in the quoins, triangular windows and decorative pilaster strips of stone, which the Saxon masons loved to use. The massive tower arch dominates the nave. The late 12th century N arcade has wonderful crocketed capitals; in the N aisle also is the quite beautiful late Saxon sculpture of Christ in Majesty. A 15th century work of art - a carving of the Annunciation - can be found in the Lady Chapel. Magnificent early 13th century font - all superlatives here. In the chancel, admire the unusual tracery of the superb E window,

Barnack

c.1325, and the elaborate piscina and sedilia watched over by little medieval faces. A particularly fine memorial to Francis Whitestones is signed by the sculptor, Thomas Greenway of Darby, 1612. Outside, take another look at the Decorated style tracery of the E window. Many good headstones in the large churchyard, some late 17th century, but make sure you see the astonishing fallen palm tree: a memorial to a Gentleman Cadet who died, aged 21, in 1868.

BARRINGTON *All Saints* [D7]
The church overlooks the largest village green in England. The base of the tower is 13th century; but you can see the later building styles and materials as the tower was built. The belfry windows are in the Perpendicular style of the 15th century, the battlements are later still. Admire the handsome 17th century pulpit, complete with sounding board and the massive parish chest. In the S arcade the 15th century wall-painting of "The three

living and the three dead" is still quite vivid; and now look up and admire the marvellous 14th century nave roof. William Dowsing had so much work to do here destroying statues and glass during his Puritan route of destruction, that he noted in his journal that he would need twice the usual payment. In 1871 Edward Conybeare became rector and for the next 27 years did much to restore the church including the restoration of the peal of six bells. Make sure you read his lively instructions to his bellringers displayed in the tower. The metalwork screen was made by village youths taught by Mr. Conybeare. Quite an eccentric - he would ride about the village with his wife perched precariously on the handlebars of his tricycle. Reredos, crucifix and candle-sticks by Comper, early twentieth century.

Bartlow

BARTLOW *St. Mary* [F8]
Do visit St. Mary's. There are only two churches with round towers in Cambridgeshire, and here is one; the other is at Snailwell. So first admire the Norman tower then go inside to admire the 15th century wall- paintings. You are greeted by a majestic St. Christopher, carrying the Christ-Child on his shoulder. St. Michael is also here, weighing the souls of the dead; the devil tries to weight the scales but Our Lady uses her influence on behalf of the sinner. On the N wall, the spectacular dragon must be quite relieved that he has finally lost his St. George. The building is mainly early 14th century but has two nice Perpendicular doorways with quatrefoil decoration. The churchyard boasts a splendid 18th century urn and also an art-nouveau metal gravehead, 1908.

BARTON *St. Peter* [E7]
A much smaller building stood here in the 11th century, but nave and chancel were rebuilt *c.*1300, tower and porch perhaps a century later. The porch, heavily restored, is quite unusual with two large lancets to lighten what may once have been an upstairs room. The many 14th century wall-paintings give us a good idea of how colourful the medieval churches were: over the N door St. Michael weighs the souls of the dead, watched by a devil and also by the Virgin Mary who weights a scale with her rosary. There is St. Christopher, St. John the Baptist and little birds watching over St.Francis of Assisi. Two more birds can be found in the central opening of the Rood Screen, which carries the arms of Thomas Arundel, Bishop of Ely 1374-88. The grand Jacobean pulpit, dated 1635, contrasts with the simplicity of the Norman font. The tower is one of five in the area, all possibly designed by the same mason and built during a forty year period, about 1400. The external limewashed rendering is a 20th century attempt to recreate a medieval exterior, in this case to protect the wall-paintings.

BASSINGBOURN *St. Peter and St. Paul* [D8]
The handsome Early English tower owes much to a major renovation by the Victorians. Attractive timber medieval porch opens on to the light and spacious 14th century interior. The chancel is a beautiful example of the Decorated period. The ogee arch is introduced everywhere: above the doorways, sedilia and really lovely triple piscina. Forty years ago the medieval rood screen was repainted, some said too brightly, but the church seems happy to accept it now. There are small windows to N and

S of the chancel arch, no doubt to throw more light on the rood group; their quatrefoil shape is most unusual. No expense was spared in the 14th century building, even the bases of the octagonal piers have fluted decoration. Poignant seventeenth century marble effigy in chancel floor. Outside, on the chancel N wall, a piscina and door remain from another chapel; and everywhere gargoyles: over windows, doors, under the turret of the outside roodstair and guarding drainpipes. In 1497 money was needed for a new tenor bell, so ten church-ales were held here during the year, no doubt the equivalent of our church fetes today.

BLUNTISHAM-CUM-EARITH *St. Mary* [D5]

The 14th century Decorated chancel is a very uncommon shape for the period: instead of being rectangular, the eastern wall forms a polygonal apse. The nave and aisles are Perpendicular but all was much restored by the Victorians. Under the tower you can see part of the medieval rood screen, with the painted figures of St. George and St. John the Baptist. Lovely font with leafy carving including the ubiquitous Green Man whose face was often used by medieval masons and by painters of pub signs today.

Bottisham

BOTTISHAM *Holy Trinity* [F6]

A wonderful place. Enter through the W porch or Galilee, perhaps the parish church version of the elaborate Galilee at Ely cathedral. The effect of light and space is enhanced by the tall 15th century stone chancel screen, making this a spectacular interior. All largely completed much earlier, between 1300 and 1320, the Decorated period. Many memorials to the Jenyns family, including the romantic Sir Roger holding the hand of Dame Elizabeth, she of the "unblemished reputation". In her memory he endowed the schooling of 20 poor children and the sculpture on the wall of the S aisle commemorates this. More fine memorials behind the parclose screen in the N aisle; here you can also see a

Falconer

unique fragment of a 15th century effigy of a falconer, showing clearly his glove and the bird's tail feathers - who was he and why was he remembered in this way?

BOURN *St. Helen and St. Mary* [D7]

A crooked lead spire tops a very fine 13th century tower with graceful arcading round the belfry. The earliest part of the original church is the fine late 12th century arcade. Notice the extra window added to the clerestory in the 15th century to shed extra light on the rood screen, as at nearby Litlington. Marvellous carving on the medieval pews: notice the Bourn Hall pew near the screen. A window in the N transept shows an Annunciation scene signed by Ninian Comper (1947) with his "strawberry plant" symbol. Reredos and E window are also by Comper. The vestry table, with fine marquetry work, is a former sounding board from the pulpit.

BOXWORTH *St. Peter* [D6]

Particularly attractive view of this neat embattled church if you approach from School Lane. A storm in 1636 necessitated major rebuilding, particularly of the chancel, though the 14th century chancel arch was retained. Records tell of a medieval altar dedicated to St. Katherine. William Cole visited in 1745 and wrote "This is a tolerable handsome church with... a lofty and heavy stone spire." The spire is now no more. Another restoration was necessary in the 19th century and the battlements were added at this time. All the windows, except the E, are by Kempe, resulting in a rather dark interior, but the rather strange windows in the S aisle roof lighten up the interior of this lovingly cared for village church. The stately pulpit, 1682, stands high on its wineglass stem. In the churchyard a large Cheviot rock near the S porch makes an unusual memorial.

BRAMPTON *St. Mary Magdalene* [C5]

Very handsome building with many splendid gargoyles and the interior is just as rewarding. Rebuilt in the 14th century replacing an earlier Norman church. Church building generally slowed dramatically after the Reformation, but this tower was rebuilt in 1635 and is a particularly fine example of the period. Several members of Samuel Pepys' family were buried here though only the tombstone of his sister remains, now in the wall of the S aisle. Three 13th century stalls have exceptional misericords, especially the harvesting scene. The Lady Chapel was made by local craftsmen in 1920, and will be of interest to anyone with an interest in heraldry. You are watched everywhere by quizzical faces in the roof.

BRINGTON *All Saints* [A5]

A secluded church with an early 14th century tower similar to others in this area of Huntingdonshire; notice the quatrefoil frieze just below the spire. The window to the W of the porch is a lovely example of the flowing Decorated style; the window to the E of the porch is a more severe design of the same period. Much restoration of the large chancel was necessary during the 19th century but the double aumbry and the squint beside the arch remain from the earlier medieval building. There is a memorial to members of the United States 303 Bombardment Group who were stationed at nearby Molesworth.

BRINKLEY *St. Mary* [G7]

A little owl sits on one of the gateposts outside this little flint church with its unusual brick medieval porch. Flint flushwork frieze around base of tower. The chancel was rebuilt in 1874 but the E window remains from an earlier building, *c.*1300. 17th century pulpit. Poignant memorial near the font to two infants: a girl who lived for four months and a boy who died whilst being christened when only four days old.

BROUGHTON *All Saints* [C5]

The newly-restored 15th century wall-paintings are quite lovely. The Day of Judgement, or Doom, above the chancel arch, must have been a sobering message for any nervous villagers. On the left, naked figures rise from their tombs on Judgement Day and to the right the damned are being driven into Hell; one unfortunate soul is suspended over a cauldron. On the S arcade Adam and Eve are expelled from the Garden of Eden. The nave roof holds carved angels with musical instruments. Most of the building periods are here: the Norman font, the Early English chancel, the Decorated arcades, the tower and most of the building are Perpendicular and the Communion Rail is 18th century.

BUCKDEN *St. Mary* [B6]

This lovely church stands out against the red brick of the Palace, which belonged to the Bishops of Lincoln when that diocese stretched from the Humber to the Thames. The two-storeyed S porch dates from the late 1400s and no expense was spared in its decoration, especially its S face. It has a curious frieze of animals over the doorway, more little faces above and even on the weathered pinnacles. Even the battlements above the doorway are decorated too. The vaulted porch roof has a central boss of the Virgin Mary. The interior 'framing' over the small porch windows is similar, though on a grander scale, to that at Easton and Buckworth. The Perpendicular windows of the main body of the church are spectacular from the outside and, with their clear glass, wonderfully lighten the interior; and there is much to admire. It is almost all mid-15th century, but the medieval masons retained the Early English sedilia, piscina and the two priests' doorways in the chancel. Jacobean pulpit and lovely 16th century Passion scenes in the panels of the Readers' desks. Now look up; everywhere there is something to see and admire: angels in nave and chancel, strange grotesques and others in the S arcade. Laurence Sterne (1713-1768), author of *Tristram Shandy* and publisher of many volumes of sermons, was ordained here in 1736.

BUCKWORTH *All Saints* [B5]

Lovely in its isolation - you are unlikely to happen upon it by chance - but do seek it out. It has a particularly lovely 13th century steeple, best seen when approaching from Leighton

Bromswold when the three tiers of lucarnes give a delicate, almost fragile look to the spire. Notice the Early English details on the W wall of the tower, especially the rose window and Y-tracery of the bell-openings; also admire the sweeping view which the gargoyles have long enjoyed. The large porch has a stringcourse, stone seats and arcades 'framing' the windows similar to those at Easton. Restoration has been carried out recently and the brightly

Buckworth

painted bosses in the roofs catch the eye. In the N aisle, read the memorials to villagers who died as far apart as Ladysmith and the Vimy Ridge. A small congregation takes great pride in its large church.

BURROUGH GREEN *St. Augustine* [G7]

This large flint church is a complicated sort of building, so do walk all the way around: surprising gables and large windows of the seventeenth century, and other earlier blocked windows and doorways. You can see where chapels once stood against the N and S walls, perhaps built in the 14th century when the tower was

in the course of construction. The chancel is earlier: the decoration of the sedilia and double piscina, as well as the lovely east window, are about 1300. The pulpit looks Jacobean but in fact is work of Victorian craftsmen. Effigies of the de Burgh and Ingoldesthorpe families, who were Lords of the Manor here.

Burwell

BURWELL *St. Mary* [F6]

Majestic, magnificent - this "most perfect example in the county of the Perpendicular ideal of the glasshouse" (Pevsner). Wonderful feeling of light and space in this spectacular 15th century building, probably designed by Reginald Ely, the first master mason of King's College Chapel. Remarkable nave roof, 1464, with a whole host of animals, angels, dragons and more. In the chancel still more wonderful figures and faces in oak and stone. It has been much restored but admire the elaborate niches with some of the original paintwork. A remarkable brass in the chancel floor shows the last Abbot of Ramsey who was well rewarded with a generous pension when surrendering his abbey. The brass, made in his lifetime, portrayed him in richly decorated vestments; later it seems he thought it more prudent to have the brass reversed and the new portrait shows him as a simply dressed cleric. You must look at the tower for evidence of the earlier building, there is a blocked Norman window and also a blocked bell-opening.

BURY *Holy Cross* [C4]

The tall lancet windows of the 13th century tower are lovely examples of the Early English style. A century later another porch or chapel stood here and remains of it can still be seen. The 12th century chancel arch with strong Norman carving and the large primitive font both remain from an earlier building. Most medieval churches had one low-side window, usually to the S of the chancel; here there are two, and both retain their wooden shutters. The small 14th century lectern is still in use today; it is a lovely delicate piece of craftsmanship and stands on a 13th century stone base. Dedications to the Holy Cross are usually found with churches of Saxon origin. 16th century wills refer to the churchyard of Our Lady at Bury; the dedication may have changed at the Reformation, or perhaps the now demolished chapel or an altar was dedicated to St. Mary.

BYTHORN *St. Lawrence* [A5]

Contrast the steep pitch of the earlier chancel roof with the flat nave roof, which became fashionable in the late Middle Ages. On the W wall of the tower is an unusual triangular shaped window of the Decorated period. The 14th century spire was declared unsafe after the last war and the villagers now have to live with a very strange looking affair. Vibrations caused by the vast numbers of aeroplanes in this area were said to have caused the damage; but some who saw it being pulled down testify that the spire was still quite safe and that it stubbornly resisted each stone being removed. Inside, notice the differing styles of thearcades; in the N the piers are alternating round and octagonal and to the S they are quatrefoil. Both built about 1300, though the N may be a little earlier. In the chancel the piscina is now at ankle level as a result of the Victorian trend of raising the floor for the High Altar. Before you go, walk around outside to see the little whiskered face over the N doorway.

CALDECOTE *St. Michael and All Angels* [B4]

If you are interested in towers then you might like to know that this is thought to be one of five in the area, possibly designed by the same mason; the others are Barton, Coton, Hatley St.George and Knapwell. All were completed during a forty year period about 1400. The outside moulding of the W window is supported by two little faces; one looks just about to sneeze. A simple aisleless church. There is a little Decorated niche by the chancel arch with more medieval faces and traces of original paintwork. Attractive 18th century headstones in the churchyard with cherubs and roses struggling through moss and ivy.

CAMBRIDGE *All Saints* Jesus Lane [E7]

Designed by Bodley in 1864. The growing parish needed a larger building to replace the medieval church of All Saints in Jewry. This stood opposite Trinity gate, where the Saturday craft market is now held. Inside, the stencilled wall decorations and delicately painted roofs are by the William Morris workshop. Superb E window by Morris, Burne-Jones and Ford Madox Brown and many other good examples of 19th century stained glass throughout. The wheatsheaf symbol of Kempe can be seen here, and note also the peacock wings he often gave to his angels; panels on the pulpit are also by Kempe. All Saints is now in the care of the Redundant Churches Fund.

CAMBRIDGE *St. Andrew the Great* St. Andrew's Street [E7]
A very imposing church by Ambrose Poynter, 1842-3, replacing an earlier medieval building. Sadly no longer in use as a parish church. There is a monument here to Captain Cook, his wife and six children. His wife lived to the age of 94 and is buried here with two of her children.

CAMBRIDGE *St. Andrew the Less (The Abbey Church)* Newmarket Road [E7]
This little church was built early in the 13th century for the villagers of Barnwell by the Augustinian canons of Barnwell Priory. It is a lovely Early English building and was once the mother church of a large parish which still bears its name. In the last century it fell into great disrepair and was restored by the Cambridge Antiquarian Society. An elegant rood screen divided nave and chancel until at least 1845 but nothing remains of it now. From outside the E window is a simple triple lancet, but inside is decorated with slender columns of Purbeck marble.

CAMBRIDGE *St. Augustine of Canterbury* Richmond Road [E7]
Built in 1890 as a dual purpose building for school and church. Resembling more a large and friendly home, St.Augustine's is an active community centre as well as a place of worship and is now one of the five churches of the Parish of the Ascension.

CAMBRIDGE *St. Barnabas* Mill Road [E7]
A church which recently had the welcome problem of needing more seating for the growing congregation. The interesting solution was to move the altar to a raised dais at the West end and the benches into a collegiate arrangement. No major structural alterations were necessary to this yellow brick church, built 1869-88. A porch has recently been added at the E end of the chancel and the Victorian wall decoration has been retained.

CAMBRIDGE *St. Benedict (St. Ben't)* St. Benet Street [E7]
Believed to be the oldest church in Cambridgeshire. The tower was built about 1025 and Saxon 'long and short' work can be seen at the quoins, or corners, supporting the massive chancel arch.

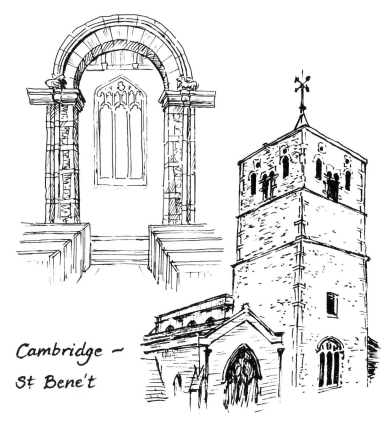

Cambridge — St Bene't

Two lion-like animals support the arch itself. The nave and chancel are typical of a Saxon church, but the pointed arches of the arcade are from the 13th century rebuilding. Nicholas Toftys from nearby Landbeach was responsible for the 'new' roof here in 1450. Many colourful figures in the roof of the N aisle with crowns and shields, and cheerful angels in the nave. A modern masterpiece stands in the N aisle - a bronze crucifixion by Enzo Plazotta.

CAMBRIDGE *St. Botolph* Trumpington Street [E7]
Dedicated to the patron saint of travellers, this church stood by the Trumpington Gate of medieval Cambridge and for a while was chapel to Pembroke College. Mainly 14th century building. Tower, *c.*1400, is topped by figures of the four evangelists. The

21

splendid font and cover will catch your eye, but also look up and admire the 19th century stencilling on the roof by Bodley. Perhaps not so admirable is the Plaifer monument, 1609, which Pevsner describes frankly as "absurdly bad". Outside there is yet another Cambridge churchyard/garden with summer flowers in profusion which do not quite conceal the interesting headstones.

CAMBRIDGE *Christ Church* Newmarket Road [E7]
The red brick exterior with large pepper-pot towers seems to be a 19th century echo of King's College. The church was built to the design of Ambrose Poynter in *c.*1837. Recently some innovative remodelling took place and the tall interior has been made into two floors. The parish hall now occupies almost the entire ground floor with the church 'upstairs' and so it is still possible to enjoy the brilliant stained glass in the E window. There are handsome central and galleried side pews and the original pulpit and lectern. An inscription on the font cover tells that it was "purchased chiefly by penny subscriptions from 1200 children in 1834."

CAMBRIDGE *St. Clement* Bridge Street [E7]
A 13th century interior remains, but the exterior walls are a result of rebuilding in the early 16th century. Wall-painting on E chancel wall of the Lord in Triumph; St. Clement seen with the Anchor of his martyrdom. Since 1986 the Anglican congregation has shared the church with the Greek Orthodox Parish of St. Athanasios and four large icons now enrich the nave. The tower, 1821, replaced a "disgraceful wooden steeple."

CAMBRIDGE *St. Edward King and Martyr* Peas Hill [E7]
This dedication is usually evidence of a pre-conquest church as Edward was declared a martyr in 1001. The lowest stage of the tower may well be Saxon. St. Edward's was rebuilt after the disastrous city fire of 1174. The graceful piers and arcades are from another major rebuilding about 1400; a little later, in 1446, the chancel aisles were added to provide chapels for the colleges of Trinity Hall and Clare. Three martyrs of the Reformation preached from the handsome linenfold pulpit: Latimer, Barnes and

Bilney; they are also remembered in a window in the S aisle. More fine linenfold panelling on the Nightwatchman's chair in the chancel. Close by the medieval 'angel' font in the S aisle is a memorial to Frederick Maurice, the 19th century preacher, writer and social reformer. A tranquil church, with a delightful little churchyard where the headstones are almost lost to view in the summertime amongst roses, flowering shrubs and trees.

CAMBRIDGE *St. George.* Chesterfield Road [E7]
The Chesterton area of Cambridge grew rapidly during the Thirties and in 1932 a small church was built for the expanding community. In 1938 Thomas H. Lyon was commissioned to design this rather grand building. Thirty years previously he had designed a very similar church, also with a tower, in South Australia. Contains several works by the talented sculptor Loughnan Pendred (1902-1980) who lived in nearby Milton.

CAMBRIDGE *St. Giles* Chesterton Lane [E7]
The Saxons built a Minster church here but the Priory moved out to Barnwell. Picot, the first Norman Sheriff of Cambridge, and his wife are said to have built a church here in 1092, as an act of Thanksgiving after his wife had almost died. The chancel arch of this little church remains as the arch between the S aisle and chapel. There is some 'long-and-short' work on the lower part of the jambs, usually a sure indication of a Saxon building. The church was rebuilt in 1875 by Healey of Bradford; the stained glass is all Victorian; the E window is a particularly fine example of Kempe's work.

CAMBRIDGE *Church of the Good Shepherd* Mansel Way [E7]
A large handsome brick church designed in 1954 by S. E. Dykes Bower using the Early English Style throughout, including the font and altar. The S chapel is dedicated to Nicholas Ferrar (1592-1637), founder of the religious community at Little Gidding in Huntingdonshire. The first vicar here was a member of the Oratory of the Good Shepherd, a religious order founded at Little Gidding in 1913.

CAMBRIDGE *Great St. Mary* Senate House Hill [E7]

An outstanding example of the late Perpendicular style, perhaps by John Wastell, the last master mason of King's College Chapel. It is quite similar to the churches at Saffron Walden and Lavenham and the same masons may have been involved. The tower took just over 100 years to complete and was not finished until 1600. The church is a tribute to the local merchants who paid for the building and furnishing; though the oak timbers in the roof were the gift of Henry VIII. Churchwardens' accounts show that the W face of the screen was to be copied from that of Thriplow, and the loft itself to be 8 feet wide; the work was finished *c.*1523. Cranmer, Latimer and Ridley all preached here. The Puritans destroyed all the medieval glass, which was replaced in the latter part of the last century. The galleries were designed by James Gibbs in 1734 for the growing number of students and the ingenious sliding pulpit was installed 100 years later. The quality of the interior emphasizes that this is the University Church.

CAMBRIDGE *Holy Sepulchre (The Round Church)* Bridge Street [E7]

In 1140 local members of the "fraternity of the Holy Sepulchre" asked the Abbot of Ramsey for land on which to build their church. Many of the 11th and 12th century churches were paid for by small local communities in this way, but it is only when records survive, such as those kept at Ramsey, that we have any detailed accounts. Jerusalem had been captured by the Turks 40 years earlier, hence the dedication. The dome roof, part of the Victorian restoration, rises above the massive Norman pillars; the gallery above is also Norman. Medieval ceilings remain in the choir and north aisle. The "candlesnuffer" was added to the tower during the restoration in the 1840s, and the S aisle added at this time. Other round churches which survive are in Northampton, the Temple Church in London, Little Maplestead in Essex and the castle chapel at Ludlow.

CAMBRIDGE *Holy Trinity* Market Street [E7]

A major fire in 1174 destroyed much of the city including an earlier building here. The present church is impressive and the tall 14th century nave adds to the light and space. The transepts were added a century later and the vast clear windows are wonderful examples of the Perpendicular style. Holy Trinity has long been associated with the Evangelical Movement and the memorials on the chancel walls make fascinating reading. Look at the tower arch, supported by flying buttresses when the elegant nave was built, and still larger buttresses to support the later 15th century roof.

CAMBRIDGE *St. James* Wulfstan Way [E7]

Designed by David Roberts and dedicated in 1955; already three additions have been necessary to fulfil the needs of an active parish. The Focus Institute opened here in 1976. It has a pleasant white-washed interior and St. James' proves that a church does not have to be ancient to have a special atmosphere of peace and welcome.

CAMBRIDGE *St. John the Evangelist* Hills Road [E7]

A large red brick church designed in 1896 by Gordon, Lowther and Gunton in the Decorated style much favoured by the Victorians. The E window is particularly fine. Most of the carving throughout the church was done by two local craftsmen who were regular worshippers here. Painting of the Transfiguration by R. Wearing, 1985, in S aisle.

CAMBRIDGE *St. Luke* Victoria Road [E7]

A large church built in 1874 by W. Basset-Smith close to an equally large United Reformed church. In 1988 it was decided to pull down the United Reformed building and modify St. Luke's for the use of both congregations. The first joint service was held on Christmas Eve, 1989. The early 14th century style used by the Victorians remains. Victorians raised the chancel floors to increase the importance of the altar; now the lovely piscina and sedilia hang suspended as decoration only since the floor has been lowered to the level of the nave. The handsome western gallery and the rails in front of the organ came from the United Reformed Church. The apse, transepts and easternmost part of the nave are now used for worship. The western end of the nave now has two floors and all the modern amenities needed by two busy city congregations.

CAMBRIDGE *St. Mark* Barton Road [E7]
A very handsome building both inside and out. Designed by Philip Day in 1901, using the Early English style with lancet windows, blank arcading and a large apsed chancel complemented by a low stone screen. St. Mark's replaced an earlier iron and timber church designed by Richard Rowe of Cambridge (who made no charge for his services) and built in 1871 as a mission church in the parish of Grantchester.

CAMBRIDGE *St. Martin* Suez Road [E7]
A church hall was built here in 1932 but it was not until 1961 that funds were raised to build St. Martin's. The architects were Paterson and Macaulay and the A-frame triangular design is carried throughout the interior. A community centre was completed in 1972 and in 1980 this active parish built a daughter church, St.Thomas, in nearby Ancaster Way.

CAMBRIDGE *St.Mary the Less* Trumpington Street [E7]
Consecrated in 1352 when known as St.-Peter-without-Trumpington-Gate, and the college chapel to Peterhouse until 1632. No chancel arch, no arcades but wonderful Decorated style details throughout. The windows are identical to those in the Lady Chapel at Ely, so perhaps the hand of Alan of Walsingham, Sacrist of the Cathedral, was at work here too. Churchwarden's initials are engraved on the font cover, 1632. George Washington's great-uncle is remembered here, and the Stars and Stripes, together with the eagle, are plain to see. Pulpit with sounding board, 1741. The High Altar is by Sir Ninian Comper (1913) who also designed the Mendel Cross and the lower part of the E window; the remainder of the window is by Kempe. The simple Lady Chapel was added in 1931. Make sure you see the garden here at Little St. Mary's, it is delightful all year round.

CAMBRIDGE *St. Mary Magdalene (Leper Chapel)* Newmarket Road [E7]
It would have been isolated when first built, but still within a reasonable walk of the medieval city. Almost certainly being used as a hospital from about 1150 and not only for lepers. The chancel would have been reserved for the priests and the hospital area, perhaps with straw pallets on the floor, would have been in the nave. The large corbel in a N window looks rather out ofplace, and may well have come from Denny Abbey much later. The simplicity of the interior is enriched by the marvellous decoration of the chancel arch. The round W windows are typical of the period but the larger window was put in by Sir Gilbert Scott during the restoration in 1867. The Chapel has had many uses: as a barn, a cattle shed and for a long time as a storehouse for the Stourbridge Fair, once one of the most important Fairs in Europe.

CAMBRIDGE *St. Matthew* St. Matthew's Street [E7]
Designed by Richard Rowe in 1866 and a very bold interior presents itself. In the shape of a Greek cross, with four equal arms; the spacious central area rises dramatically to the octagon lantern. Rowe had worked at Ely with Gilbert Scott c.1850 and had been responsible for detailed drawings of the octagon. Later, c.1873, when Surveyor to the Dean and Chapter, he supervised the restoration of the octagon. One of the windows is dedicated to his wife Sarah. Only 3 of the original stained glass windows remain behind the altar, two being destroyed when bombs dropped nearby during the last war. Just behind the church the new vicarage is also of innovative design.

CAMBRIDGE *St. Michael* Trinity Street [E7]
Built in the early 14th century by Hervey de Stanton, the founder of Michaelhouse College, to serve both the college and the surrounding parish. The S chapel is in true Decorated style; notice the highly elaborate niches each supported by a worn little angel. The chancel retains the elegant 14th century piscina and sedilia; the 18th century choir stalls are thought to have come from Trinity College. A fire necessitated a major restoration in the last

century by Gilbert Scott. In 1966 the church was united with Great St. Mary's and the nave is now used as St. Michael's Hall.

CAMBRIDGE *St. Paul* Hills Road [E7]

A large red brick church designed by Ambrose Poynter in 1841 using the Perpendicular style for the window tracery. The aisles and transepts were a later addition. Attractive E window replaces the one blown out when bombs dropped nearby in World War II.

Cambridge ~ St Peter

CAMBRIDGE *St. Peter* Castle Street [E7]

A small tranquil place, parts of which date to the 11th century. It fell into total disrepair and was rebuilt in 1781 using the original stone. The arch in the N wall is from the original building. Almost devoid of ornament except for the quite remarkable font, with mermen at each corner, which may well have stood in that early church; it is supported by a 14th century base. Now safe in the care of the Redundant Churches Fund, St. Peter's provides quiet welcome for all.

CAMBRIDGE *St. Philip* Mill Road [E7]

The present, Early English style, brick building was built in 1890 by William Wade of St. Neots, at a cost of just under £2,000. It replaced an earlier wooden chapel nearby. Nicely carved pulpit. The western end of the large nave has recently been converted into pleasant parish rooms and offices.

CARLTON *St. Peter* [G7]

No spire here to guide you but medieval bells hang in the double bellcote. The walls are patched with plaster and lean outwards rather alarmingly. The E window has recently been restored following the design of original tracery, but the church cannot have changed too much over the years. The 15th century font has symbols of the Resurrection. There is an early 17th century pulpit and a single tie-beam and kingpost roof. The medieval rood screen has been moved to the W end of the nave. In the chancel a monument recalls a vicar and his wife, and their seven children who all died in infancy.

CASTLE CAMPS *All Saints* [G8]

Attractively located on high ground, half a mile or more from the village. The church once stood within the outer bailey of the castle built in 1068 by Aubrey de Vere, Earl of Oxford, and was probably the garrison chapel. Nothing remains of the original wooden church, nor of the elaborate fortifications which once covered at least eight acres. The 13th century S doorway and piscina are the oldest parts of the present church, though building continued over the next two hundred years. Extensive restoration was necessary around 1850 when tower and porch were rebuilt.

CASTOR *St. Kyneburga* [B3]

This church must have been one of the very finest in the country when it was built in the 12th century; perhaps that is why the actual dedication date in 1124 was carved above the priest's door on the S chancel wall; very few such carved records have survived. Bands of rich arcading surround the magnificent central tower which is topped by a 14th century spire. The interior is splendid too: the decoration on the piers supporting the tower; the

Castor

CATWORTH St. Leonard [A5]

14th century for the most part, the large-windowed clerestory is later. There are faces everywhere, inside and out and a fine Early English S doorway. In the chancel a disfigured piscina dates from the same era; it must once have been double but has been crudely cut. Nicely carved wooden gate, flanked by unusual stone walls. Nave roof and rood screen were restored in 1939. The elaborate chandelier came from Brasenose College, Oxford. An interesting churchyard, with a lovely memorial to a young boy, standing with cricket bat in hand.

CAXTON St. Andrew [D7]

Another church, like Old Weston, that now stands quite apart from the modern village. The chancel was built in the 13th century. The piscina is original, also the strange stone seat which has an 'armrest' with a single small star design similar to that on the stone seat at Houghton. The E window is a memorial to Dr. August John Wright, Surgeon, who died in 1849 and must have been much admired by the donors, who were 430 patients and friends. In the 17th century the church was in such a ruinous state that the roof had fallen, but it was rebuilt and in 1672 two new bells, by Christopher Graye, were hung. Again in the last century the church was only saved by a national appeal and a major restoration took place 1863-9.

wall-paintings, particularly that of St. Catherine; the late medieval roof with painted angels; a small Saxon sculpture in the chancel, not unlike that of St. Peter at Wentworth. St. Kyneburga, a Mercian princess, was the foundress and Abbess of the convent here. She died c.680 and her relics were later translated to Peterborough.

CHATTERIS *St. Peter and St. Paul* [D4]

Set back from busy Market Hill. Much restored in 1909 by Blomfield, thanks to the generosity of a sexton's son who made his fortune in the New World. Very little remains of the 14th century church except for the lower part of the W tower and the nave arcades. 20th century faces, as well as more ancient figures, gaze curiously down from the roof. Lovely carving on the pulpit in memory of the vicar's son who fell at Flanders. Stained glass window dedicated to a former choirboy who was posthumously awarded the Victoria Cross.

CHERRY HINTON, Cambridge *St. Andrew* [E7]

A wonderful interior; the height, light and simplicity of this 13th century church must be seen. It is all so elegant - in the chancel lovely triple sedilia and an equally lovely double piscina with dogtooth moulding. Stone faces stare down from the nave roof. Medieval benches remain in the N aisle and above them hangs a sculptured oak panel, formerly the altarpiece in St. Andrew the Great in Cambridge. Monument in chancel by Flaxman, to Walter Serocold (1794), of whom it was said "the king has not a more meritorious captain". Recently a community hall has been added to the N.

CHESTERTON, Cambridge *St. Andrew* [E6]

The Manor of Chesterton originally belonged to the King and in 1217 Henry III presented the church and living to Cardinal Guava, in gratitude for rescuing England from almost certain civil war during the previous reign of King John. The advowson remained with Vercelli Abbey until 1436, when Henry VI finally retrieved it and gave it to Trinity college. There is much to admire here. 15th century benches with carved arm-rests as crouching lions, griffons, dragons and other beasts. The roofs are full of carved faces and angels and there is a spectacular late 15th century Last Judgement above the chancel arch. Lovely piscina and triple sedilia with little faces supporting the vaulting in each one. On the wall of the N aisle, near the porch, read the memorial to the "daughter of the African". Interesting headstones in the large churchyard.

CHESTERTON Nr. Peterborough *St. Michael* [B3]

The handsome Early English tower is easily seen, but to reach the church you must find the 'daisy lane' between the bus stop and post box. The S doorway is also Early English but much of the interesting interior is early 18th century, notably the chancel, many windows and the small baluster font. Fine monument in N aisle to the Belville family, 1611 - the couples facing each other and the children clustered below, kneeling on tasselled cushions.

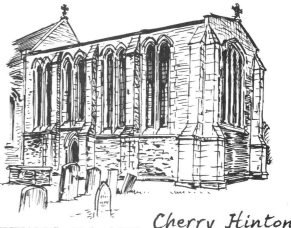

Cherry Hinton

CHETTISHAM *St. Michael* [F4]

A lovely country church, with wooden porch, shingled bell-turret, and a highly polished interior. A brick wall surrounds the churchyard and all is lovingly cared for. A 13th century, Early English, building with no chancel arch. The roof is painted in the style of the Arts and Crafts Movement of the late 19th century, when considerable restoration took place. Fragments of Norman sculpture are kept in the vestry.

CHEVELEY *St. Mary and the Holy Host of Heaven* [G6]

A church dedication unique in the country, although dedications to St. Mary alone are by far the most common. A cruciform building with central tower of the early 1300s. The octagonal top was added a little later and is best seen from the S, away from the stair turret. Walk all around and notice windows of three periods: simple Early English lancets, flowing tracery of the Decorated period and the more formal Perpendicular style. Inside, stand beneath the crossing to see the deep grooves left by the bell ropes on the arches. Angels carrying shields support the chancel roof and there are nicely carved bench ends on some of the choir stalls. Splendid font with shields depicting the Instruments of the Passion and Signs of the Evangelists.

Chippenham

CHIPPENHAM *St. Margaret* [G6]
Land here was given by Richard I to the Knights Hospitallers about 1190 and although most of the church dates from the 13th century, some evidence of the Norman building remains; notably the window in the chancel, now blocked. Medieval graffiti can be found on many of the piers, particularly in the N arcade; some of it is thought to be very early. Mrs. Pritchard in her book *English Medieval Graffiti* suggests that a scratched drawing, which is upside down on the pillar next to the N parclose screen, may be a caricature of Richard I, making it *c.*1190. An Indulgence for rebuilding the church after a fire was granted in 1447 and no doubt much stone was reused at this time. A spectacular wall-painting of St. Christopher on N wall, and remains of colour on piers and arches throughout. At first glance the Rood Screen appears to be decorated with delicate scrolls and leaves, but closer inspection reveals little faces on almost every cusp, and also on the pinnacle-like decorations as well. Similar faces and pinnacles can be seen on the rood screen, now in the N aisle, at St. Andrews, Soham - the same craftsman maybe. Very fine monument in chancel to Thomas Revet (d.1582) with his two wives and four children.

CHRISTCHURCH *Christ Church* [E3]
Large Victorian church designed by John Giles in 1864. Attractive interior with white painted apsed chancel and cheerfully coloured roof. Until this church was built, the area was known as Brimstone Hill as the vicar of Upwell was supposed to have chased the devil away from his village to this spot.

COATES *Holy Trinity* [D3]
Designed in 1840 by J. Wild in the Norman style; the aisles were added later. Unusual in having a NE tower. This is one of the so-called Commissioners' Churches which were built to provide churches for the new urban areas as a result of a Parliamentary Commission of 1818.

COLDHAM *St. Etheldreda* [E2]
A tidy little church built, in the Decorated style, in 1875. The pews slope alarmingly to the outside walls, as do many others on the soft fenland soil, but no doubt it is all safe enough. The Victorians insisted on the elaborate piscina and sedilia, and notice the scenes on the three large tiles in front of the altar.

COLNE *St. Helen* [D5]
Rebuilt by William Fawcett the Cambridge architect, using many materials from the original church which had collapsed in 1896. The low pitched roof is attractively painted. Several memorials from the earlier church remain, including an interesting board dated 1690 showing the generosity of several parishioners with their bequests of loaves of bread and money for the poor. The original church stood a little distance away; only parts of the crumbling porch survive.

COMBERTON *St. Mary the Virgin* [D7]

An interesting church and churchyard. Inside, the pointed arches of the Early English S arcade contrast with the wider flat-topped arches of those of the Perpendicular period of the N arcade. Thomas Baron (d.1525) paid for the building of the N aisle and his initials are on one of the medieval bench ends. One small window in the chancel holds all that remains of the medieval glass, thanks to a visit by the tireless William Dowsing. He was appointed by Parliament in 1643 to destroy whatever might be offensive to the Puritans. He kept a diary and here in Comberton he wrote that he broke down "a crucifix, 69 superstitious pictures .... 36 cherubims, and gave order for the remainder, with the steps, to be taken down". Villagers rescued some of the angels' wings and defiantly nailed them back in the N aisle.

CONINGTON Nr. Cambridge *St. Mary* [D6]

Approaching through the large, well-tended churchyard, the progress of different building periods of St. Mary's can be seen: the tower is 14th century, nave 18th century, chancel rebuilt in 1870. Inside, extensive restoration was lovingly carried out in recent years by a dedicated priest-in-charge, an indefatigable church warden and many equally tireless villagers. One of the most impressive collections of monuments in East Anglia commemorates a long line of Lords of the Manor: the Cottons, Askhams, Hattons and Gardeners. Grinling Gibbons signed his elaborate memorial to young Robert Cotton who died in 1697, aged 14. The chancel is dimly lit through the Victorian glass. One of the four bells is reputed to be the oldest in the county, *c.*1365. A contented, peaceful place.

CONINGTON Hunts. *All Saints* [B4]

An important example of the mature Perpendicular style of the late 15th century. The Cotton family were Lords of the Manor from 1460 and this large church, then dedicated to St.Mary, was probably largely built by Thomas Cotton (d.1505). Many fine monuments including one to David, King of Scotland, whose family were Lords of the Manor here during the 12th and early 13th centuries; many Cotton and Heathcote memorials; also a

Conington

remarkable very early marble effigy, *c.*1300, of a young Franciscan. Beside the 13th century font lie memorials to a brother and sister who died in infancy. A detailed guide is provided by the Redundant Churches Fund which now cares for All Saints.

COTON *St. Peter* [E7]

A lovely village church with two small late medieval porches. Two small round-arched windows survive from the Norman building; also the massive font with each side decorated with primitive designs. Few of the medieval craftsmen are known, but here inside the tower on the S wall is written in Latin 'Andrew

Swynow... began the arch on St. Wulstan's day 1481'. The woodwork is largely Jacobean, and the lock on the screen doors is dated 1622. The organ was moved to its present position 20 years ago and now stands, cheerfully repainted, in the S aisle. Memorial to Dr. Andrew Downes (d.1627) one of the translators of the King James Bible and "the foremost Greek scholar of Europe ...." The tower is one of five in the area built during a period of forty years about 1400, possibly designed by the same master mason; the others are Barton, Caldecote, Hatley St. George and Knapwell.

COTTENHAM *All Saints* [E6]

A splendid building complete with battlements. A gale destroyed most of the tower and it was rebuilt in pale pink brick from 1617-19. The bulbous pinnacles were added at this time. Many of the donors' names can be seen on the S face, and a sundial warns us that "Time is Short". Many gargoyles including a shaggy-maned lion. The tall Perpendicular windows and large clerestory make for a light interior. In the chancel, the lovely 15th century piscina with shelf above and triple sedilia are enhanced by a delicate quatrefoil frieze. The bench ends, by a local craftsman, are a 19th century addition.

COVENEY *St. Peter-ad-Vincula* [E4]

The church stands on a ridge, almost hidden by trees. The nave and chancel are mostly 13th century; the tower, with its open base, a little later. The interior is a little gem. Athelstan Riley was Patron of the living here and generously endowed the church with its present furnishings. His initials are carved on the rood screen (1896). Fine stained glass in E window by Geoffrey Webb (1937), his work easily distinguished by his 'spider web' symbol. The reredos, *c.*1500, is of German origin. The pulpit (1706), with painted panels of the apostles, came from Denmark. In the nave some medieval benches remain and carved poppyheads include the keys of St. Peter and the cockerel. Fine views from both sides of the churchyard. An inscription on the lych gate commemorates those who gave their lives "to keep their country free from the chains of a foreign yoke". If you walk a little way N along the

Coveney

ridge you will understand why the majestic Ely cathedral is called the Ship of the Fens.

COVINGTON *St. Margaret* [A5]

A compact little church on the county's south-western edge. A fine example of a Norman door on the N wall with the carving of the tympanum looking almost as fresh as it must have done in the 12th century; another round-arched doorway in the S chancel wall. The font is Norman too with low decoration on the bowl and base; attractive modern font cover. More Norman fragments are built into the chancel wall. The S doorway, chancel S windows and piscina are all 13th century. Outside on the nave S wall is a blocked window which must have been inserted to throw light on the medieval rood screen. There is also evidence of an earlier chapel on the S side also, and the blocked archway remains.

CROXTON *St. James* [C7]

Once the centre of the small village but now stands alone following the landscaping of the park in the 18th century. Madingley and Wimpole are other examples of this fashion, largely due to the influence of Capability Brown. Late

Perpendicular tower with good, though crumbling, decoration. The interior is quite unspoilt. There are still two sofas in the family chapel. The servants' pews were to the W and the remaining pleasantly careworn benches are 15th century. Cromwell's troops are said to have been billeted here and perhaps took notice of the roundel in the SW window, warning the military not to steal the church plate. Most of the medieval glass has gone but large angels remain in the roof. Interesting churchyard with an ornate tomb of the Rev. William Cavendish Bentinck (d.1865) grandfather of the Queen Mother. A strange box-like stone remembers an "honest and valued servant ... 62 years in employment".

CROYDON *All Saints* [D8]
A simple unspoilt country church, but it is quite alarming to see the angle of the 14th century S arcade and walls. The large Norman font stands immediately inside the entrance. Niches in the S chapel on either side of the window and a little ogee-arched piscina. Sir George Downing, founder of Downing College (d.1749), is buried here. His grandfather, Sir Charles Downing, had an unsavoury career, serving Cromwell or the King as it best suited him. However, he is well known today: he leased a piece of land in London, built houses on it and gave his name to the street.

DIDDINGTON *St. Lawrence* [B6]
You must walk across fields to reach this interesting church. The chancel and N arcade are Early English and the lancet windows remain; the low-side window is early 14th century. The brick tower and porch were built during the reign of Henry VIII. This was a rare occurence during that troubled era when monasteries were being destroyed all over the country and little rebuilding was undertaken. Some lovely medieval bench ends survive too. Good 15th century stained glass and continental glass of a later date.

DODDINGTON *St. Mary* [D3]
The tower and nave are 14th century. The chancel is earlier and a large royal Coat of Arms dominates the N wall. Lovely angels in the medieval nave roof. Here also a window from the now demolished Benwick church has been reused. A famous rector here was Christopher Tye, musician to four monarchs. He composed for Henry VIII, Edward VI and Mary Tudor until he retired to Doddington during the reign of Elizabeth I. E window in N aisle is from the early school of William Morris, *c.*1865. Many 18th century headstones in the churchyard and the tall cross at the entrance stands on a 14th century base.

DOWNHAM-IN-THE-ISLE *St. Leonard* [F4]
A sturdy Norman tower and a wonderful doorway; the pointed arch from the late-Norman or Transitional period of the late 12th century. This leads on to the typical 13th century lancet windows and alternating (round and octagonal) arcades. The Coat of Arms of George III dominates the W end of the nave. In the N aisle hangs an 'Act of Parliament Clock' (so called because Pitt the Younger imposed a tax on clocks and watches in the late 18th century, and it became more economic to rely on public clocks). In the N aisle a chapel is dedicated to Ovin, steward to St. Etheldreda.

DRY DRAYTON *St. Peter and St. Paul* [D6]
The church was owned by Crowland Abbey from the 9th century until 1543. An attractive building standing at the edge of the village. The exterior is largely the result of 19th century rebuilding, though the 14th century style of the medieval church was followed. Very worn sedilia stand next to the chancel wall; perhaps the chancel was shortened resulting in the loss of the piscina. Weathered corbels, one with handsome moustache. The 19th century E window is dedicated to the Smith family; father and son were both rectors here. The glass is by Willement, who marked his work with his initials T.W. in a shield. Beautiful brass of Thomas Hatton and his wife, with their four sons and seven daughters, *c.*1540.

DULLINGHAM *St. Mary* [G7]
Very handsome N porch with a flushwork frieze, and two good gargoyles holding the down spouts; the frieze continues around the N aisle. The chancel still has the pointed arches of the 13th

century, but the rest of the church was built in various stages from 1399 to 1525. The large green marble pulpit (1903) comes as somewhat of a surprise. The font is dated 1622 but looks earlier. Several good monuments by Westmacott (father and son) to members of the Jeaffreson family. Lt.Gen. Jeaffreson, whose "heart teemed with kindness", died in 1824. Outside you can see the blocked priest's door in the chancel; also notice on the S side how strangely the tower buttress stands against the chapel. Several early 18th century headstones.

Bear   Boar

Lions.

Duxford - S⁺ Peter

DUXFORD *St. John* [E8]
No longer used as a parish church, it is now in the care of the Redundant Churches Fund; the wall-paintings being gradually restored by students from the Courtauld Institute. The strongly carved moulding of the doorway is Norman, but the unusually shaped cross may be earlier, as it resembles those seen on Anglo-Saxon buildings. Inside, massive Norman piers support the crossing tower. Graffiti here also, including a 'swastika pelka', or Solomon's Knot, which Mrs. Pritchard has found to be common in many churches.

DUXFORD *St. Peter* [E8]
Attractive flint church with 12th century tower and some windows remaining from the Norman period. The chancel is almost as large as the nave and was embellished with much tiling during the restoration in 1883. The stone faces of the corbels in the nave roof are quite startling, with a fiendish grinning boar and a far from benevolent lion. In the Lady Chapel the two modern, brightly painted saints, stand comfortably in their 15th century niches supported by medieval angels.

EASTON *St. Peter* [B5]
Perpendicular broach spire similar to that at Ellington. The porch has stone seats, windows which are 'framed' with arcading on the inside, and a stringcourse matching that of the tower, all very similar to the porch at Buckworth and to some extent like Old Weston. Fragments of a Norman window have been built into the N wall. In the S aisle more 12th century sculpture and what may be a later medieval Consecration Cross. A simple oak rood screen of the 15th century. The nave roof is prominently dated 1630. Above N door are listed the Charitable Donations of 1826.

EATON SOCON *St. Mary* [B7]
Fire destroyed the interior of the medieval building in 1930, though much of the outer shell remained. Funds were swiftly found and this fine new church, designed by Sir Albert Richardson, was consecrated in 1932. It is light and airy and has impressive woodwork throughout, especially the reredos and stalls. The loft above the elegant rood screen is reached by a spiral staircase in the N aisle. Some of the old corbels remain in the N aisle, but elsewhere you are watched by the 20th century

faces of local people involved with the rebuilding. The square font is Norman, with typical decoration of intersecting arches.

ELLINGTON *All Saints* [B5]

A slender Perpendicular tower with battlements and happily weathered gargoyles. The E and N chancel windows are all *c.*1290, the tracery was restored by Sir Gilbert Scott in 1863. The aisle, clerestory nave and N porch are all Perpendicular. On a bright day the interior is flooded with light and the 15th century carvings in the roofs can be appreciated - apostles and angels with outstretched wings. Notice also the altar rails and benches, which are the work of Victorian craftsmen.

Elm

ELM *All Saints* [E2]

Wonderful Early English tower, with three tiers of blank arcading and lancets of the 13th century; you need to stand away to appreciate the breadth of the base. The W doorway has an earlier rounded arch. Inside, the size of the tower arch is quite breathtaking. Practically all the interior is Early English including the unusually early clerestory windows. Notice the old roofline above the tower arch. The 13th century string course continues in the chancel where the windows have been heavily restored. The lovely nave roof is late medieval and names of the churchwardens are written in the N aisle roof as a reminder of a restoration in 1620.

ELSWORTH *Holy Trinity* [D6]

As you enter by the N porch, the high arcades and imposing tower create a feeling of great space. The chancel, although much restored in the last century, must be the oldest part. The piscina and sedilia echo the delicate tracery of the windows, all late 13th century Decorated. There is one distinctive Perpendicular window in the chancel, and below it a small low-side window. The handsome stalls are late 15th century, early Tudor, and have unusual lockers under the bookrests. The large reredos has been removed from behind the high altar and is now at the W end of the nave.

ELTISLEY *St. Pandionia and St. John* [C7]

The elegant spire can be seen from afar. Most of the church is Early English, 13th century, including the very fine doorway with dogtooth ornament of about 1200. The chancel was demolished in 1841 and was rebuilt using a yellow brick. St. Pandionia is thought to have been a daughter of a Scottish prince; she died at a Benedictine nunnery nearby in 904. Her body was translated into the church in 1344 and many miracles occurred. St. Pandionia's Well stood outside the chancel until the 16th century when it was demolished for being used for "superstitious purposes".

ELTON *All Saints* [A3]

A particularly fine late Perpendicular tower, *c.*1500, with quatrefoil friezes, a large sundial and gargoyles all around. The chancel arch, *c.*1270, has nailhead decoration. Some 16th century benches, some with linenfold panelling and in the N aisle an 18th century German vestment cupboard. Much fine glass of the Arts and Crafts era and later. Several by William Morris and Burne-Jones, with marvellous colours in the W window of the S aisle. The Te Deum or All Saints E window is by Clayton & Bell, 1893. Many memorials to members of the Proby family, including an Admiral, Colonel, Lord Lieutenant and others. The pulpit was the gift of Fr. Faber, when he was the incumbent here, before he seceded to Rome and founded the Brompton Oratory.

Ely – St Mary

ELY *St. Mary* St. Mary's Street [F4]

Superb N doorway, thought to have been made in the nearby monastery workshop during the late 12th century. Tall arcades dominate the elegant interior and lead to the Early English chancel. The chapel has an interesting window showing the martyrdom of St. Edmund and St. Etheldreda and a detailed picture of the cathedral. For another superb view of the octagon and roofs of the cathedral, walk around to the garden to the S side. A Saxon font and ancient coffin stand here, in front of the handsome hexagonal parish room, built in 1985.

ELY *St. Peter* Broad Street [F4]

The widow of Canon Edward Boyer built this church as a memorial to her husband; it was dedicated in 1890. This was then a densely populated area of Ely, with much river traffic as well as the railway which had arrived in 1845. A very neat building, lovingly cared for by a small congregation. There is a beautiful painted Rood Screen, by Sir Ninian Comper; angels either side of

the Rood Group are balanced delicately on wheels, a device often used by Comper to indicate their ceaseless motion.

Etton

ETTON *St. Stephen* [B2]

St. Stephen's has changed little since it was built and is a superb example of the Early English period. The 13th century tower has a frieze of little heads and a horizontal sheila-na-gig figure. On the N wall of the chancel the outline of an earlier chapel and its piscina can still be seen. The long, narrow chancel has 13th century Y-tracery windows with trefoils. Over the low-side window is a lovely flowing arch; it must be a little later though it is still not quite the ogee of the Decorated period. It could be the same date as the early 14th century quatrefoil windows of the clerestory. There is a plain octagonal font with 17th century cover. Careful restoration was carried out in the 19th century; but the tiled chancel floor inserted at this time has considerably shortened the priest's doors. Medieval wall-paintings have recently been uncovered in the S aisle.

EYE *St. Matthew* [C2]

Building of this cruciform church began in 1836 using the Early English style. It was designed by George Basevi, who died after falling from scaffolding on Ely Cathedral. A spire was added some ten years later, but was removed *c.*1982/3 and replaced by the saddle-back you see now. The lancet windows are filled with Victorian glass; the E window, 1863, by Gibbs. The font and piscina are from the original 14th century building.

Eynesbury

EYNESBURY *St. Mary* [B7]

Many fine things to admire in this rather plain brown cobble building, outwardly in the Perpendicular style. The Early English doorway opens on to a much earlier interior. The round piers of the N arcade are Norman, *c.*1100. The stoup was once the base of the medieval town cross of St. Neots. The early 15th century carving of the bench ends is quite superb and is known locally as the Eynesbury Zoo. There are human heads, a camel and a pig with an orange in his mouth. Then the pulpit - a beautiful example of late 17th century work and may have come from a London workshop influenced by Christopher Wren. A memorial in the nave floor to 'The Eynesbury Giant', said to be the tallest man in England. The tower was struck by lightning and rebuilt in 1687 but the Norman arch survives. In the vestry are memorials to former rectors - the passing of the Revd. William Palmer was "regretted by all classes", thanks perhaps to his generosity in regularly distributing a pint of brandy to his parishioners. A detailed account in the porch of a Colonel's numerous battles and wounds in the Napoleonic wars: no wonder he called his son William Wellington Waterloo.

FARCET *St. Mary* [C3]

Walk round outside the tower to see the 12th century rounded lancets in the lower stages; it was completed about 100 years later at the same time as the nave and S arcade. Low-side window on N wall of chancel - they are more often found in the S wall. The rare 13th stone seat resembles those at Houghton and Stanground; here there is an original flower-like design on one arm, the other is a more recent copy. An older roofline can be seen on the E face of the chancel arch. The N aisle, roof and clerestory date from a restoration in the 1850s but some medieval carvings remain. Handsome Early Renaissance pulpit with linenfold decoration.

FEN DITTON *St. Mary* [E6]

A rowing eight tops the weathervane, oars stand in the nave and further links with the river Cam are found in the new (1989) W window. It recalls Wick Alsop (d.1987) who for many years, at the Annual Oarsmen's Service, would read a passage from "The Pilgrim's Progress." The tower is 13th century, N

Fen Ditton

aisle and chancel are Decorated (early 14th); the rest mainly 15th century Perpendicular. Cole's records tell of glass in the E window with the arms of Bishop Hotham (1316-37); so it could be true that Alan of Walsingham, creator of the Octagon at Ely c.1330, was responsible for building the scissor-beam chancel roof here. The font is late 14th century, with mutilated arms of Bishop Arundel (1374-88) and the arms of Ely (3 crowns); it came from the Cathedral in 1881. Major restoration was carried out in the late 19th century and much of the glass is from this period. In S aisle Kempe has signed his window with his usual wheatsheaf motif, but unusually he has put it at the very top. Outside there are some good early 18th century headstones with skulls, weeping angels and swags of roses. Read of the Willys family in the chancel - Ann, mother of 13 children, died in 1685 and thirty years later it seems that four generations died in a very short period of time.

FEN DRAYTON *St. Mary* [D6]
Lovely little brown cobbled church. The low tower has windows and bell-openings in the Decorated style of the early 14th century, and the various stages of building, using slightly different material, can easily be seen. The tiny window in the N wall of the chancel is something of a mystery; perhaps an anchorite or hermit had a cell here and thus was able to see the high altar; from the inside it looks like a squint. Pevsner suggests it may be Saxon. Two box pews are preserved in the chancel, but sadly little remains of the rood screen though one of the delicately carved panels now hangs in the S aisle.

FENSTANTON *St. Peter and St. Paul* [D6]
Turn at the King William IV and make your way past thatched cottages to this neat and attractive church. The chancel, surprisingly large and with an impressive E window, was built by William of Longthorne, rector here from 1345-1352. Much of the remainder is of the later Perpendicular period. Elegant monument with an eloquent inscription to Capability Brown, the illustrious landscape gardener. He was lord of the manor here and died in 1783. The dark wooden roofs of both aisles have many handsome

angels, now without wings, but still clutching their once brightly painted shields. Before you leave the village, look at the little brick jail house, built about 1600.

Fletton

FLETTON *St. Margaret* [B3]
A peaceful churchyard despite the surrounding bustle of Peterborough. Late 13th century, Early English, tower with broach spire. Rather severe square windows on S aisle and clerestory are 17th century. It is the Anglo-Saxon sculptures that are the great treasure here. Until quite recently (1981) the lovely frieze now set safely behind the altar was built into the E buttress of the chancel. The work is thought to be early 9th century. On the S wall of the chancel are two carvings of Saints, perhaps

Norman, early 12th century. We are fortunate that the church is standing at all today, as arsonists almost destroyed it in 1983. The charred pages of the Visitors' Book show where they defiantly wrote "The Destroyers", but the blaze was seen in time and the fire was contained.

FOLKSWORTH *St. Helen* [B3]

Dedicated to the mother of Constantine, the first Christian Emperor. Delightful unspoilt churchyard, filled with cowslips in the spring, where William Cockerill "waiteth for a glorious resurrection" beneath an unusually early headstone of 1611. Walk around to the N to find a small Norman doorway with what looks like a portcullis above it; this in fact should be more grandly known as a

Folksworth

tympanum of 'gridiron and pellets'. A gargoyle of particularly vindictive appearance faces you at eye-level at the porch. The massive Norman arch quite dominates the nave; the chancel beyond is a product of Victorian rebuilding and zealous restoration in the 1850s.

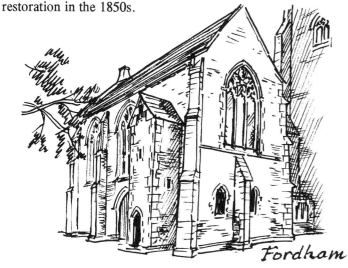

Fordham

FORDHAM *St. Peter* [G5]

The pride of this medieval church is the two-storied Lady Chapel in the Decorated style, early 14th century. Once quite separate from the church, but now joined to the N aisle. Round-headed Norman windows remain here but most are 15th century Perpendicular. Early English chancel, 13th century, with lancets and typical dogtooth ornament on the chancel arch. The medieval stalls here, some with misericords, may have come from Fordham Abbey. It is the wall-paintings which really stand out - not at all the medieval ones you might expect, but a happy blend of Edwardian colour on medieval stone. The artists were two sisters, Edith and Minnie Townsend, who completed the work in 1905.

FOWLMERE *St. Mary* [E8]

A handsome flint cruciform church. A fine string-course of ballflowers ornaments the N transept as this was, and remains, the 'show' side which faces the village street. A massive door opens on to an impressive interior. The chancel is Early English with original double piscina and low-side window. The large memorial on N wall is to William Mitchell (d.1745). Mr. Mitchell was related to the Bennetts of Babraham, two of whom have a remarkable 17th century monument. The E window here is by Clayton &

Fowlmere

Bell who also made the prettier window by the font. The transepts are later, and the ogee arch of the Decorated period takes over in the niches, though no statues remain. The ogee arch is repeated in the elegant rood screen. Part of a Norman capital can be seen in the porch but little survives of the earlier church.

Fulbourn

FOXTON *St. Laurence* [E8]

Three distinct types of window to be seen as you approach. Three 13th century Early English lancets of the chancel, the Decorated windows of the N aisle a little later, and the 15th century Perpendicular in the clerestory. Indulgences were granted here for rebuilding in 1456. Marvellous interior with screen and wooden chancel arch, all much restored. The upper doorway of the rood stair indicates how far forward was the roodloft. The 15th century chancel roof has carved wooden angels bearing shields. A particularly destructive visit from William Dowsing in 1644 resulted in the church becoming a "neglected wreck" during the next 30 years. Happily subsequent restorations have been sympathetic and St. Laurence still gives a good idea of a village church before the Reformation.

FRIDAY BRIDGE *St. Mark* [E2]

An alarming sight, as the tower leans at a dramatic angle and appears to be taking the west front with it. Villagers are undismayed as apparently this happened soon after it was built in 1864 (designed by J.B. Owen). Victorian glass, one window signed Alex Gibbs, London, 1868.

FULBOURN *St. Vigor* [F7]

An unusual dedication to a 6th century missionary who became Bishop of Bayeux (514-538) and converted many violent Norsemen to the Christian faith. A second church once shared this graveyard, while serving a separate parish. All Saints tower collapsed during a storm on Trinity Sunday 1766; a private Act of Parliament allowed it not to be repaired. The churches almost touched each other, closer even than the two you may still see at Swaffham Bulbeck; if you can find the tomb of Elizabeth March you will be inside what was once All Saints. The pulpit you see now, with the beautiful panels of St. John and St. Elizabeth of Hungary, may well be early 14th century. The panels are thought to have come from the rood screen of All Saints. Notice the lovely carving of owls and other birds, rose hips, bluebells and little human faces supporting delicate arches. In the chancel a tomb recess with cadaver is a memorial to a 15th century rector. Large brass (1377-86) in chancel floor. Several other good brasses; don't miss those let into the wall in the S aisle, near the splendid 17th century monument to Mr. Wood and his lady.

GAMLINGAY *St. Mary* [C7]

Marvellous cruciform church of local russet-coloured stone which was quarried just outside the churchyard. A stately 15th century exterior with battlements and gargoyles. A small lancet remains in the N aisle from an earlier building. Elaborate two-storey vaulted N porch and tall single-storey S porch. Light floods the interior, where you will find an Early English font of *c.*1200 and a fine Rood Screen of the late 14th century. The chancel has triple Decorated sedilia, the piscina perhaps a little later; the roof holds large angels with wings outstretched. In the S aisle notice the tall narrow cupboard, used since medieval times, to hold the

processing banners. In the N transept, a little squint is set quite low down, but would once have given a good view of the high altar. Interesting graffiti throughout. Several of the choir stalls, c.1442, have misericords, and the panelling behind retains some original colour.

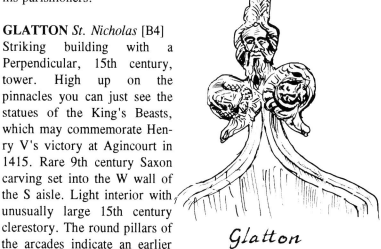
Glatton

too. In the N aisle hangs an imposing list of Donations and Benefactions dated 1853; the rector seemingly more generous than his parishioners.

GLATTON *St. Nicholas* [B4]
Striking building with a Perpendicular, 15th century, tower. High up on the pinnacles you can just see the statues of the King's Beasts, which may commemorate Henry V's victory at Agincourt in 1415. Rare 9th century Saxon carving set into the W wall of the S aisle. Light interior with unusually large 15th century clerestory. The round pillars of the arcades indicate an earlier date, about 1200, though they would have been lower then. Fine poppyheads on the benches, particularly the man carrying a woman's head under each arm. Several wall-paintings c.1500 and a tall, elegant rood screen.

GIRTON *St. Andrew* [E6]
Various building stages can be seen in the differing colours and types of materials used. Before you go in, notice the base of the tower: it is rectangular, not square and the lower part, with herringbone pattern, was built in the 11th century. On the tower E wall can be seen the faint outline of the roof of the Norman nave. A 20th century statue of St. Andrew stands above the entrance to the medieval porch; it has an upper room which may have been added at the same time as the clerestory and battlements. The N wall of the chancel has two blocked windows watched over by a particularly cheerful lion. There is a strange blocked window in the E wall of the chancel

Gamlingay

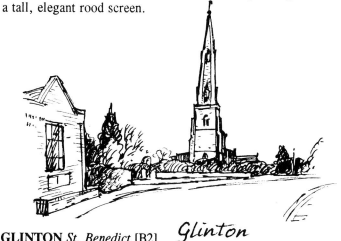

GLINTON *St. Benedict* [B2] *Glinton*
Beautiful spire (c.1510), very tall and slender, with pronounced entasis, rising from the battlements of the 15th century tower. The

gargoyles on the S clerestory are worth a mention. There are three quite ordinary ugly faces and one "reverse view", supposedly put there by the disgruntled mason when his wages remained unpaid. Two 14th century figures in the porch, the lady still elegant despite her worn appearance; opposite is a forester with his horn. Inside, traces of wall-painting survive on either side of the chancel arch. Notice the 19th century carving of bench ends with all manner of beasts and angry faces. The poet John Clare, who lived in nearby Helpston, attended the school in the Lady Chapel here in the early 1800s.

GODMANCHESTER St. Mary the Virgin [C5]

A stately church built for a large and prosperous medieval town. A rare Saxon Mass Dial is set into a buttress on the S chancel wall. The Norman church had a central tower and an outline of an earlier roof can just be seen above the chancel arch. Major rebuilding took place in the 13th century; the church was lengthened and the tower built at the W end. In the late 14th century the wealthy merchants again enlarged their church. The

Godmanchester

tower fell into disrepair and was rebuilt in 1623 using much of the original 13th century material. Small 14th century N porch, but enter through the more elaborate S porch. Inside, much remains of the Early English building. The 15th century choir stalls may be from Ramsey Abbey; some have beautifully carved misericords: a fox and goose, a rabbit and a deer rubbing its nose; the initials W.S. refer to William Stevens, vicar here 1470-1481. Several windows by Kempe and one by William Morris and Co., 1911. In the S chapel the reredos and altar rails are by Martin

Travers, who is buried in the churchyard. Many interesting headstones and tombs, particularly that of Mary Ann Weems who was murdered by her husband in 1819.

GOREFIELD St. Paul [E1]

An attractive flint church built in the Early English style, thanks almost entirely to the energies of the Revd. Andrew Beck, rector here from 1870 to 1901. The chancel, 1903, is dedicated to his memory. There is a handsome stone pulpit and oak lectern in the nave. The building is beautifully maintained and stands in a pleasant churchyard.

GRAFHAM All Saints [B6]

An unusual tower that becomes octagonal, and then has little 17th century pinnacles. The single bell dates to c.1400. The body of the church is mainly late 13th century, All Saints would then have been surrounded by woodland, but since the 1960s the large open space of the Grafham Water reservoir has quite altered the landscape. A quiet simple church but with a particular welcome about it. Chancel and N arcade remain from the Early English period. The S arcade, and the font, came a little later, in the Decorated style. Interesting memorials to members of the Puckle family.

GRANTCHESTER St. Andrew and St. Mary [E7]

Before entering, walk round to the S porch; beside it you will see evidence of much earlier buildings: a small Saxon window and interlace panels, Norman zigzag patterns, and two little 12th century faces. The tower can be dated by one of the shields on the lower window, that of Bishop Fordham of Ely, 1388-1426. The 15th century nave is rather gloomy but the chancel is quite spectacular. Pevsner suggests it may have been the work of craftsmen from the Lady Chapel workshop at Ely. It is certainly a wonderful example of the Decorated period: the ogee arch is used everywhere. An elaborate tomb recess in the N wall is surely that of the donor. There is also a large Norman font and a Jacobean pulpit. Corpus Christi College has been Patron here since 1380; their Coat of Arms, featuring the pelican (a symbol of

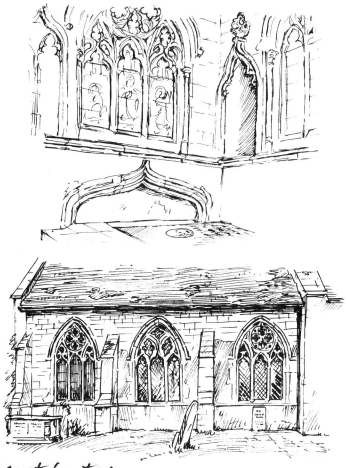

Grantchester

self-sacrifice) and lilies (purity) can be seen in the chancel and churchyard.

GRAVELEY *St. Botolph* [C6]

A unpretentious welcoming church, its chancel still lit by candlelight. Four cheerful little gargoyles greet you above the W door. Outside you can see what remains of the N aisle, perhaps taken down in the 18th century when the Rev. Henry Trotter undertook major restorations and "rebuilt and beautified the chancel". He died in 1766 and his memorial, telling of his generosity, is in the chancel. A more recent memorial to those who served with the Pathfinder Force at RAF Graveley in World War II. A picture dated 1748 shows a S porch and very different windows in E chancel wall. Read the memorial on the S wall of the chancel to Mary Warren; when only two years old, her family brought her back to England from India. She survived the journey, including crossing Egypt by camel, only to die at the rectory here at the age of three.

GREAT ABINGTON *St. Mary* [F8]

Approached down a long lane, beyond the thatched cottages in open fields. A flint and rubble church, mostly 13th century; with a group of three lancet windows in the tower and more lancets in the chancel. A later addition is the small window inserted to throw light on the rood screen. The rood loft has now long gone, but the worn steps which once led up to it remain. In the chancel, Sir William Halton (d.1639) rests resignedly on his elbow. He lies facing the organ with its striking case of dull reds and golds. The font is partly built into the pier of the tower arch.

GREAT CHISHILL *St. Swithin* [E9]

Beautifully situated in a lovely part of the county. Mainly built of flint. The porch was once two-storeyed; the staircase remains and the outline of the upstairs doorway. The base of the tower and the chancel arch are early 14th century but curiously they are not in line with the present nave. Beside this rather small chancel arch is an unusually broad squint. The organ, early 19th century, is by G.M.Holditch, who built the pedal organ in Lichfield Cathedral. There is a large graffito of two keys.

GREAT EVERSDEN *St. Mary* [D7]

The church was struck by lightning in 1466. An Indulgence was given in the same year for its rebuilding and work was carried out at the end of the 15th century, and much of the old material was reused. The piscina may also date from this time. Lovely timber porch dated 1636 and the pulpit is perhaps of slightly earlier date. Two misericords in the chancel, one with the arms of the

Beauchamp family. Admire the lovely modern design for an altar cloth, using local wild flowers.

GREAT GIDDING *St. Michael* [B4]

As you approach, notice the windows in the chancel - good examples of the three different styles: Early English (central, triple lancets); Decorated (to the left, early 14th), and the larger Perpendicular window on the right. The S doorway, 1250, is perhaps the earliest part, but the nave and chancel, with lancets, are still 13th

Great Gidding

century. By 1400 the church was almost as you see it now, with clerestory, aisles and porch. The chancel boasts a particularly fine Decorated piscina, a Communion Rail of 1640. On the S wall is a wooden panel, dated 1614; on it is a remarkable word square such as was used by the first Christians in Rome. Fearsome gargoyles on N nave and smiling cherubs on some of the 18th century headstones in the churchyard.

GREAT GRANSDEN *St. Bartholomew* [C7]

An impressive church with grand battlements and startling gargoyles. Almost entirely in the Perpendicular style of the 15th and 16th centuries. Inside there are more handsome carved figures and bosses in the roof. In the chancel is a beautiful 15th century piscina, complete with shelf. Barnabas Oley (1602-1686) was the much loved rector here for 53 years, although his royalist connections forced him to flee north for some years. He was a great admirer of George Herbert and published many of his poems. The carillon and chimes were added to the splendid clock to honour his 50th year in the parish. The lych gate is a memorial to those who died in the Great War and a remarkable stained glass window was given in 1989 in memory of those that died flying from Gransden air field during World War II.

GREAT PAXTON *Holy Trinity* [C6]

Approaching from the north, the church appears quite low and sits comfortably into the landscape; it gives little preparation for the breathtaking height and space of the interior. This was a Minster church, built *c.*1020 and is said to be "the most ambitious building of the 11th century". Pevsner describes the N transept arch as being "thrown across at a height unparalleled in early English architecture". It is all quite spectacular and certainly worth a detour. Notice the bulbous capitals and the huge stones used in the wall-like piers to the E of the nave. The simple

Great Paxton

grandeur of it all will justify any time spent looking for the key. The chancel is 13th century with original piscina and double sedilia. The iron hinges and strap work on the S door are also the work of 13th century craftsmen.

GREAT SHELFORD *St. Mary* [E7]
A Norman church once stood here, but it was entirely rebuilt between 1396 and 1411 at the expense of Thomas Patesely, rector at St. Mary's and also Archdeacon of Ely. His brass lies in the chancel. A very fine two storey porch, and among the bosses in the roof is the pelican (symbol of piety) and a Green Man too. In 1798 part of the tower collapsed, together with the five bells; interesting inscriptions on the tower S wall date from the rebuilding. Delicate Parclose screen in N aisle. The rood screen has two more little Green Men facing the E window - was it supposed to face the other way? Splendid chancel roof with large bosses and much gilding, and the hammerbeams of the nave roof are supported by eight, now wingless, angels. Above the chancel arch, the painting of the Last Judgement or 'Doom', *c.*1400, is one of the finest in the country and probably dates from Patesely's building. A damned soul can be seen clutching at St. John's robe.

GREAT STAUGHTON *St. Andrew* [B6]
A very dignified church in a lovely setting, full of interest inside and out. Nothing remains of the church mentioned in the Domesday Survey but rebuilding began in the late 13th century; the aisles, porch and clerestory were added during the next 200 years. The pinnacled tower with two handsome quatrefoil friezes was added *c.*1470 and its buttresses obscure the aisles' W windows. Very unusually, the sanctus bell survives above the E wall of the nave. The N chapel, *c.*1455, contains many good monuments. On N chancel wall to the Dyers, one of whom was Lord Chief Justice; opposite is a memorial to the Conyers' infant son and daughter, watched over by cherubs. In the S aisle Valentine Wauton lies with his head on a red and gold pillow - he married Oliver Cromwell's sister, and was one of the regicides: his story is here for all to read. Also memorials and a window to members of the Duberly family, long associated with the village.

Great Shelford

Great Shelford: Screen and pulpit

GREAT STUKELEY *St. Bartholomew* [C5]
A lovely position with panoramic views of the surrounding countryside from the churchyard: it is said that seven spires can be seen from here on a clear day. Of the original Norman church only fragments remain, now set into the walls. The arcades are late 12th century or early 13th, the Transition period from Norman to Early English. Only one pier has typical Early English 'stiff-leafed' decoration, from the same period as the lancets in the

chancel. Don't miss the truly splendid corbels in the tower. Also notice the medieval mason's use of recycled materials: old coffin stones were reused here when building the clerestory. Stand in S aisle and look N; at the top right hand corner of the easternmost window. (Somewhat complicated to find but certainly unusual.)

GREAT WILBRAHAM *St. Nicholas* [F7]
Walk round the outside first to appreciate fully this large cruciform church, built mainly during the Early English period of 13th century. Three tall lancet windows and one small round-headed Norman window on the N wall. To the S, the chancel has one flat-headed Perpendicular window and remains of another lancet. There is a substantial 15th century tower, with battlements and pinnacles. The lovely flint porch has seats either side and the grand S doorway has good examples of dogtooth ornament. The font is earlier and would have stood in the Norman church; it also has ornate decorations, each side a 'sampler' of 12th century decoration. The 14th century chequerboard painting on the crossing arches is still bright enough to give us an idea of the strong colours in medieval churches.

GUILDEN MORDEN *St. Mary* [C8]
The elegant spire can be seen from afar. The exterior of this large church seems to be entirely in the 15th century Perpendicular style. Inside, however, the nave is in the Decorated style of the 13th century; part of the S arcade a century earlier. The beautiful rood screen is a rarity, a blending of two or three 14th century designs. Much of the paintwork may be original: St. Edmund is shown with the crown and arrows of his martyrdom; he was killed by the Danes in 870 for refusing to renounce his Christianity. The Bishop depicted is Erkenwald, brother of Etheldreda the foundress of Ely Cathedral. The inscription begins "In death's dark hour, Jesu have care of me...". The chancel is full of light from the Perpendicular windows and has a marvellous hammerbeam roof where four pairs of angels overlook the more earthly figures of the corbels below. The 12th century font has pretty scrolling decoration over the lip of the bowl.

Guilden Morden

GUYHIRN *The Puritan Chapel* [D2]
Over the doorway, inscribed in stone, is the date 1660, the year in which England reverted to a monarchy, following the death of Cromwell and the end of the Commonwealth. It is said to be a Puritan building but in fact may be a simple Anglican chapel. It is quite unspoiled and has happily escaped any over-enthusiastic restoration. No light or heat, a simple communion table and narrow uncomfortable pews to encourage concentration on lengthy sermons. Wooden hat pegs remain on the walls. It is now in the care of the Redundant Churches Fund and the Friends of Guyhirn Chapel of Ease.

GUYHIRN *St. Mary Magdalene* [D2]
Remains of a medieval church were discovered when foundations were dug in 1877. The "new" church was designed by Gilbert Scott, built in yellow brick in the Early English style. There is a pleasant timber porch and fine Victorian work throughout, with angels either side of the chancel arch. The church was consecrated in 1878. The lectern was carved by the wife of the original benefactor. There is a triple bell-turret and quite recently a memorial cross was erected in the churchyard.

HADDENHAM *Holy Trinity* [E5]
This fine medieval church was almost a ruin in the 19th century. A massive restoration took place about 1876 and the architect, R.R. Rowe, paid much attention to the original details. Walk round outside to the W wall of the tower: there is little room to admire the restored early 14th century work, with typical ballflower but also the dogtooth decoration which is more usually found in earlier 13th century work. St. Etheldreda's steward, Ovin, may have built a church in Haddenham in the 7th century. A replica of his memorial cross is here but you must go to Ely cathedral to see the original. It was found in the village in the 18th century, being used as a mounting block. The chancel floor has tiles depicting the ministry of Christ. 15th century brass to John Godfrey and his wife. A fine window engraved by David Peace, 1969.

HADDON *St. Mary* [B3]
A churchyard filled with headstones and flowers in almost equal profusion. Stand away from the W wall of the tower and you will see the faintest outline of the steep roof of the Norman church, which would have had a bellcote only. Inside, the elaborate chancel arch is of the early 1100s and one round-arched Norman window survives. Large lancet windows in the transepts and the arcades are all 13th century. 15th century wall painting above the chancel arch, and more paintings are hidden behind the white plaster walls.

HAIL WESTON *St. Nicholas* [B6]
A lovely church of cobbles, very different from its neighbours. It has a large tiled roof and a timber tower, covered in shingles, which is the only one in the county. Inside, look at the ancient timbers in the roof: roses are carved along the length of one. A lancet window in the chancel remains from the 13th century building. Only the lower half of the rood screen has survived, but the reredos was added as recently as 1963. Some medieval benches survive in the W end.

HAMERTON *All Saints* [B5]
A peaceful setting, with fields on two sides of the churchyard. A fine church, mostly Perpendicular, with battlements on both sides. The porch has 13th century windows which were perhaps reused as they appear to predate the porch itself. The S doorway and much of the interior date from the 1300s. Here is another church with two low-side windows, similar to those at Bury. The medieval roof has carved angels, apostles and central bosses. The large 15th century font stands on three steps. The hand-pumped organ is one of the treasures here. Monument in S aisle to poor Mawde Bedel, who bore 5 sons and 5 daughters before she died in 1597, aged 37.

HARDWICK *St. Mary* [D7]
The church is mainly 15th century and stands in a tree-lined churchyard. The tower is 14th century and an ogee arch on the W doorway is evidence that the building began at the beginning of the century while the Decorated style was in fashion. The chancel has few furnishings except a massive parish chest. No screen survives but the stair doors are unusually tall. Both chancel and nave have 15th century queen-post roofs. A memorial slab under the tower arch to Thomas Barron who died in 1762: his earlier namesake (d.1525), was a benefactor to the church at Comberton. Small patches of wall-paintings remain. A major restoration was carried out in 1987.

Harlton

HARLTON *Assumption of the Blessed Virgin Mary* [D7]
A common dedication in the Middle Ages but most survive today as St. Mary. A splendid interior and an important example of the transition between the Decorated and Perpendicular periods. Built mainly during the second half of the 14th and into the first part of the 15th century. The chancel is dominated by the superb E window with canopied niches on either side. The stone reredos is

a happy blend of original niches which now hold figures of the 12 apostles carved in 1934 by H.J. Ellison, son of a former rector here. A fine stone rood screen; few of these have survived. William Cole, in the 18th century, described the Fryer monument as "most beautiful and magnificent" and so it is to this day. Sir Henry Fryer died in 1631 fighting a duel in Calais, so he kneels with hand on sword, flanked by his father in doctor's robes and his mother; his stepmother lies below.

HARSTON *All Saints* [E7]
Delightful situation with the River Rhee bordering the western end of the churchyard. The sturdy battlements, porch and conical stair turret give All Saints an air of importance as you approach from the N; (the entrance is more usually to the S). If you walk around to the S here you will notice that expensive battlements were not wasted on the less public side. All Saints is largely the result of 15th century building. Notice the typical lozenge-shape piers; this N-S elongation is often found in arcades of the Perpendicular period. There is a simple rood screen and a Jacobean pulpit stands on a wine glass stem. Notice the small transept in the N aisle, and also the unusually narrow aisles; perhaps the result of 15th century rebuilding when the nave may have been widened at the expense of the aisles. The chancel andvestry were rebuilt in 1853. The present peal of six bells was hung in 1937.

HARTFORD *All Saints* [C5]
A delightful setting on the riverbank. A timber church in Hartford was referred to in the Domesday Survey. This was replaced by the Normans and the arcades and massive font survive from their building. The Norman style chancel arch is almost entirely the work of Victorian craftsmen during a restoration in 1861; unusually the arch is decorated on both sides. The tower was built during the 15th century but restoration was needed in the late 1800s and six bells were hung. The highly decorative pulpit is a lavish Victorian addition. In a corner of the churchyard is a triangular pillar, set up in 1735 when earlier monuments and headstones were moved to enable the burial ground to be reused.

HASLINGFIELD *All Saints* [E7]

A very striking 15th century tower with quatrefoil frieze at the base, embattled turrets and wooden spire. Both porches are 14th century, though the S porch was rebuilt in 1746 and the churchwardens' names can be seen on the roof. The interior is mainly Decorated but the dogtooth moulding is earlier. Stone faces everywhere and particularly fine 14th century roofs in both aisles, with delicate tracery. Interesting monuments in the chancel; that of Thomas Wenday, 1612, and his family was recently restored. It was returned to the church in 174 different pieces but now once again stands as a proud memorial to the physician to Elizabeth I. Works of art are still being created - look at the altar kneelers which are designed and worked by a parishioner in the very finest detail. Notice also the painted chancel roof, restored by a 19th century rector.

HATLEY St. GEORGE *St. George* [C7]

An unusual appearance since the chancel was pulled down in 1966. The tower is one of five in the area (the others are Barton, Caldecote, Coton and Knapwell) built during a forty year period about 1400, and possibly designed by the same master mason. The clear E window lights the delicately carved angels in the fine hammerbeam roof. Heraldic arms of the St. George family line the walls. Marble monument to Thomas Quintin, 1806, by E. Gaffin. A loving memorial to Elizabeth Quintin who died in 1801, 32 years before her grieving husband. Several brasses, including one of Baldwin St. George, 1425.

HAUXTON *St. Edmund* [E7]

As you approach the S doorway, notice the Mass dials on either side of the handsome Norman entrance. Once inside there is more evidence of the 12th century church, particularly the massive chancel arch.

Hauxton

47

Altar recesses on either side of the arch, *c.*1229. One of them holds the earliest surviving painting of St. Thomas Becket, dated about 1250, only 80 years after his martyrdom. The villagers must have taken trouble to hide it during the reign of Henry VIII, when an order was made in 1538 that all representations of Becket should be "put down or defaced".

HELPSTON *St. Botolph* [B2]

Saxon foundations of "long and short" work are reputed to support tower; total rebuilding of the tower *c.*1865 reused medieval material. Much of the early 13th century interior remains. The chancel with sedilia and piscina is somewhat later, about 1300; the low-side window retains its iron grating and perhaps the original hinges. One deep medieval squint remains. A modern version of the squint can be seen beside the organ: a television screen which gives a very clear picture of the high altar. What may be two stone bench ends remain on either side of the chancel, not unlike the arms of the stone seat in Farcet, but here are strange primitive heads and no simple star design. The mosaic tiles in the chancel floor may well have come from the Roman villa nearby. The interior is dominated by the E window of Christ in Majesty, by Francis W. Skeat (1983). Outside the S wall of the chancel is the tomb of John Clare, the "Peasant Poet". He was born in Helpston in 1793 and died in Northampton in 1864. His family are buried close by. There are many finely worked kneelers in the church and John Clare's house is shown on one of them.

HEMINGFORD ABBOTS *St. Margaret of Antioch* [C5]

The Abbots of Ramsey were Lords of the Manor here and the village is thus distinguished from the Hemingford which once belonged to the Grey family. There is a very fine steeple with battlements, turrets and gargoyles, which replaced an earlier central tower. The main body of the church is of brown cobbles except for the chancel, built rather surprisingly in yellow brick about 1800. The font, with its decoration of round Norman arches, survives from the 12th century building and the glass screen, engraved by David Peace, celebrates the church's millennium in 1974. The 15th century roof is full of angels, some clasping musical instruments, others with shields. The medieval St. Christopher barely survives, but the new St. Christopher, at the Heming Ford, was completed in 1978.

Hemingford Grey

HEMINGFORD GREY *St. James* [C5]
Beautifully situated on the banks of the Ouse. The rather curious design to the upper part of the tower is the result of a hurricane in 1741 which destroyed the spire. The base was levelled and eight large balls placed on the angles. The interior is spacious and light. The centre arch in the N arcade is practically all that remains of the original Norman building which also had a central tower, as did Hemingford Abbots. The chancel is later, mid 13th century and was lengthened when the central tower collapsed. Notice the elaborate Early English double piscina, of the same design as those at Jesus College, Histon, St. Ives and other local churches. Outside on the S buttresses are two medieval Scratch dials and a large painted 18th century sundial on the clerestory.

HEYDON *Holy Trinity* [E8]
Above the N doorway is the history of Holy Trinity - its founding, near-destruction and renewal. On the S side there is a massive door to the porch, which must have been the main entrance at one time, with an equally impressive lock. Notice also, beside the chancel arch, the worn steps of the clunch stairway which once led up to the rood loft. Much Victorian restoration in the chancel, and the highly coloured reredos would have been added at that time. After being hit by a bomb in the 2nd World War, the church was rebuilt in the 1950s, but this has not altered its ancient and welcoming feeling.

HILDERSHAM *Holy Trinity* [F8]
A lovely situation overlooking meadows leading down to the Granta. The 13th century tower has been considerably heightened in the past 100 years. The ladder is said to have been here since it was first constructed! The windows are filled with Victorian glass and at first make it difficult to appreciate the brightly coloured Victorian murals in the chancel. All was planned by two Goodwins - a father and son rectorship lasting 94 years. The work was carried out, about 1890, by Italian craftsmen working at Pampisford Hall. Four good brasses, all of the Paris family. The nave is surrounded by arms of Lords of the Manor. The Jesse window in N aisle is by Clayton and Bell, 1860.

HILTON *St. Mary Magdalene* [C6]
Lovely approach through tree-lined paths to this large and stately church. The tower is 14th century but the rest of the building is later. A once-beautiful niche of the Decorated period in the S aisle. Most of the glass is 19th century with two windows by Kempe. Outside on the green, look for the stone pillar marking the intricate grass maze that has been challenging visitors since it was first cut in 1660, the year of Charles II's restoration.

HINXTON *St. Mary and St. John* [E8]
The church dates back to 1150, but there may have been a church here as early as 1080. The lower part of the sturdy flint and rubble tower is Early English, but the upper stage and elegant

spire is a 15th century addition. The S door was added at this time; notice the corbels, their faces rather worn - perhaps the 19th century porch was built to protect them? Inside the Victorian pews sit rather primly, many with their original half doors. The stairway beside the Jacobean pulpit lead to what must have been a particularly large rood loft. John of Gaunt's steward, Sir Thomas Skelton (d.1416) is remembered on a fine brass in the Lady Chapel. The Norman N doorway, now blocked, is better seen from the outside.

HISTON St. Andrew [E6]

A cruciform church. Outlines of earlier steeper roofs can be seen on the central tower. Inside, the entrance to the rather dark nave gives little suggestion of the splendid Early English transepts beyond; they are without question the finest in the county. The elaborate double piscinas in both transepts are just like those in Jesus College, and copied in several churches in the county. Pevsner

Histon

suggests that the designer of the Early English work here must have come from the lodge working at St. Radegund's Nunnery and Jesus College in the latter part of the 13th century. Elegant blank arcading continues around the walls. The chancel too is Early English, but rather over-restored by Gilbert Scott. A tall niche in the S transept once held a statue of St. Catherine but only her wheel survives. A large angel stoops under an eagle's talons to provide an unusual lectern. Stained glass in S transept by Clayton & Bell, 1872.

HOLME St. Giles [B4]

Records tell of a church here in the 12th century but the present building, by Edward Browning of Stamford, dates only to 1862. A pleasant interior in the Decorated style. In the chancel, a fine gilded reredos and a particularly large and handsome chandelier. In the 19th century an enterprising rector established a floating church from here to serve those living along the canals in the more remote areas of his large parish.

HOLYWELL CUM NEEDINGWORTH St. John the Baptist [D5]

There has been a church here since 969 and a major rebuilding in the 13th century resulted in this fine building. The chancel is a good example of the Early English period with double lancet windows. The tower came much later, in 1547, constructed from stones retrieved from Ramsey Abbey after the Dissolution. In the nave are carved wooden figures which were originally with others in the roof. The medieval Rood doorway in the chancel arch now opens on to a 20th century screen. Try to be here for the colourful annual Well Dressing Ceremony, held towards the end of June. Interesting churchyard with good headstones, one particularly nice 18th century one with an angel holding crowns and swags of roses.

HORNINGSEA St. Peter [E6]

A massive restoration was undertaken last century by the energetic Fr. Chapman, parish priest for 54 years, and less than a decade ago more major repairs were needed. Records tell of a

Minster church here in 9th century but nothing can be seen of it now. Enter through the 14th century porch: the two huge lions as gargoyles are still startling, though sadly worn. As recently as 1985 there was no electricity here but now there is a choice of oil lamps, candles or electric light, and no longer any need to hand-pump the organ. Several interesting features: the fine pulpit with sounding board *c.*1600; a strange wide pillar attached to the remains of a wall in S aisle; early 13th century font. No rood loft remains; however, a piscina 12ft above the floor is evidence that the rood gallery must have been substantial enough for a small altar. Few rood lofts had such altars and piscinas, though another example can be found at Maxey.

Horseheath

Horseheath

HORSEHEATH *All Saints* [G8]

Spare some time for All Saints. The building is 14th century but there was a church here earlier still. The interior is beautifully light and airy, thanks to the large Perpendicular windows. The medieval rood screen has a little of the original paintwork and roses still decorate the doorway to the roodstairs. The church was probably complete by about 1524, when money was left to complete the battlements. William Dowsing no doubt destroyed much stained glass and statues when he visited here in 1643. Major rebuilding was necessary in the 18th century and again in 1891. Very fine monuments to the Alingtons in the chancel. Also a lovely brass of Sir William Audley, 1365, who is watched over by an angel very similar to the medieval angels which have survived in the E window above him.

HOUGHTON *St. Mary* [C5]

Elegant brown cobbled church standing beside the narrow road leading down to the water mill. Unusual tower with octagon, battlements and stone spire. The pinnacles were badly damaged during the hurricane of 1741 when the spire at Hemingford Grey was blown into the river. The chancel is 14th century Decorated, and here is another very early double piscina, perhaps about 1300 (similar to piscinas at Histon, Arrington and Hemingford Grey). The rare stone seat in the chancel resembles those at Stanground and Farcet but with a small star-like rosette on the armrest. Read the epitaph beside the porch; similar verse is found on blacksmiths' memorials in other parts of the country.

HUNTINGDON *All Saints* [C5]

The church dominates the small market place and much of the 14th century building remains. Opposite the church, the Cromwell Museum retains the Norman arches and blind arcading of about 1190, when it was part of the Hospital of St. John; later a Grammar school where Oliver Cromwell and Samuel Pepys were both students. Cromwell was baptized in All Saints, and Mary Queen of Scots' body rested here in October 1612 on the way to Westminster. The N arcade is Early English, and unusually the tower is in the NW corner. Much Victorian glass; the W window of the N aisle shows Cranmer, George Herbert, Newton, Queen Victoria, Prince Albert, Handel and the Duke of Wellington too. The W window is by Kempe (look for his wheatsheaf symbol); the E by his successor Tower (his symbol is easy to remember). Musical angels are everywhere: outside the N doorway, inside on the choir stalls, on the lovely organ and in the painted roof of nave and chancel.

HUNTINGDON *St. Mary* [C5]

A very grand late-Decorated tower, built between 1380-90; some rebuilding was necessary in the 17th century and the names and initials of donors can be seen on the upper stages, and the dates 1672 and 1677. The W doorway is quite elaborate, a frieze of grotesque little faces and niches on either side. At the top is a quatrefoil frieze, battlements and pinnacles. The interior is largely 13th century with one rather alarming 'leaning' pillar in the S arcade. The chancel was originally much larger as can be seen by the position of the priest's door which is now "too near" the E end. The High Altar and rails are by Comper, 1920. Beside the pulpit a stone recalls R. Cromwell, father of the Protector.

Huntingdon - St Mary

ICKLETON *St. Mary* [E8]

Make a detour if necessary to see this church. In 1979 an arsonist almost succeeded in destroying it and the tower's painted ceiling was ruined. However, some good came of it all because it was during the restoration that the extensive wall-paintings were discovered. They were painted between the 12th and 14th centuries and executed in true fresco, though most of the linework has gone and we are left with the block colour. They give a marvellous idea of the brightness and colour enjoyed by the medieval worshipper. But first look at the church itself. The magnificent arcades and small clerestory windows remain from

51

Ickleton

IMPINGTON *St. Andrew* [E6]

Remains of the earlier Norman church can still be found: a small carved head on the S wall of the chancel and chevron markings on several stones. The timber porch is medieval and once inside you will marvel at the wall-painting of St. Christopher. Close by, in a delicate niche surrounded by twenty tiny rose bosses, is a modern carving of the Crucifixion. Modern craftsmen also created the oak chest, decorated with simple oak leaves, which stands in the chancel. Brass of John Burgoyn and his family, 1504. Recent restoration is nicely recorded on rain pipes.

ISLEHAM *St. Andrew* [G5]

Dedicated in 1331 and a lovely example of the Decorated period. The 500 year old lych-gate is said by Claude Messent to be the oldest in East Anglia. A grand two-storey porch with blank arcading opens onto the very fine nave. Major rebuilding in the 15th century resulted in the elaborate decoration above the arcades, filled with shields of the Peyton family. The unusually high clerestory and angel roof were given by Chrystofer Peyton in 1495; the S transept has recently been restored by his descendants. Several superb brasses, but especially that of Thomas Peyton, 1484, and his two elegant wives. There are a

the Early Norman building *c*.1100. Notice the unusual cushion capitals which are typical of the period. The four end columns may have come from a Roman building and perhaps stood in the Saxon church here. The arcades are partly faced with Roman tiles and the salmon pink colour of the mortar was achieved by the use of crushed Roman brick. A large Roman villa and basilica once stood close by and the red tile on the outside W wall of the tower is more evidence of the reuse of Roman materials. Several medieval poppyheads survive on the benches, notably St. Michael weighing the souls, and an ox, the symbol of St. Luke. The wall-paintings certainly deserve lengthy appreciation and the excellent Guide Book describes them in detail. Outside, carved medieval coping stones have been incorporated into the churchyard wall.

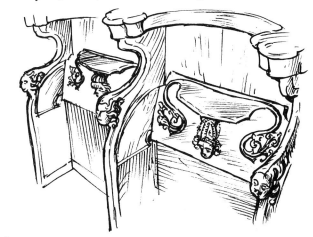

Isleham

52

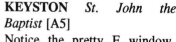

Isleham

large number of tombs, especially the two splendid six-poster
Renaissance memorials to Sir Robert and Sir John Peyton. In the
N transept read the memorial to Revd. Peachey Clerke, 1683. The
piscina here is angled into the wall. No chancel arch remains but a
little picture shows the rood gallery in place. Much to admire:
brasses, misericords of *c.*1450 and lovely carved bench ends with
poppyheads, shields and animals. Before you leave the village,
notice the secularised 11th century Norman Priory Church; a
lovely unspoiled example of the period with herringbone masonry
and typical small windows.

KENNETT *St. Nicholas* [G6]

Someone at the little Post Office knows the whereabouts of the
key. The church is hidden at the end of a long grassy lane.
Almost entirely an Early English building with large triple lancets
in chancel. A lovely little double piscina with slightly large
Victorian decoration. The tower and N arcade are Perpendicular
and the W window has attractive stained glass.

KEYSTON *St. John the Baptist* [A5]

Notice the pretty E window, trefoils in the circle beside the tulip-like tracery. Now walk around to the W face of the tower: the elaborate doorway and window are lovely examples of the early 14th century Decorated period; but the design of the broach spire is earlier, similar to other 13th century spires in the area. The reason is that, during a major rebuilding in 1882, the Early English style was preferred. Continue round to the N wall of the chancel, perhaps not so interesting but you can see the work of various masons over the centuries - old rooflines, a blocked doorway, an Early English lancet and a later Perpendicular window. Lively faces in stone and wood in the porch and nave roofs. The 13th century chancel has a fine piscina, sedilia and priest's door. In the N aisle lies a grim 15th century cadaver.

Keyston

53

Kimbolton

KIMBOLTON *St. Andrew* [A6]

This tower and broach spire was completed in the early 1300s; there is an unusual frieze of tiny heads at the top. Handsome S porch in Perpendicular style. Inside, the round piers of the S arcade may precede the alternating round and octagonal piers of the N arcade; a progression from the early to the late 13th century. There are marvellous figures in the aisle roofs and stone corbels in the chancel. The lovely medieval screens with painted panels are more often seen in Norfolk and Suffolk. There is much to see here: from Cromwellian bullet marks in the door to the delightful monument (1912) to Consuelo, Duchess of Manchester; Tiffany glass, 1902; a plaque commemorating the 379th Bomber Group of the US Air Force. The font may be Saxon or as late as the 12th century (Pevsner considered it to be "very uncouth").

KING'S RIPTON *St. Peter* [C5]

A simple early 14th century building. The tower was added a century later and has a very high interior arch. Later still the chancel was refaced and the porch added. The piscina comes from an earlier building and is probably about 1260. Large E window, reset by the Victorians. A memorial (1837) in the chancel, to a presumably harassed parson, remembers that "his lot, alas, was not so envious here."

KINGSTON *All Saints and St. Andrew* [D7]

The church was rebuilt following a disastrous fire in 1488. The outline of the earlier roof can still be seen on the E face of the tower. The rood screen and the extensive wall-paintings date from that "new" church. In the N aisle the painting of the Wheel shows the Seven Acts of Mercy with the "Laying out of the Dead" at the top; a particularly lively Devil watches from below. Victorian restoration usually raised chancel floors to enhance the importance of the altar; however, here you must step down into the chancel. Village lore says that it was the stabling of Cromwell's horses here that caused the floor to be so low. More paintings in the chancel and a monk can be seen between the S windows. The base of the font is delicately carved; perhaps it was once used as the bowl itself.

KIRTLING *All Saints* [G7]

Set quite apart from the village, on the Newmarket side of Kirtling Towers and not very easy to find, at the end of an unmarked lane. But a rewarding place to visit. A handsome Norman doorway, with a 12th century tympanum of Christ in Majesty; the iron strapwork may be almost as old. A small window to the W of the porch and, inside, the round arches of the S aisle also remain from that early church. The remainder is mostly Perpendicular although blocked 13th century lancets remain. The North chapel is crowded with elaborate monuments and tomb-chests of members of the large North family. In his will, dated 1521, Richard Pytchye left money to pay for major refurbishment. The bowl of the font rests on top of a capital. A brass, dated 1553, remembers Edward Myrfin who travelled far in

Kirtling

his short life, to Greece, Armenia and Syria, but returned home to die at the age of 27.

KNAPWELL *All Saints* [D6]
Another secluded church lying well hidden from the road. The neatness of the flint and rubble exterior is the result of the restoration in 1866 by William Fawcett of Cambridge. The tower is one of a group of five in the county (Barton, Caldecote, Coton and Hatley St. George) which are thought to be the work of the same master mason, built within a forty-year period *c.*1400. The building fell into a ruinous state in the 18th century and the chancel collapsed. It was shortened and rebuilt in 1753. The decay continued until the Revd. Henry Brown revived its fortunes when he was appointed curate in 1861. The interior is largely Victorian with decorative red and black brickwork and apsed chancel. Notice the primitive faces on the font and the round-arched decoration on the stem. The Revd. W. V. Awdry, of *Thomas the Tank Engine* fame, was rector here 1946-55.

LANDBEACH *All Saints* [E6]
Alarming gargoyles greet you outside but the nave roof holds welcoming angels. Recently fragments of Norman masonry have been discovered, showing that a 12th century stone church once stood here. Jack Ravensdale details the church's history in his book *The Domesday Inheritance* and tells of tithes from All Saints being made over to the Augustinian canons at Barnwell in 1119. There is much fine woodwork: the Rood Screen; the pulpit with painted panels which came from Jesus College in 1787; medieval

Landbeach

benches, one with the blacksmith's symbols; two 14th-century misericords in the choir stalls. The lovely roof may well have been built by Nicholas Toftys who lived in the village: it is known that he built the roof of St. Benet's in Cambridge in *c.*1450. A distinctly unusual angel carries the lectern on his back (perhaps 17th century Dutch craftsmanship). Traces of delicate vine-like painting remain behind the pulpit. The truly massive parish chest is early 14th century.

LANDWADE *St. Nicholas* [G6]
Delightful unspoilt country church, moated and surrounded by fields. Difficult to find but worth persevering (turn up Landwade Road then first right, it's hard to see as there is no welcoming spire). Built about 1445 for Sir Walter Cotton, and if you enjoy family histories you will enjoy reading the tablets and monuments recounting the lives and deaths of the Cotton family, Lords of the Manor here since the 15th century. One son died from a fall from his horse at Secunderabad, another in Colombo. In the N aisle you will find Sir John (d. 1593) and Dame Isabell and read of their 13 children; look at the details of the figures, her feet peeping out from beneath the many-layered petticoat. Admire also the delicate work of the faded 15th century Rood Screen and the medieval glass (*c.*1450) which has survived.

LEIGHTON BROMSWOLD *St. Mary* [B5]
The church is visible for miles around, standing as it does on the ridge that parallels the road between Huntingdon and Oundle. The massive square tower was rebuilt in *c.*1640, possibly designed by Inigo Jones. The church had been in a ruinous state when the poet

Leighton Bromswold

George Herbert (1593-1633) was appointed Prebend in 1626 and took on the task of rebuilding and furnishing it. Much of the interior dates to this period, including the roof which had collapsed. Herbert insisted on the identical pulpit and reader's desk, emphasizing the equal importance of preaching and prayer. The benches in the chancel are not choir stalls but seats for the celebration of communion, as the communion table then stood lengthwise in the centre of the chancel. The congregation went up into the chancel for the Holy Communion which followed Matins, for which they would have been in the nave. Light floods in through the large clear windows, though the dating of those in the chancel is difficult. Some are 15th century and others may be the result of the 17th century restoration, using an earlier style. The elaborate piscina remains from the Early English building, and is one of the best examples of this design. Similar piscinas are found elsewhere in the county, including Jesus College, Arrington, Burrough Green and Histon. After he died, George Herbert's poems were published by his friend Nicholas Ferrar, leader of the nearby community of Little Gidding.

LEVERINGTON *St. Leonard* [E1]

This handsome church dominates the surrounding Fenland. The lower part of the tower is Early English and the elegant spire rises above an embattled belfry and four octagonal turrets. The early 14th century porch is quite stunning, almost shrine-like and somewhat reminiscent of the Slipper Chapel near Walsingham. The chancel with triple sedilia is Early English, the S chapel a little later with the softer flowing lines of the Decorated period. Nave arcades and clerestory are Perpendicular. The late medieval colourful lectern is supported by six cheerful lions and the magnificent font has saints surrounding the bowl, angels below and more figures around the stem. The 15th century Jesse window in the N aisle was beautifully restored in 1900. Many memorials in the chapel, mostly to the Swaine family. Interesting headstones in the churchyard, one with a crowned head and weeping angels; another 1701-18 to Susanna Griplin and her children.

Leverington

LINTON *St. Mary the Virgin* [F8]

Tucked away from the busy main street and overlooked by lovely medieval buildings. The unusual round clerestory windows are the result of a late medieval heightening of an earlier Norman clerestory, some of which can still be seen. The church was largely rebuilt in the 14th century, though the four-arched S arcade remains as a good example of the Early English period. The N arcade is perhaps 100 years later, by which time the masons needed only a three-arched span. The tower was built about 1300. Splendid monument, signed by Wilton, to Elizabeth Bacon and her brother Peter Standly (1792). A ledger slab in the floor of the S chapel is badly defaced, dated perhaps 1538, and reads "Pray for the souls of ..." the remainder is illegible, doubtless erased during the period of the Commonwealth. Also read the small brasses of 20th century worshippers here.

LITLINGTON *St. Catherine* [D8]

Handsome long flint and rubble building with a low tower and flushwork decoration in the buttresses. The strongly carved Norman doorway in the chancel is blocked, and is almost all that remains of the 12th century church. A major rebuilding, including the clerestory, took place during the early 14th century, the Decorated period. The lovely font has elaborate but worn carving of angels and animals. Tall rood screen overlooked by extra windows either side of the chancel arch to throw more light on the rood itself. Fascinating graffiti in a S aisle window refer to Francis Drake's ambitious voyage in 1570; and in the N aisle near the organ is scratched in Latin "As on sea so on land" and signed by Robert Bownest 1594.

LITTLE ABINGTON *St. Mary* [F7]

Lovely situation looking across the fields to St. Mary's in Great Abington. Large stones in the E of the nave may well be reused from the Saxon church which once stood here. Both doorways have round Norman arches and the nave may be early 12th century, leading on to the 13th century building of the chancel. Major restoration by J. P. St. Aubyn in 1885 no doubt saved it all from total ruin. The chancel floor would have been raised at this time, which puts the Early English piscina, with its dogtooth decoration, in an awkwardly low position now. One window depicting the Adoration of the Magi is by Kempe (1901).

LITTLE CHISHILL *St. Nicholas* [E9]

Country churches are usually easy to find but you can easily drive past St. Nicholas as the tiled roof and low tower are almost hidden, tucked away in a very unspoiled part of the county. The S porch is decorated with shields and worn corbels; there is seating on either side and decorative strips of blank arcading beside the windows. A round-headed window remains from the Norman chancel but the piscina is from the 13th century building. Several memorials to members of the Crossman family; the reredos in memory of one brother who died in the Great War; the younger brother in World War II. The E window by Kempe and Tower (c.1916). Much of the remainder is in the Perpendicular style of the 15th century, including the rather nice N door with its worn quatrefoil decoration to the outside.

LITTLE EVERSDEN *St. Helen* [D7]

Simple country church with a lovely medieval timber porch. An earlier, steeper roofline can be seen on the E wall of the 15th century tower; walk round to the W wall of the tower and see the two quaint heads as corbels on the typical Perpendicular window. Inside, the walls are whitewashed, in stark contrast to the dark and stately choir stalls which came from Queens' College, Patron here since 1549. Dedications to St. Helen are unusual in the county; only Colne, Folksworth and Bourne are dedicated to the mother of the Emperor Constantine who was converted to Christianity at the same time as her son, in 312.

LITTLE GIDDING *St. John the Evangelist* [B4]

It is so unexpected compared with the large medieval churches with their grand spires in the neighbouring villages; the community at Little Gidding worships in what at first sight appears to be a rather plain diminutive

Little Gidding

Little Gransden

Little Gidding

brick building. Nicholas Ferrar installed the panelling in 1626, but it was extensively restored in 1714. The brass tablets behind the altar, the lectern and the unique brass font were all put here by Ferrar; the lid of the font is still twisted as a result of being thrown in the nearby pond during the raid of 1646. Nicholas Ferrar died in 1637 but the community continued until the death of his brother 20 years later. It was not until the late 1930s that interest was again shown in the importance of the Ferrar Community, and T. S. Eliot wrote "Little Gidding", the last of

LITTLE GRANSDEN *St. Peter and St. Paul* [C7]

Less imposing than its neighbour at Great Gransden, and the exterior is largely the result of extensive restorations by the Victorians. The tower is 15th century and much of the interior 13th century. The medieval screen has been restored and repainted, but one or two strange worn heads survive: a small face, perhaps a Green Man, and what looks like a benign hippopotamus; a sheaf of wheat and a bunch of grapes too, symbolizing the bread and wine. Some wall-paintings survive over the chancel arch. Beside the W door a graffito shows a man with a sword, but he is upside down - a deliberate mistake when reusing stone, or a medieval workman in a hurry?

LITTLE PAXTON *St. James* [B6]

The tympanum, over the S doorway, is Norman, and shows Christ the Good Shepherd with the lamb, to the left of the Cross, and to the right is what may be a wolf pursuing a lamb. Another reminder of the 12th century is the top of a round-headed window in the S wall of the chancel. In the nave, notice the tower buttresses are inside the church, so the tower was built before the nave itself. Beside a window in the chancel S wall, you can see some remarkable medieval graffiti - especially that of a horse which looks remarkably like a fine example of our Suffolk Punch horse today. Originally this church may have been a Chapel of Ease to the Minster church of Great Paxton so that the priests would then have had to ferry between the two.

LITTLEPORT *St. George* [F4]

Mainly 15th century with a fine tower which once had a passageway through its base, probably because it was built to the edge of the churchyard. A second nave and N aisle were added in 1857 and have

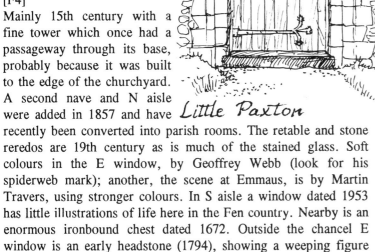

Little Paxton

recently been converted into parish rooms. The retable and stone reredos are 19th century as is much of the stained glass. Soft colours in the E window, by Geoffrey Webb (look for his spiderweb mark); another, the scene at Emmaus, is by Martin Travers, using stronger colours. In S aisle a window dated 1953 has little illustrations of life here in the Fen country. Nearby is an enormous ironbound chest dated 1672. Outside the chancel E window is an early headstone (1794), showing a weeping figure seated by a tree.

LITTLEPORT *St. Matthew* [F4]

A small Victorian church built in the fen in 1879, away from the town. The attractive and well proportioned Rood Screen has been moved to the W end of the nave where it now frames the font. The First World War memorial has many names on it from this small community. Small side chapels to N and S are cherished by the parishioners.

LITTLE SHELFORD *All Saints* [E7]

The Norman doorway and the N and S chancel walls remain from the 12th century building. However, a double-splayed window high up in the S wall of the chancel is pre-Conquest and the interlace pattern panels may be reused from a 10th century building. The church is filled with memorials to members of the de Freville family. Sir John (d. 1312) may have been responsible for the rebuilding and his effigy lies under an elaborate canopy in the chancel. Panelling (*c*.1450) is brightly painted with the de Freville arms. 17th century pulpit with sounding board; de Freville brasses in the chancel floor. The fine 15th century chantry chapel has two charming brasses, the couples holding hands and watched by three little dogs, symbols of loyalty. The two alabaster statues were found beneath the chancel floor in 1854.

LITTLE STUKELY *St. Martin* [C5]

The church was thoroughly restored during the 19th century by Robert Hutchinson, who went to great lengths to preserve parts of the 12th century building. Norman column-shafts are set into the S wall of the tower; more fragments are displayed inside the tower and on the S arch of the N chapel. Much carving of corbels survives and a large winged man is the first to catch the eye. On the SE pier notice the scene of an unfortunate individual being devoured by a monster, now used to support the hymn numbers. The *Old Hundredth* is written high in the S aisle and it looks as if the painter was working on an unsteady ladder and also without any guide lines to help him. A fine small brass of William Halls in clerical dress (1617).

LITTLE THETFORD *St. George* [F5]

Small, low and attractive with all the details of a 14th century church when seen from the outside. Attractive flat-headed Decorated windows in nave. The W end of the nave is now used regularly for various village groups. The medieval font on an octagonal stem still retains a little of its original colour and worn carved heads on the four panels.

LITTLE WILBRAHAM St. John [F7]

A large Saxon cemetery was found close by but if there was a Saxon church here, nothing remains of it now; the chancel and nave are both 13th century. A tiny Norman round-headed window survives in the S aisle looking out on to the huge base of the churchyard cross. Rather lovely 15th century S door with shields of the Burgh, Lisle(2) and Bourchier families. Major restoration was carried out about 1850 including renewal of the roofs; three of the original medieval figures have been retained. There is a large squint N of the chancel arch but it no longer has a view of the High Altar. In the chancel floor a fine brass of William Blakway (d.1521). The 14th century tower is certainly unusual with almost-flying buttresses supporting the arch; outside from the W notice its large base, with tapering later stages. Recent repair work has unveiled a large flintwork cross in the N outer wall of the N aisle. It resembles a Maltese Cross and the Revd. Brian Kerley suggests that, bearing in mind the dedication of the church, it may be connected with the Knights of St. John; or perhaps it may be a Bishop's dedication cross for the massive N aisle.

LODE St. James [F6]

A carefully tended churchyard and a path of yew trees leads to this attractive Victorian church designed by Rhode Hawkins. No tower, but a little bell-cote and a welcoming timber porch. The clock, by Dent of London, was installed when the church was completed in 1853. A beautiful Italian 18th century silk embroidered altar frontal. The Lady Chapel was built by the Fairhaven family in 1960-62 and the memorial here to Lord Fairhaven (1966) reads "lover of all things beautiful."

Lode

Lolworth

LOLWORTH All Saints [D6]

A fragment of dogtooth decoration is almost all that remains of the 13th century church. A small piece of frieze shows the ballflower ornament used during the Decorated period of the early 14th century; Pevsner compares this fragment with that seen at St. Mary's, Over. In 1393 Thomas of Walsingham recorded that "lightenings and thunders did much damage" and caused most of the village and the church to be burned; the field adjacent to the church is still known as Burnt Close. All Saints was rebuilt without aisles, though the blocked arcades can still be seen, and it was rededicated in 1406. The 14th century font has survived and beside it is the base of the medieval churchyard cross. The 16th century panel painting in the chancel, showing the Raising of Lazarus, was found in a ruined Belgian church during the Great War. The Rood and Stations of the Cross were given to All Saints by Revd. E. J. Dredge, rector here from 1926-31.

LONGSTANTON All Saints [D6]

Built largely in the Decorated style; the tracery in the windows of the S transept is a joyful example of the period. The ogee arch of the early 14th century is used over the triple sedilia in the chancel; but a small N window must have been in the earlier chancel. There were low-side windows to the N and S; both are blocked now but they retain the iron grating. In the N aisle is a handsomely carved 16th century family pew. The S transept contains many memorials to the Hatton family, Lords of the

Manor since the days of Elizabeth I. Sir Francis Drake's ship *The Golden Hind* was named in honour of the crest of his patron Sir Christopher Hatton. An elaborate monument to Sir Thomas Hatton (d. 1658) shows Sir Thomas and Lady Hatton; her hand is in a partly open purse, perhaps as a mark of her generous nature. Heraldic glass here also as Hatton memorials. Do make a point of looking at the Perpendicular font: its eight panels are carved as a sampler of the different styles of window tracery of the period. The tower and S porch are a little later, in the Perpendicular style.

LONGSTANTON St. Michael [D6]

Not far from the parish church of All Saints is this lovely little 13th century building. Carefully restored in 1884, it is a rare and unspoiled church built in 1286. It retains its thatched roof on nave and aisles and a simple interior, except for the elaborate double piscina, similar to those at Jesus College in Cambridge, Histon, Arrington and Caxton. The well under the large chestnut tree was used for baptisms for centuries; tradition has it that the sun must shine through the open cross in the brickwork before the mark could

Longstanton - St Michael

Longstanton - St Michael

be made on the baby's head. (It may have been restored incorrectly, as it doesn't seem possible the way it is now.) St. Michael's is now in the care of the Redundant Churches Fund.

LONGSTOWE St. Mary the Virgin [D7]

A very attractive church now; but like many others it fell into great disrepair and the medieval tower was used as a dovecote during the 18th century. It now stands comfortably beside the Victorian nave and chancel, rebuilt by William Fawcett of Cambridge in 1864. In the N chapel two remarkable monuments crowd into each other. Below lies Anthony Cage, with his 6 sons and 4 daughters. He was the builder of Longstowe Hall and died in 1603. The effigy beside him may be from another tomb, as the style of the lady does not correspond with that of the baronet. William Cole, the 18th century historian, saw the original Cage tomb when it was in the chancel. It was so enormous that the altar was off-centre and the Bishop unsuccessfully demanded its removal. Sir Anthony now gazes up at the remarkable allegorical memorial to Sir Ralph Bovey (d. 1679). A lovely sculpture by Hans Feibusch is a memorial to Temple Bevan (d. 1981); it shows St. Michael carrying the soul to heaven. A 14th century bell hangs in the tower.

LONGTHORPE (Peterborough) St. Botolph [B3]

Dedicated to the patron saint of wayfarers. This lovely, simple, 13th century church is one of the oldest buildings in Peterborough. Permission to rebuild was given in 1263-4 by the Abbot of Peterborough to Sir William de Thorpe and the tall narrow lancets are typical of the period. The interior is noteworthy for 20th century craftsmanship; much of the handsome woodwork was given as memorials during and after the Great War, including the reredos, the rood and the communion rail. A window in the N aisle commemorates a Parish warden who spent "40 happy years" here. Statues beside the altar are of St. Botolph, holding the church, and Peada, the founder of the Abbey at Peterborough in 654.

Madingley

MADINGLEY St. Mary Magdalene [D6]

The church stands at the entrance to Madingley Hall. The medieval village which once surrounded the church was moved out of sight of the Hall, as a result of extensive reshaping of the landscape in the 18th century. The 12th century bowl of the font may be the oldest visible remains of an earlier church; the base on which it stands is later. A lancet window remains from the Early English period; the chancel, nave and elegant tower arch are mainly 14th century Decorated. Bishop Alcock, Comptroller of the King's Works to Henry VIII, is remembered by his rebus here as a corbel. Lovely 17th century Communion Rail originally from Great St. Mary's in Cambridge. Sir John Cotton, Lord of the Manor, spent £300 rebuilding the chancel in 1770-80, shortening it by 12 feet and re-setting the E window. Interesting monuments: Jane Hinde (1692), reclining on a cushion; an anchor memorial to Sir Charles Cotton, Admiral of the White (d. 1812), by Flaxman; and Mrs. Jane Cotton, kneeling and partly hidden at the W of the N aisle (d. 1707). Edward VII stayed at the Hall during his student days and his Coat of Arms hangs inside the church.

MANEA St. Nicholas [E4]

Completely rebuilt in 1875, by Peter Ruddle of Peterborough. Some interesting interior brickwork, especially the false arcading in the nave. 19th century glass in the E window. Much evidence throughout of the Victorian stonemason: notice the font and lectern, also the angel corbels in the chancel. A 17th century altar remains from the earlier church.

Madingley

MARCH St. John the Evangelist Station Road [E3]

Designed by T. H. Wyatt in 1871 when the population of March was expanding with the building of the railway. Rock-faced exterior with bellcote and tiny spire. Victorian glass throughout.

MARCH St. Mary Westry [E3]

An attractive church designed by T. H. Wyatt in 1873. It serves a large rural area and stands surrounded by a large open churchyard on the Wisbech Road about a mile from the town. The bellcote is topped with a small tower. There is a prettily painted pulpit and, in the porch, a small stained glass window of "The Sower."

MARCH *St. Peter* High Street [E3]
A large rock-faced building on the High Street. Designed in 1880 by T. H. Wyatt, the architect for two other churches built in March during the previous decade. Here there is a large broach spire rising between four turrets. Wide arcades and all generally in the Early English style.

MARCH *St. Wendreda* High Street [E3]
Above all, allow yourself time here to admire the astonishing "angel roof" of *c*.1500, more correctly known as a double hammerbeam roof. If the light is bright enough, you can distinguish some of the figures: to the N Christ with hand raised in blessing, opposite St. Matthew holding a globe. The excellent guide booklet explains it all. The building is in the Decorated and Perpendicular styles, except for the chancel which was rebuilt in 1872. A passage through the base of the tower was necessary as it was built over a public right of way. A papal indulgence was granted in 1343 to those donating towards the cost of the "new building." The remains of St. Wendreda were returned here the same year. Towards the end of the 15th century another costly building period included the porch, chancel arch, clerestory with flint and flushwork, quatrefoil friezes and battlements, and of course the "angel roof." Happily the roof was spared by the commissioners of Edward VI, when they visited March in 1546. They may have considered the roof to be too recent to justify its destruction. It is recorded that they were well wined and dined when they visited the town. Good 16th century brasses also survive, possibly of important donors towards the rebuilding campaigns.

MARHOLM *St. Mary* [B2]
Lovely rural setting and sheltered by majestic cedars. The low tower is Norman, and arcades and chancel arch remain from a major rebuilding towards the end of the 13th century. Usually the tower dominates the outline of a church but here the tower is only

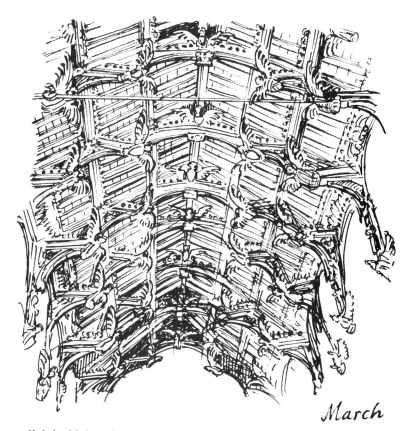

March

slightly higher than the chancel roof. This impressive chancel is the result of ambitious rebuilding by Sir William Fitzwilliam of Milton. He died in 1534 and expressed a wish that he should be buried in the chancel "lately edified" by him. Splendid monuments here to several generations of his family, many of which have been recently restored. Another Sir William died in Ireland in 1599 "worn out by the fatigues of the war and state there"; he lies now holding hands with his wife Anne. Read the inscription on Edward Hunter's memorial (d. 1646). There are many more. In the S aisle the fine effigy on the altar tomb is thought to be that of Sir John de Wittelbury, Lord of the Manor of Marholm at the end of the 14th century. Interesting heraldic glass of the Fitzwilliam family. An unusual font, quite plain except for two large roses.

MAXEY *St. Peter* [B2]

The church now stands isolated from the village. Originally it stood equidistant from the three parishes it served; two have long vanished and Maxey was the only one to flourish. The substantial Norman tower was probably built by the master mason responsible for that at nearby Castor. The 12th century church here was large; both aisles date from the Norman period and the small round windows of that clerestory can be seen from inside the nave. In the tower arch two Green Men, their faces surrounded by foliage, gaze down from the tower arch. The Lady Chapel (*c.*1367) is separated from the N aisle by an elegant archway; nearby a shelf is supported by a grinning, whistling face. A magnificent rood screen and loft once graced the chancel arch. It was donated by Margaret of Lancaster, the mother of Henry VII. The loft was large enough to hold an altar and the piscina can still be seen high on the S wall, a very rare feature. (Another can be seen at St. Peter, Horningsea, near Cambridge.)

MELBOURN *All Saints* [D8]

A handsome building of flint and rubble, with flushwork decoration around the base on the south and west walls only; an economy found necessary in many churches. Parts of the 13th century building remain, including the lancets in the chancel and the double piscina. A little later, about 1300, came the Decorated style typified by the ogee arch, found here above the priest's door in the chancel. About 1500 a major rebuilding took place when the style now known as Perpendicular came into fashion. Most of the windows, which make this interior so light, date from this time; the tower was also rebuilt and the decorative bases added. Two members of the Hitch family bequeathed money towards the cost of the elegant rood screen: Robert (d. 1504) and Thomas (d. 1508). The marvellous nave roof can also be dated by the rebus (a cockerel) of Bishop Alcock of Ely.

MELDRETH *Holy Trinity* [D8]

There is much to admire. The tower is late 12th century, the transitional period between the Norman and Early English. A walk round to the N reveals three elegant Decorated windows of

Meldreth

the early 14th century; also a small late 12th century doorway. Inside, remains of extensive wall-paintings can be seen. Medieval pulpit and rood screen. The earliest part is the chancel with 2 round headed Norman windows; the E window is a 19th century addition. The splendid "finger and barrel" organ was bought from Bassingbourn in 1866 for £100; it is thought to be the only working model in the county.

MEPAL *St. Mary* [E4]

A lovely little church surrounded by fields. Although it was heavily restored three times between 1849 and 1905, the lancet windows remain in the chancel and tower from the 13th century building. The simple Early English piscina is from the same period. There is a round-headed low side window in S chancel wall. Small 14th century niches under ogee arches on either side of the E window. A memorial tells of the interesting life of James Fortra, a refugee from Brabant, who became a courtier.

MILTON *All Saints* [E6]

Turn beside the Jolly Brewer and you will find the medieval church tucked away beside the new Children's Hospice. The Saxons built a timber church here but the oldest part of All Saints must be the solid Norman chancel arch. A major restoration was carried out in 1864 and the chancel was largely rebuilt, including the E window. The Communion Rail came from King's College Chapel in the 17th century. Interesting brass (1553) in the chancel to "the great Judge Coke". Also a fine marble monument to Mrs. Knight (d. 1800) by Flaxman. More recently a modern extension has been added to the north. Outside the chancel E wall a tablet placed by "his Master and Mistress for his faithful service" recalls Thomas Cannon who died in 1726.

MOLESWORTH *St. Peter* [A5]

The steep chancel roof dominates the flat aisleless nave, similar to that at nearby Brington. The chancel was rebuilt in 1884 and the blank arcading around the windows and the large chancel arch were put in, following the original Early English style. 16th century wall-paintings with St. Christopher on the N wall; opposite can just be seen St. Anthony and his pig. The E window was given by the widow of the Revd. Henry Penzer (d. 1929); he is shown kneeling in a purple cassock and in the lower windows are shown his churches at Molesworth and Keyston. A hundred or so yards away from St. Peter's churchyard, on private land, is a Pets' Cemetery where all manner of animals were buried in the early part of this century; little headstones remember "Dear Bobbie - Jim's Chum" (1909) and "Dear Jumbo" (1910).

MORBORNE *All Saints* [B3]

An early 17th century brick tower stands happily beside the medieval nave and chancel. The Norman chancel arch has been dated about 1140, followed by the N arcade about 1240 and the S arcade later still. Three small recesses above the 13th century double piscina were perhaps to hold the communion vessels. A wall-painting can just be seen in the N window in the chancel. The early 13th century effigy in the S aisle may be the Abbot responsible for bulding All Saints; his feet rest on two human heads. The square font now lying in the S aisle looks even earlier than the 12th century font now in use.

MURROW *Corpus Christi* [D2]

A simple red brick church built in 1857 in the Early English style. A brightly painted chancel, shining pews and the lovely little 19th century organ are all lovingly cared for. Very elegant 18th century font.

NEWBOROUGH *St. Bartholomew* [C2]

A small brick church built in the mid-19th century to serve the needs of the newly established community in the Fens. There are Commandment Boards beside the entrance to the chancel and a very attractive E window by A. K. Nicholson dated 1938.

NEWTON Nr. Cambridge *St. Margaret* [E8]

The earlier church was cruciform, i.e. with transepts north and south. A 13th century lancet, a piscina and a fragment of a wall-painting remain in the S transept. About 100 years later aisles were needed as the congregation grew, and the transept roofs were raised. The tower is late 14th century. Dowsing visited here in 1644 on his voyage of destruction. William Cole wrote in 1742 that the chancel was "new". Some very good monuments; many of them memorials to the Pemberton family. Christopher, an early war journalist, died at the Battle of Sedan in 1870. An unusual Art Nouveau memorial (1900). There is a massive 13th century font which Norman Scarfe compares to the very similar example at Shepreth. In the churchyard the Poynter mausoleum, 1922, is a memorial to the Walston family.

65 *Morborne*

NEWTON-IN-THE-ISLE
St. James [E1]

St. James is the patron saint of pilgrims, but the original dedication here was to St. Catherine. Stout round piers in the nave remain from the Norman building; the arcades were raised during the 1300s, perhaps at the same time as the tower was built. The clerestory and Perpendicular windows of the chancel are a century later. In 1879 a major restoration was necessary; a vestry was added and bells and belfry repaired. The rood screen is a late 19th century replacement; notice the unusual embattled walkway at the top of the medieval rood stairs. A large font with blank shields. Window in N aisle is signed by Easton, 1931, using his distinctive symbol. Interesting headstones in the churchyard.

Newton-in-the-Isle

NORTHBOROUGH *St. Andrew* [B2]

A very interesting place to visit, although it does give a first impression that the builders left abruptly without completing their task. The ambitious building, S of the chancel, of the elaborate Delamare chantry chapel, designed to be part of a greatly enlarged church, was never completed, and this small parish had not the means to do so. The exuberant craftsmanship in the lavish Decorated style is much in evidence; the ballflower frieze and flowing window tracery is all typical of the early 14th century

mason. Compare the quite plain W end of the church and belfry which remain from the much simpler 12th century building. Fragments of wall-paintings in nave and S aisle. Oliver Cromwell's widow, Elizabeth, is buried here.

OAKINGTON *St. Andrew* [E6]

Very attractive church with uniform Perpendicular windows on the N side; part of a much earlier window can be seen in W wall of S aisle. The tower was built about 1300, and on the E wall is the outline of a steeper nave roof. The lancets in the chancel, and both arcades, are part of the Early English building. The medieval screen no longer stands in the chancel arch but parts of the dado remain in the N aisle. Attractive 15th century niches either side of the Perpendicular window in N aisle. Much rebuilding was necessary during the 19th century. Close to the font is a simply carved stand for the Visitors' Book, given by members of 7 Squadron RAF, one of the valiant Pathfinder squadrons of World War II. Outside, parts of the older building have been reused in the S aisle. On a sundial are carved the words "God always cares."

OFFORD CLUNY *All Saints* [C6]

The Abbots of Cluny in Burgundy were Lords of the Manor here until the 15th century. The arcades and chancel arch remain from the Early English 13th century building. The Perpendicular embattled tower has three quatrefoil windows. A plain Early English doorway remains in the N wall. The short brick chancel was built in 1726; a faint outline of the earlier chancel roof can just be seen. Look up to admire the silent congregation here: six large figures in this medieval "angelic roof", their hair bound by cross and diadem. Pulpit is Elizabethan, the lectern Jacobean. The medieval font was found in pieces about 70 years ago; it now holds flowers in the churchyard.

OFFORD DARCY *St. Peter* [C6]

Standing all too close to the railway line and no longer in regular use; but it is worth finding the key to see the simple interior. Lovely ballflower frieze around the top of the S nave wall, typical of the Decorated period of the early 14th century. Inside, the N arcade is Norman; the chancel is later, i.e. Early English. Notice the unusual angle piscina in the S arcade. The rood screen is also of the Decorated period; few such early screens survive. Interesting early 15th century brasses and several monuments here. Notice the one to Richard Nailour (d.1616) surrounded here by his two wives, two sons and six daughters. The church is now in the care of the Redundant Churches Fund.

Old Hurst

OLD HURST *St. Peter* [D5]

A lovely little church and an unspoiled example of the Early English period, as you see from the lancet windows and the pointed arch of the S doorway. No tower, just a double bellcote. The font is of the same period. An unusual pillar piscina, in a corner of the chancel, is perhaps Norman and therefore earlier still. The stone altar slab has also survived. Outside, notice the weathered faces on corbels on S wall. A tablet on the E wall marks its rebuilding in 1903.

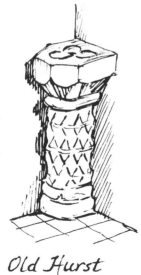

Old Hurst

OLD WESTON *St. Swithin* [A5]

Now almost isolated though until ⁀⁀⁀⁀s there were many houses around the church. The porc. _ ⁀ ⁀atching that of the tower; perhaps the porch which may _. room, was moved when the S aisle was added. The N ᴜᴏᴜ. be as early as 1200 and outside has rough nailhead decoration. The chancel is late 13th century and the finer nailhead decoration on some of the arcades indicates these were completed about the same time. In 1895 a series of wall-paintings were discovered, three layers deep in some places. The dedication is unique in Cambridgeshire although there are 58 other churches in the country dedicated to St. Swithin. His relics were translated into Winchester cathedral on July 15th 971, when miraculous cures occurred and heavy rains fell, as further testament to his powers. His shrine at Winchester became a famous pilgrimage centre until it was destroyed at the Reformation; it was restored in 1962.

ORTON LONGUEVILLE *Holy Trinity* [B3]

Lovely tracery on the E window greets the visitor. A handsome church with battlements on tower and chancel. The building dates largely from 1280-1300; the flowery hinges on the priest's door are thought to be *c.*1320. A quatrefoil window remains in the Decorated porch, restored in 1675. The chancel is mainly Decorated and the ogee form is used as well as some ballflower ornament. Strangely, a small blocked lancet frame is set low on the N wall; shallow niches with seats either side of the arch. Interesting monuments especially in N chapel; notice also the memorial in the S aisle to Sir Charles Cope (d.1781).

ORTON WATERVILLE *St. Mary* [B3]

Attractive 13th century stone porch and S doorway. Inside, notice the good example of 'stiff leaf' decoration on one of the capitals in the S arcade. Early 14th century, Decorated, windows in both aisles but the more simple lines of the chancel windows are 17th century. The Elizabethan pulpit is extravagantly carved and is said to have come from Great St. Mary's in Cambridge. The royal arms of the Stuarts are finely carved and hang over the tower

He had been tutor to the young Richard II, but was impeached and beheaded in 1388. The wonderful roof was reconstructed by an 18th century Rector here and the colours restored again in 1883. Late medieval choir stalls, many with misericords, may have come from Trinity College. Interesting memorials to several Masters. The clock (c.1616) is perhaps the oldest working public clock in the country; this also came from Trinity College in c.1740. In the S aisle is a mutilated but still exquisite statue of the crucifixion; carved in the early 14th century, it was hidden away to escape the excesses of the Reformation and only discovered in the 19th century. Unusual Royal Arms (1686) for King James II.

Orton Waterville

Orwell

doorway. 15th century pinnacles once topped the tower, but were taken down in 1929 and still lie forlornly on the grass.

ORWELL St. Andrew [D7]
This lovely church stands high above the road and holds much of interest. In the porch notice the fragment of Saxon carving with the interlace design; another carving dates from the 12th century. Most of the interior is 14th century. The magnificent chancel, in the early Perpendicular style, was built in 1398 by the Rector as a memorial to the Lord of the Manor.

Orwell

OVER *St. Mary* [D5]

Before you enter, walk around to the N and notice the quite grand aisle built in the early 14th century. The large Decorated windows are impressive, and the ballflower ornament completes the lavish appearance. On the W face of the tower is a deteriorating medieval carving of the Assumption of the Virgin Mary. To the S and see more ballflower decoration and the splendid porch still in the Decorated style. Wonderful gargoyles: an owl, and many grotesque faces; the lion and water-bearer to the E of the porch perhaps had some astrological significance. Inside there are carvings everywhere; little faces around all the capitals including one head with three faces, rather like a Toby Jug. The choir stalls on the S wall of the chancel came from Ramsey Abbey and the 3 rams' heads can be seen on one of the misericords. Fine Jacobean pulpit; tucked away underneath are heads representing the seven deadly sins. The medieval screen retains its coving on the chancel side only. Some very decorative wall-painting in the S aisle. The spire and tower were badly damaged in the 1987 hurricane.

Pampisford

PAMPISFORD *St. John* [E8]

Described by William Cole, the antiquary, in 1742, as "a very neat pile of building". The W wall of the tower shows the three stages of its building beginning in the early 14th century. The S doorway is much older and above it is a remarkable Norman tympanum, detailing, from right to left, the life of John the Baptist. It includes a font symbolizing the baptism; Salome; John,

winged as an angel; the severed head. The building is largely 13th century but much restoration was carried out in the 19th century, under the direction of Revd. Brocklebank. The vestry was added, nave roof renewed, a family pew added with curved front to allow access to the vestry. Windows are filled with Victorian glass, some by Kempe. A window in S aisle (1982) recalls Brytnoth, Earl of Northampton, a Saxon noble who led the English forces against the Danes and died in 990 at the Battle of Maldon. In 1978 a new peal of six bells was installed.

PAPWORTH EVERARD *St. Peter* [C6]

Rebuilt in the 19th century after it had fallen into a ruinous state. The tale of destruction was helped no doubt by a visit from the infamous William Dowsing, the zealous Parliamentary Visitor in East Anglia (*c.*1640). He carried out his instructions to destroy all adornment and icons with considerable success and here he recorded the defacing of wall-paintings and statues of the four evangelists. The tower was demolished later by the hurricane of 1741, which caused a huge amount of damage in the area. A new tower was not built until 1870. The church enjoys happier times now and all is lovingly cared for.

PAPWORTH St. AGNES *St. John the Baptist* [C6]

The church is covered with attractive chequerwork and is a fine example of a 19th century rebuilding. Only the tower arch remains from another major restoration in 1530, initiated by Anthony Mallory. Notice the lions' faces on the downpipes and guttering. Declared redundant in 1976 and only narrowly escaped demolition; but thanks to much determination by the villagers, it is in use once more and in the care of the Friends of Friendless Churches.

PARSON DROVE *Emmanuel* [D2]

Created out of the large Leverington parish in 1870, at the same time as Gorefield and Southea with Murrow. Built in 1872, by the Ecclesiastical Commissioners, in the Early English style. An apsed chancel. Red brickwork throughout with bands of black. No tower but a bellcote between nave and chancel.

Parson Drove

PARSON DROVE *St. John* [D2]
The Redundant Churches Fund has carefully restored this lovely building. The 15th century Perpendicular tower has a vaulted roof and impressive tower arch. The interior is light and spacious, thanks to all the plain glass and large clerestory windows. No chancel; it was washed away in a flood in 1613. A late 16th century communion table, with bulbous legs, stands under the 15th century window in the S aisle. The N aisle is older and has a curious shallow 13th century porch. The large font has elaborate decoration on bowl and stem.

PASTON *All Saints* [B2]
There is still a village-like feeling about the church despite its urban situation. The tower (*c*.1300) has a massive though narrow arch supported by two large crouching figures, perhaps monk and nun. The chantry chapel to the N of the chancel is earlier still. The low side window in the chancel is blocked now, but you can see where the hinges once hung and part of the catch remains. The medieval rood screen was removed during the last century and when it was replaced the lovely carvings at the top were mistakenly made to face away from the congregation. In the S aisle are fragments of sculpture with round Norman arches, possibly part of an elaborate reredos of an earlier church.

PEAKIRK *St. Pega* [B2]
Dedicated to Pega, a hermit at "Pega's kirk" or church, who died in 719. Pega's brother was St. Guthlac, one of England's most popular pre-Conquest hermit saints, who founded nearby Crowland Abbey in Lincolnshire. Much of St. Pega's church remains as it was in Norman times: the lovely S doorway, W wall and bellcote. The N arcade with round piers and arches is 12th century, the S arcade a century later. Important 14th century wall-paintings include the Quick and the Dead (with gruesome corpses and insects) and a Warning to Gossips (two women with a devil between them). The rare 14th century lectern stands on a slender eight-shafted stem with original stone base. The E window (1913) is by Kempe and recalls the 59 years of service by the rector here.

Peakirk

PETERBOROUGH *All Saints* Park Road [B3]
The foundation stone was laid on All Saints' Day, 1886. The architect was Temple Moore. Exactly one year later, the first

service of worship was held in this handsome, Decorated style, church. Canon Richard Ball, having been 17 years at St. Paul's in Peterborough, then came to All Saints and remained for 20 years. He and his family were responsible for much of the furnishings in the new church. The oak lectern was given in memory of Canon Ball and also designed by Temple Moore, as is much of the carving here. A panel with a 15th century Della Robbia design hangs near the font.

PETERBOROUGH *St. Barnabas* Taverners Road [B3]
Built in 1900, by W. Bryer. A large brick building with some chequerboard decoration. Built as a daughter church of St. Mark's necessitated by the expansion of this area of the city. The church is now shared with the New Testament Church of God and the two congregations join for several services throughout the year.

PETERBOROUGH *Christ the Carpenter* Central Avenue [B3]
An unusual dedication for an Anglican church. The exterior is typical of the 1950s (the building was consecrated in July, 1958). The interior has warmth and sparkle. It has been called the poor man's Coventry Cathedral because of its distinctive shape and the orientation of the windows. The stained glass was added in the 1970s. Over the entrance is etched glass representing the Carpenter's tools. The statue of the Resurrection is by Oliffe Richmond, a pupil of Henry Moore.

PETERBOROUGH *St. John the Baptist* Cathedral Square [B3]
This very fine Perpendicular church was dedicated in 1407. It replaced an earlier 11th century building and much of the material was reused. Lovely S porch with vaulted ceiling and carved bosses of the Trinity, Annunciation and Crucifixion. The interior is light and spacious with tall, slender 15th century arcades. The large octagonal font has typical Perpendicular quatrefoil panels. Several good monuments, one by John Flaxman, 1826. Much restoration took place in the 1880s and the E window was inserted then. N aisle window by Kempe. Most of the woodwork is 20th century, including the rood screen and group.

Peterborough
-St Jude

PETERBOROUGH *St. Jude* Atherstone Avenue [B3]
Consecrated in July 1984, St. Jude has a dignity and warmth not always found in contemporary churches. The remarkable belltower may have been inspired by continental examples and holds three bells and a bat box. In the early 1960s a RAF hut was the only place for worship here, and a modest church hall was

71

built in 1968. The church now standing here was designed by 'Jo' Robotham and built by local craftsmen. It has acquired many interesting treasures in its short existence: the statue of St. Peter from Vèzelay in Burgundy; the rood group from a church in Teddington; the terracotta Stations of the Cross are the work of the Community of Little Sisters of Jesus at Walsingham and the statue of St. Jude was sculpted by Mother Concordia of Minster Abbey in Kent; the doorway and font are from the now demolished church at Benwick. There is also a peaceful walled garden.

PETERBOROUGH *St. Mark* Lincoln Road [B3]
Designed in 1856 by E. Ellis, when the arrival of the railway stimulated major expansion in the area. In fact St. Mark's was the first new church in the city since St. John's was rebuilt over 400 years before. The Victorians chose to use an early Decorated style. The tower is sited on the NE corner where it can best be seen from the road. The balustrading under the clerestory is unusual and the dormer windows (definitely not early Decorated) were added in 1906.

PETERBOROUGH *St. Paul* Lincoln Road, New England [B3]
Designed in 1868 by James Teale using the Early English style. Built to serve the "new" Great Northern Railway settlement. Impressive interior with sturdy apsed chancel. Tall lancets of the central tower lighten the unpainted rood figures and screen. The Stations of the Cross are beautifully crafted. The font is certainly quite ancient, but not even the 92 year old parishioner knew from whence it came.

PIDLEY *All Saints* [D5]
Attractive setting at the N end of the village. Rebuilt by William Fawcett, the Cambridge architect, in 1864. A drawing of the earlier church can be seen in the tower. The lovely old-fashioned churchyard has large lilac trees and headstones leaning in every direction. A particularly lovely early 18th century headstone under the E window.

PONDERSBRIDGE *St. Thomas* [C3]
Spacious Victorian church which replaced an earlier chapel nearby. In the early 1970s it was in such poor repair that it was closed for three years; but the efforts of a very small but loyal congregation raised enough money for the necessary rebuilding to be carried out. The acoustics are particularly good and it is regularly used for concerts as well as a place of worship.

Prickwillow

PRICKWILLOW *St. Peter* [F4]
The exquisite white marble font, with cherubs, pearls and shells, is reason enough to come here. It was given to Ely Cathedral in 1697 and has been here on loan for a hundred years. The church was built by Richard Rowe, the Cambridge architect and engineer in 1868. Stained glass by Heaton. Rev. Kingdon was rector here for 30 years until the end of World War I. The unusual shingled spire is a local landmark.

Rampton

Rampton

Rampton

was rebuilt during the early 14th century, when the ogee arch of the Decorated period was extensively used, and is seen here in a recess in the N wall. Very unusually the low-side window still has the original grille and wooden shutters; it may be that these windows were used to provide fresh air for the smoke-filled interiors, and were not used for ringing the sanctus bell or hearing confessions. The pulpit is Elizabethan and in the 18th century the brick S porch was added and the Communion Rail acquired.

RAMPTON *All Saints* [E6]

There is a real feeling of peace and age about All Saints. The thatched roof is uncommon in Cambridgeshire and the medieval wall-paintings inside remind us of how colourful our churches once were. Most building periods are evident: fragments from Saxon coffin lids; a blocked Norman window and the jambs of the chancel arch are exceptionally wide apart for a 12th century village church; tower and S arcade Early English. The chancel

RAMSEY *St. Thomas of Canterbury* [C4]

Perhaps the finest Norman building in the county. Building began *c.*1190 and proceeded from E to W. It was intended as a hospital or guest house to the Abbey and was not dedicated as a church until *c.*1237. The sheer size of it all is awesome (*see picture over page*). Originally eight bays, now only seven: the W door has probably been reset. The font may well have been in this first church. The nave is magnificent with bold carving on the capitals. Both N and S aisles are much later and the windows are in the Perpendicular style of the 15th century. Many windows (*c.*1920) from the workshop of Morris & Co.; also some 16th century continental glass. The tower is a late 17th century addition, but there is evidence of the reuse of 13th century materials.

RAMSEY St. MARY *St. Mary* [C4]

A large Victorian church, built in 1858 at the expense of Miss Emma Fellowes. Corbels in the roof of kings and queens. Good font with scenes from the life of Christ, and large angels support the chancel arch.

REACH *Holy Trinity* [F6]

A chantry chapel dedicated to St. Etheldreda is recorded in Reach in 1378. Little is known of that building until 1768 when a drawing showed the chapel in ruins, parts of which can be seen beside the present church. Holy Trinity was built in 1861 to serve as church and school. This it did until 1909 when a separate school was built; at which time the priest-in-charge noted "Church clear of Day-school. Thank God!" The elegant 18th century font and the lectern came from the now disused church of St. Cyriac and St. Julitta at Swaffham Prior.

Ramsey ~ St Thomas

St Ives

ST. IVES *All Saints* [D]

A fine church. The graceful steeple has had an eventful existence and has been rebuilt on three occasions; the last time after a Royal Flying Corps plane flew into it in 1918. Walk round and admire the W door before entering by the N porch. The Early English piscina in the S aisle is similar to those in Jesus College, Histon and Hemingford Grey. The major part of the building was completed in the latter part of the 15th century and is a good example of the Perpendicular period. The elaborate screen, organ case and loft are particularly early examples of the work of Sir Ninian Comper, from 1893. Other windows are by Comper and Kempe. In the nave statues of saints, again by Comper (c.1897); they stand on 15th century corbels. The pulpit is Elizabethan. Before you leave St. Ives, visit the tiny chapel on the narrow medieval bridge. It was dedicated to St. Laurence and consecrated in 1426, and is one of only three such "Bridge Chapels" in the country.

ST. NEOTS *St. Mary* [B6]
A walk along the wide path surrounding the church enables you to appreciate that the church and its spectacular tower are of one uniform style: the Perpendicular period of the late 15th and early 16th centuries. The flat nave roof was a late medieval fashion. The tower, one of the very best in the county, was begun in the 1480s, and took 50 years to complete. Inside are wonderful roofs, screens, ornate carvings of all manner of angels and beasts, an elegant niche by the north door and fascinating monuments, especially the one to the Rowleys. Most of the benches are 19th century though there are several medieval ones with misericords. Much Victorian glass, especially by Clayton & Bell.

SAWSTON *St. Mary the Virgin* [E8]
Three pleasantly ugly gargoyles face the street and there are excellent corbels inside. The tall round arches W of the nave remain from the sizable Norman building. The chancel may be 13th century and there are several lancet windows. On the S side two large Perpendicular windows were inserted later but half of one lancet remains. Several good brasses, especially that of Robert Lockton and his wife (1500). Also interesting graffiti on a round pillar of N aisle: one of a man wearing a little pointed cap thought to be 12th century; one about 15 inches high of a man holding a sword, thought by T. C. Lethbridge to be connected with the hill figures he discovered on the nearby Gogmagog Hills.

SAWTRY *All Saints* [B4]
Three churches were recorded in Sawtry in the 11th century. Little remains of the ruined St. Andrew's to the East of the A1

and nothing survives of the church at Sawtry Judith. All Saints, designed by Sir Arthur Blomfield, was built in the 1880s and much material was used from the earlier church. Medieval tiles were retained as well as some of the stained glass. The superb brass of Sir William le Moyne and his wife (1404) brings many visitors here.

St Neots

75

Shepreth

SHEPRETH *All Saints* [D8]

A peaceful setting overlooking open countryside. A lovely interior: the small Norman chancel arch seems just the right scale. On either side of the arch are decorative altar recesses of the 13th century. The piscina is also 13th century but the chancel has been rebuilt on three occasions: in the 17th, 18th and 19th centuries. In 1743 the tower cracked, perhaps struck by lightning or as a result of damage from the hurricane two years previously. In 1774 the spire was dismantled and the tower lowered in 1853. The uniqueness of All Saints is perhaps not only in the bricks and mortar but in the atmosphere of it all.

SHUDY CAMPS *St. Mary* [G8]

Little remains of the 13th century church except the S door of the chancel. Most of what you see now is the result of a major rebuilding programme in the 15th century and later. The chancel arch is curiously off-centre due to the nave being enlarged to the south. The rood screen (*c.*1920) is a World War I memorial. The Dayrells were Lords of the Manor from 1702 and there are monuments to various members of the family. Over the W door of the tower are figures of the Virgin and Child and St. George.

SIX MILE BOTTOM *St. George* [F7]

The foundation stone was laid in April 1933 and this neat little church, built in flint and brick, was consecrated in December of the same year. The land was given for the church by the Delamere family, twenty years earlier. The curious twisted wooden pillars were given by Lady Delamere and may be of French origin; the lovely little font echoes the design of the canopy and pillars under which it stands.

SNAILWELL *St. Peter* [G6]

A Cambridgeshire round tower is a rare thing; the only other one is at Bartlow, though they are more plentiful elsewhere in East Anglia. The nave stands almost as tall as the 12th century tower. Inside, a picture shows a very different interior before the Victorian restoration, but the screens with gilded ornament remain from the medieval building. Early English lancets. The more elaborate design of the arch above the tomb-chest, perhaps earlier used as an

Snailwell

Snailwell

Easter Sepulchre, and the niches in the chancel are Decorated. Notice also the ornate cross set into the S arcade. Lovely hammerbeam roof with large figures of bishops on one side and saints on the other.

SOHAM *St. Andrew* [F5]
A church has been standing on this site since 650, when Felix of Burgundy built a monastery here. The 13th century church was cruciform with a central tower, and the great pillars that supported it remain. There is lavish decoration on the W side of the W arch. The superb W tower you see now was "new" in 1502 and is a very fine example of the Perpendicular period, possibly by a Suffolk architect. Notice the flushwork around the base, in particular the intricate designs on the N side, the same side as the elaborate N porch. It seems that the masons were quite unable to hold themselves back when decorating the top stages of the tower. Admire the angels in the hammerbeam roof and the lovely ogee-decorated piscina and sedilia in the 14th century chancel. Some medieval glass remains in the Lady Chapel; notice the little panes of birds in the N window. The medieval pews are now at the W end of the nave. Look closely at the fine 16th century screen in the N transept; it is the original rood screen and stood under the chancel arch until the mid-19th century restoration.

Soham

Several of the little faces are similar to those in the rood screen across the fen at Chippenham, but there is a curled up crocodile here too. A memorial in the N aisle to the railwaymen who saved this small town from a burning ammunition train in 1944; two were awarded the George Cross.

SOMERSHAM *St. John the Baptist* [D5]
The Bishops of Ely had a palace in Somersham for centuries and they may well have paid for this fine Early English church, mostly built between 1250 and 1300. In the chancel three slender lancets, the piscina and triple sedilia remain from that early building. The glass is a memorial to those who died during World War I. The medieval nave roof has splendid carved bosses, one of King Richard II and another of his wife, Anne of Bohemia; they must have been spectacular when brightly painted. There are remains of medieval wall decoration above the N door. Note too the strongly carved corbels: one man sits cross-legged, another strokes his beard. 16th century brass in chancel floor.

Southoe

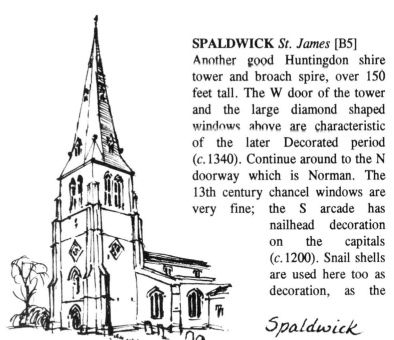

Spaldwick

SPALDWICK *St. James* [B5]
Another good Huntingdon shire tower and broach spire, over 150 feet tall. The W door of the tower and the large diamond shaped windows above are characteristic of the later Decorated period (*c.*1340). Continue around to the N doorway which is Norman. The 13th century chancel windows are very fine; the S arcade has nailhead decoration on the capitals (*c.*1200). Snail shells are used here too as decoration, as the symbol of St. James, patron saint of pilgrims. A simple glazed pitcher, used as a flower vase, is a loving memorial to a victim of the Korean war.

STANGROUND *St. John the Baptist* [C3]
A pleasant uncomplicated church built towards the end of the 13th century and consecrated in 1310. The tower has ballflower frieze decoration of the 14th century and a broach spire. Much of interest inside: nice corbels on

SOUTHOE *St. Leonard* [B6]
The more you look at the Norman S doorway the more amazing it becomes, resembling a sampler of the craftsman's skills; the 12th century mason demonstrating all the designs in his repertoire. He continued in less exuberant fashion on the interior of the doorway. The chancel arch is also Norman, but the lancet windows are later, Early English. Merton College has long been the Patron of St. Leonard's and the brickwork of the Elizabethan tower and clerestory gives the church a pleasantly formal air.

the piers - the one in the S aisle might be the work of an apprentice, and some of the menagerie on the capitals in the N aisle are rather tentative too. You can also find a splendid Green Man, and a corbel with a bald-headed man is said to represent the master mason. An unusual stone seat in the chancel, similar to those at Houghton and Farcet; also lovely double piscina and sedilia under one arch. In the tower some little brass hooks for the bell ropeswere given in 1930, one with the diesel symbol of the local engineering company. The stone cross in the churchyard is considered to be pre-Conquest.

STAPLEFORD *St. Andrew* [E7]

Lovely little flint church with chancel arch and some zigzag decoration remaining from the 12th century Norman building. The 13th century saw a rebuilding of the chancel and the Early English lancets were inserted. Modern craftsmen have left their mark here too. The glass in the E window of the S aisle is by Christopher Webb (1960); his symbol of St. Christopher can be seen. A statue of St. Andrew, by John Skelton (1963). In 1988 new tiles were laid around the font in a maze: start your journey from the centre of the W wall and when you reach the font, read the words (from T.S. Eliot's "Little Gidding") around the cover. The new organ, by William Johnson, was also dedicated in 1988. Fragments of a small Norman coffin and an earlier Saxon cross have survived from the earliest days of this lovely building.

STEEPLE GIDDING *St. Andrew* [B4]

A pleasant walk across the fields from Little Gidding brings you to this little church dating from the 12th century; the S doorway remains from that building. Walk around outside to the W and notice the unusually narrow tower and slender spire. Three curiosities here: the slit window in the W nave wall which may be a squint but seems too high; the strangely placed niche above the S belfry windows; and high on the buttress of the NE corner of the nave is a consecration cross, a rare survival of the original twelve. The Norman doorway, with round-headed outer arch and zigzag moulding, was moved during a 14th century rebuilding. Fine monument to Sir John Cotton (d.1752), recording his descent

Steeple Gidding

from David, King of Scotland. Interesting headstones in the churchyard. The building is now in the care of the Redundant Churches Fund.

STEEPLE MORDEN *St. Peter and St. Paul* [C8]

An unusual little flint church with much flushwork in the S buttresses. The original steeple collapsed in 1633 and the shingled one you see now was built in 1866. The rather casually blocked up windows of an earlier clerestory remain. Inside notice the quatrefoil design of the piers with drip moulding on the bases, late 13th and 14th centuries.

STETCHWORTH *St. Peter* [G7]

Down a quiet lane away from the village with a churchyard that is carpeted with snowdrops in early spring, an embattled tower, decorated with flushwork, bids you welcome. The strange round quatrefoil windows are from the 19th century restoration but the chancel still retains its Early English lancets. A lovely little niche in the S aisle has an angel which perhaps once supported a statue of St. Peter. A vast monument in N aisle to Henry Gorges, Superintendent of the Draining of the Great Level, dated 1674. A memorial nearby to Ashton Benyon who "drooped and died in manhood's early dawn." More cheerful reminders of earlier

Stilton

worshippers can be found in their "scratchings" or graffiti on the piers of the N aisle. A lady is shown (3rd pier from the W) wearing a very elaborate head-dress (c.1330), and an owl-like creature above her, perhaps as a somewhat mocking cartoon, with similar exaggerated attire. On the second pier, a man is shown in doublet, hose and pointed shoes as worn at the French court about the same time. Mrs. Pritchard, in her book *English Medieval Graffiti*, suggests that this may be connected with a visit of Queen Philippa, wife of Edward III, as it is known she stopped here on her journey to Norwich on several occasions.

STIBBINGTON *St. John the Baptist* [A3]
At first glance the church comes as a surprise with the three-gabled facade, a result of a major rebuilding in 1849, but the W door is Norman and inside much remains from the 12th century: the N arcade, chancel, chancel arch and octagonal font have stood here since then. Interesting memorial to Captain Wright, who fought at the Battle of Flamborough Head (1779). In the graveyard lies Canon Trollope, rector 1868-1907 and uncle of the novelist Anthony Trollope, a frequent visitor to the village.

STILTON *St. Mary* [B4]
Much restoration was carried out in the early part of the 19th century and the chancel was rebuilt. The nave and arcades are early 13th century; notice the different shapes of the piers: round on the S, and octagonal on the slightly earlier N arcade. The tower is later, the nailhead decoration on one of the capitals putting it at about 1300. Ornately carved lectern. Delightful brass to Yeoman Richard Curthoyse (1573) and his wife (1606). In the churchyard some very interesting tomb chests and headstones; French names must be of prisoners who were kept at Norman Cross during the Napoleonic wars.

STOW CUM QUY *St. Mary* [F6]
Little remains of the original small, aisleless church, but there is the outline of an earlier window in the S arcade near the chancel. The building was enlarged about 1340 and the window to the W of the N aisle has unique tracery of the Decorated period. The tower was added later that century. A short piece of dogtooth decoration from the earlier building is set into the SE pier, underneath two weary little heads. High in the nave you can just make out the remains of a medieval wall-painting of St.

Christopher. Fine brass to John Anstey (1465), still watched by his twelve sons and four daughters, although two are hidden by the pulpit steps. A memorial in the S aisle to Jeremy Collier, eminent church historian and scourge of the Restoration playwrights. Another tells of the two priests from Stow who later became Archbishops.

Stow Longa

STOW LONGA St. Botolph [B5]

St. Botolph was an Abbot of a Suffolk monastery (some insist it was in Lincolnshire); he died in 680. The tympanum with the wild-looking mermaid was carved over the priest's door in the 12th century and must remain from an earlier church. The oldest parts of the present building are the entrance doorway, which is Early Engl-ish, and the arcade. The tower is much later and can be dated, by the arms of a Bishop of Lincoln on the W wall, to 1496-1514. Two Mass dials are thought to be Saxon. There is much to admire, including the Early English font, in this interesting church tucked away at the end of the village.

Stow Longa

STRETHAM St. James [F5]

Saved from ruin in the last century when it was practically rebuilt; but much remains of the 14th century interior. Good 15th century Perpendicular rood screen, although the rood group is of the 20th century and was erected as a memorial to those who died in World War II. In the Lady Chapel read the poem by Innes Stitt who died aged 19 in the First World War. He was the rector's son, and his marble memorial is in the S wall of the chancel. Large brass to Joan Swan (d. 1497).

STUNTNEY Holy Cross [F5]

At first glance appears to be all Victorian but then you come to the S doorway: the rounded arch and zigzag decoration are all Norman. A vigorous rebuilding in the last century moved the Norman N doorway to its rather uneasy position in the S aisle; the original 12th century chancel arch was moved behind the organ at the same time. The font is also thought to date from the Norman church. Lovely stained glass window by John Hayward (1964), and nearby a 17th century alms box.

SUTTON Nr. Peterborough St. Michael [A3]

No tower, but the bellcote dates from the 13th century, as does the window below. Two rather startled faces greet you from high above the N doorway and inside more faces support the roof as corbels. But it is the rounded Norman chancel arch (c.1130) and the marvellous carving on the capitals which dominate the interior. Also note the two splendid Green Men on the capitals. In the S aisle lies a passive lion which may once have been part of a Norman doorway.

Sutton-in-the-Isle

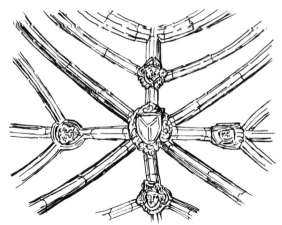

Sutton-in-the-Isle

SUTTON-IN-THE-ISLE *St. Andrew* [D5]
The distinctive "pepperpot" tower is visible for miles. In fact the octagon shape from Ely Cathedral is repeated twice in the tower. Notice that the S, or 'show' side, is the most elaborate, with battlements, gargoyles and of course the wonderful two-storey porch. The whole church was probably rebuilt between 1350 and 1370. It is a marvellous example of the progression of the late Decorated period into the Perpendicular. The elaborate tracery in the windows, extravagant carving and the ogee arch are evidence of the early 14th century Decorated style. The beautiful E window in the chancel is a very early attempt at the Perpendicular style (the modern stained glass is also impressive). The medieval work was done in three stages: nave, chancel, tower. The architect also worked on important mid-Norfolk churches at Attleborough and Hingham. Admire the vaulted roof in the tower, the two-light clerestory windows, the blank arcading around the windows. Faces grin down at you everywhere, gargoyles, grotesques and corbel heads. In the S aisle a lovely corner piscina with a sadly mutilated Madonna. Interesting churchyard; a headstone to John Youndes, who fought at Waterloo and died in 1878 at the age of 82.

SWAFFHAM BULBECK St. Mary [F6]

Three stages of building can be distinguished fairly easily as you walk up to the church. The tower with narrow lancet windows is Early English, 13th century; you can see the outline of an earlier steep roofline on its eastern wall. The chancel has more elaborate windows with flowing tracery of the Decorated period and the ogee arch of the same period is used for the sedilia and tomb recess; the aisles and clerestory were added in the 15th century and the windows take on the more severe lines of the Perpendicular period. But that all sounds rather serious: inside you will find much light-hearted medieval craftsmanship. The carving of the bench ends is spectacular! No plain poppyheads here, but camels, a whale, a merman and what looks to be a close cousin of a turkey; and all this carving was done in the 15th century. A 15th century Italian chest in the S aisle was once used as a travelling altar. Some interesting 18th century headstones in the churchyard and a 13th century coffin lid being used as a stile.

Swaffham Prior

SWAFFHAM PRIOR St. Mary. St. Cyriac & St. Julitta [F6]

A rather astonishing sight - these two large churches standing side by side high above the village street. St. Mary's is the parish church in use today. The tower was built between 1150 and 1180; so the octagon stage predates that at Ely Cathedral. Inside you will find a typical feature of the 15th century in the lozenge

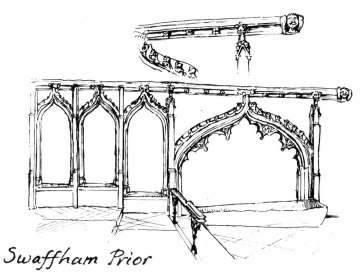

Swaffham Prior

shaped piers, elongated N to S. Some interesting portrait brasses, the oldest of John Tothyll (d. 1463). Windows in the S aisle came from St. Cyriac's. The unusual First World War memorial windows in the N aisle apparently caused "a considerable stir" when first seen. The church of St. Cyriac and his mother St. Julitta, built c.1250, was made redundant in 1972. Nothing remains of the 13th century building. The late 15th century tower is similar to that of St. Mary's - an octagon on a square base. The remainder results from rebuilding in 1809-11.

SWAVESEY St. Andrew [D6]

An impressive church in a large cedar-filled churchyard. There is some evidence of Saxon long-and-short work in the S chapel. Handsome early 14th century exterior. Inside there is a veritable forest of carved bench ends, almost all 19th century work. The smaller medieval benches are in the N aisle. Excellent misericords in the chancel include a falcon clutching a rabbit, two squirrels munching acorns and many others; all this watched over by medieval angels in the chancel roof. Contrast two very different styles of piscina and sedilia: Decorated, early 14th century with ogee arch, in the chancel; later, Perpendicular in the S chapel. Interesting Jesse Tree window in the Lady Chapel (1967), and a lovely monument by Edward Marshall (1631).

TADLOW *St. Giles* [C8]

Easy to miss this church, standing to the N of the main road, some way from the village. Mainly 13th century. The tower is later and money was left towards its building in 1472. All was restored in 1860 by William Butterfield. Inside the entrance doorway there is the almost obliterated indent of Margaret Broggrife (1493); a drawing in the tower shows her praying above her six children. William Dowsing came here in 1643 and recorded that he demolished two windows and a cross. A 17th century Archdeacon's Visitation recorded that during the sermon on Christmas Day a dog stole the consecrated bread from the Altar Table and consequently the priest did not feel he could offer Communion that day.

TEVERSHAM *All Saints* [E7]

Much remains of the Early English building. The tower is later in a typically East Anglian Perpendicular style. The capitals of the arcade have been dated c.1230. There is more bold design on the slender piers to the E. The clerestory, of the same period, once let the outside light shine through its strange oval eyes. The work of Victorian craftsmen must be admired in the chancel; their angels are linked with banners below the handsome roof. Lovely rood screen and Jacobean pulpit bought from St. Andrew's, Cherry Hinton in 1891. A tomb chest (1598) stands in the S aisle.

THORNEY *St. Mary and St. Botolph* [C2]

The first Minster was founded here in 662; it prospered, was sacked by the Danes and rebuilt in 972 as a Benedictine monastery sheltering the relics of three local saints. At the Dissolution by Henry VIII in 1530s this immense building was almost completely destroyed and its masonry and furnishings distributed throughout the county and beyond. What remains is the people's nave and the wonderful W front; the enormous 15th century window was replaced by a smaller one in 1638. The 15th century octagon turrets are linked by a series of statue-filled niches; the stairways remain from the Norman building. Walk around the outside to get an idea of the size of the arcades before the destruction took place. The interior is now tall and narrow, focusing on the rich

Thorney

colours of the E window which was installed in 1840, a copy of one in Canterbury Cathedral. The transepts were also added at this time.

THORNHAUGH *St. Andrew* [A2]

Stands high above the road in a lovely churchyard filled with early headstones carved with skulls, cherubs and urns; all now softened with lichen and moss. The low tower was built in 1889 and replaced an earlier tower which fell in the 15th century. Bright medieval decoration can still be seen on the arcades. The Early English chancel retains its lancet windows and dogtooth ornament around the piscina. In the Chantry Chapel is the splendid Russell Monument: the tomb of Sir William Russell, created the first Baron Russell of Thornhaugh in 1603. He died in 1613 in Hertfordshire and was buried here. His effigy is surrounded by his three brothers and three sisters kneeling in prayer. In 1694 this Sir William's grandson was created 1st Duke of Bedford.

THRIPLOW *St. George or All Saints* [E8]

Attractive cruciform church, easily seen long before you reach the village. William Cole visited here in 1742 and recorded several medieval stained glass windows, some "very well done", and painted panels on the screen. Later restorations have removed much of it, and only fragments of the once lovely screen, (*c.*1350) remain. It was a particularly good example of its kind and in 1518 the church of Great St. Mary in Cambridge ordered their new screen to be similar to that at Thriplow. In the chancel is a double piscina, with central flutings or grooves. The delicately painted roofs are Victorian, perhaps from the time of Gilbert Scott's restoration in 1877. Stand beneath the crossing and see the medieval faces at each corner.

TILBROOK *All Saints* [A6]

A lovely place with much of interest. The 13th century building may have had a central tower but this

Tilbrook

Tilbrook

collapsed, to be replaced by the fine Decorated W tower with a broach spire and splendid gargoyles too. Above the entrance to the porch there is a figure said to be St. Anthony and a pig. The round piers in the N arcade are Norman, late 12th century. Wonderful rood screen with some original paintwork, hinting at the brilliance and colour once enjoyed in the earlier churches. Sections of the screen are now in the Victoria and Albert Museum. A very deep opening in the N wall of the chancel may have been the chrismatory to hold the requisites for baptism.

TOFT *St. Andrew* [D7]

Lovely churchyard, filled with snowdrops in February. The neat, brown cobble church has been subject to so much restoration and rebuilding that little remains of the medieval building but there is a lovely atmosphere here. In 1647 William Dowsing and his men visited during their tour of destruction and much damage was done. In the chancel mutilated figures remain from what must have been a beautiful 15th century alabaster altar.

TOSELAND *St. Michael* [C6]

The rounded arches of the S doorway, a window and the chancel arch remain from the Norman church. The list of rectors goes back to 1232 when the patron was the Bishop of Lincoln. Like so many others, the building fell into great disrepair in the last century. In 1873 Arthur Blomfield was responsible for the sympathetic restoration. A Sarsen stone, a pre-Christian megalith, stands near the entrance and once marked the meeting place of the Toseland Hundred.

TRUMPINGTON *St. Mary and St.Michael* [E7]

A parish church built almost on cathedral scale in the early part of the 14th century. A chapel once stood against the N wall of the chancel and its piscina remains on the outside wall. The chancel was built about 1280 and the narrow late Early English windows remain. The intricate E window is in the Decorated style of the early 14th century and fragments of medieval glass have

Trumpington

been assembled in a "grande salade." All is light and space. The font has quaint early 14th century faces on the bases, but stem and bowl are later and much recut. More medieval faces now support a 17th century tablet in the S transept, the woman's headdress indicating a date of *c.*1370. The pulpit, originally a "three-decker", was bought from Emmanuel College in 1677.

Trumpington

However, it is surely the large monument and important brass of Sir Robert de Trumpington (d.1289) that bring most visitors here; it is the second largest brass in England. Sir Roger lies under an elaborate ogee canopy, also contemporary with the rest of the building. The trumpet on his shield is repeated in medieval glass in the N aisle. Much restoration was carried out by William Butterfield between 1858 and 1867, including resurfacing the exterior with Bath stone.

Tydd St Giles

TYDD St. GILES *St. Giles* [E1]

An unusual and interesting church. The Early English tower stands alone, not unusual in the fenland where the greater weight of the tower makes them settle too deep and they can begin to lean crazily, as at Surfleet in Lincolnshire. Enter through the W door and notice above it the "Walsingham Window", said to have been designed by Alan of Walsingham, sacrist at Ely Cathedral and responsible for building the Octagon there after the collapse of the central tower in 1322. The interior of St. Giles is light, with stout 12th century arcades and different decoration for almost each capital. There really is no chancel. Sir Gilbert Scott, while his brother was rector here, took down the poorly built 18th century chancel which replaced the medieval chancel which had been destroyed during a gale in 1741. The font is lovely: the carving includes a grotesque, with mouth agape, said to represent Gluttony; an angel; a small Green Man with large foliage; the three crowns of Ely; St. George's shield and the symbols of the Passion.

UFFORD *St. Andrew* [A2]

Large double E windows dominate the approach, the result of the 19th century restoration. A walk around the outside reveals the remains of a 13th century piscina and little shelf from before the demolition of the N chapel; there is a low side window and niche here too. The handsome 15th century tower is of three stages, divided by a string-course and little battlements. The battlements are repeated again on the capitals of the tower arch inside. The high grand chancel arch of *c.*1300, is flanked by doorways which once opened onto the rood loft and up into the roof. The elegant arcades are a little later with

Ufford

small corbels as heads; there is a crowned lady with veil or a gossip's scold, next to a man who appears to be doing all the talking. Lovely details on the well-carved bench ends, some of them medieval. Notice the monument to the remarkable Lady Carre (d.1621), who was 25 years Gentlewoman to the Privy Chamber of Elizabeth I, and then served King James I's Queen Anne for a further 14 years.

UPTON Nr. Alconbury *St. Margaret* [B5]

An attractive, compact church. Weather-beaten gargoyles peer down from the strangely short broach spire. The S doorway and elaborate font are both Norman. The chancel is Early English with familiar Y-tracery windows. A major restoration was carried out in 1870 by Gilbert Scott and the N aisle added at this time. Outside, the little faces on the hood-moulds are 19th century too. Several 18th century monuments in the tower. A medical student, aged 25, died in 1802 in the "flower of his youth", and his epitaph ends "Go thy way Traveller, And convinced of the instability of Human Life, Meditate upon Eternity." Remains of the churchyard cross stand near the S porch.

UPTON Nr. Peterborough *St. John the Baptist* [B2]

An earlier dedication was to St. Helen, mother of the Emperor Constantine. This is a tranquil place, set in fields north of theA47. Notice particularly the straight-headed windows of the early 17th century rebuilding. The unspoilt interior is dominated by the Norman chancel arch (*c.*1120) and then by the massive altar tomb of Sir William Dove (d.1627). He lies beside his two wives; Dame Frances' hand is closed, but Dame Dorothy's lies open as a symbol of her known generosity and kindness to the poor. There is a very fine Jacobean pulpit and Communion Rails. In a field to the south stands a large 17th century sundial.

UPWOOD *St. Peter* [C4]

Much rebuilding has been necessary over the past hundred years. However, many features of the 12th century Norman church remain: round headed windows; round piers; a rounded chancel arch. The S arcade is later. Some medieval glass fragments also survive. Above the S door read the will of the generous Mrs. West. A "plague pit" is said to lie west of the churchyard. William Cromwell, cousin of Oliver, is said to have brought the plague to the area when he had a piece of cloth sent to him from London in 1666.

WANSFORD *St. Mary* [A3]

Wansford

This attractive stone village straddled the Great North Road for centuries and the stone bridge over the Nene has seven arches surviving dated 1577, others from 17th and 18th centuries. The handsome church stands surrounded by lovely weathered headstones; one dated 1672 stands at a corner near the chancel E wall. The tower is 13th century but a triangular topped Saxon window survives in the W wall. The S doorway is c.1200 and the font is even earlier, about 1120. It is quite spectacular, with figures carved under the round Norman arches. It was found nearby at Sibberton Lodge being used as a cattle trough, on the site of a village abandoned after the plague. Rebuilding of the nave and porch was carried out in 1663 and the chancel was rebuilt in 1902.

WARBOYS *St. Mary Magdalene* [D4]

The handsome tower and broach spire, one of the very finest examples in the area, were completed by the end of the 13th century; the details of the bell openings and lucarnes are especially fine. Marvellous Norman chancel arch with bold zigzag decoration. The arcades are typical 13th century, with alternate round and octagonal piers in the N, S all rounded. The chancel was rebuilt in 1832, rather surprisingly in yellow brick. The

priest's door has what may be a rare 12th century door knocker of a lion's head and two dragons entwined in battle. Two good 18th century monuments by Bacon; one for Elizabeth Strode (1790), whose "anxious Endeavours to relieve Distress were not less judicious than liberal."

WARESLEY *St. James* [C7]

In 1724 the church was destroyed by "a tempest" and rebuilt four years later. It was again in poor repair in the last century and was replaced by the building you see now, designed by William Butterfield in 1856. The chancel is a fine example of his work. Contemporary stained glass; strong colours of the N aisle window in the Burne-Jones style. The church's battle with the elements continued when in January 1988 the entire spire was torn off during a violent storm. Less than six months later, as a result of heroic fundraising and labour, a Thanksgiving service was held to celebrate the rebuilding of Butterfield's elegant oak shingle spire. The Duncombe Mausoleum connects with the church to the south.

WATERBEACH St. John [E6]

Completed in the 13th century, and pillars in the N arcade have the stiff, upright leaves of c.1200. The S aisle and clerestory were 15th century additions. Early in the 19th century the spire collapsed for a second time and prolonged restoration took place. The chancel was completely rebuilt and the colour and decoration is typical of this Victorian period. The pulpit (1883) has elaborate mosaic panels. The Communion Table is by Rattee & Kett (1879), using a slab of Purbeck marble thought to be 11th century and found beneath a Tudor floor. The Revd. William Cole was Curate-in-Charge here from 1767 to 1770. He travelled tirelessly throughout the county and beyond, documenting and drawing the parish churches. Walk about 100 yards to the east to the Garden of Remembrance, there you will find the original 14th century font.

WATER NEWTON *St. Remigius* [B3]

The most picturesque way to approach this church would surely be by boat along the Nene. Ermine Street, the Roman road from

Water Newton

London to Lincoln, crossed the river not far from here. On the W face of the tower a niche holds a small kneeling figure, and the inscription below asks you to pray for the soul of Thomas Purdew. Early English tower and much of the interior as well. The list of rectors goes back to 1245. Restoration was carried out in the 17th century and most of the windows are from this period. Notice the carvings on the choir stalls, some with very aquiline profiles. There is a the stone effigy (c.1300) in the S aisle. The unusual dedication must refer to St. Remigius, the 6th century Bishop of Rheims who baptized Clovis, King of the Franks and all his followers. In 1975 a hoard of late Roman Christian silver, probably 4th century, was found at Water Newton. So a Christian community existed here before that. Simon Cotton suggests that a sub-Roman Christian community may have persisted here; or perhaps Remigius was an import of the Saxon period, or the dedication of an earlier church may have been changed to Remigius by 11th or 12th century Normans. To the S of the chancel lies the tomb of Admiral Edward Edwards (d. 1813); as Captain Edwards, he went out to capture the mutineers of the Bounty. He was shipwrecked and made a passage of 1000 miles to safety in an open boat.

WENTWORTH *St. Peter* [D5]
Two Norman doorways, the S being more elaborate than the N. In the chancel is an important early Norman sculpture of St. Peter, the figure very fresh looking. The font is 13th century with stiff-leafed decoration below the bowl. The Revd. Oswald Henry Moseley made the simple cross above the screen in 1890 and was buried in the churchyard in 1899. In the tower a small tablet (1809) remembers Peppercorn Sanxter but does not tell us why.

WERRINGTON *St. John the Baptist* [B2]
A largely Norman building with a little twin bell-cote between nave and chancel roofs, zigzag decoration on the S doorway and nailhead ornament on some of the capitals. The chancel is Decorated and has a lovely E window; but it was all much restored in 1901-2. The porch, with stone seats, is also Decorated. A tablet on W end of the nave marks a restoration of 1680 and then again in 1884.

WESTLEY WATERLESS *St. Mary the Less* [G7]
This was the third church with a round tower in Cambridgeshire until it fell in 1855 (two others remain at Bartlow and Snailwell).

Wentworth

The church is justly famous for the exquisite brasses of Sir John Creke and his wife (1325) with "engraving of the highest distinction" (Alec Clifton-Taylor). Most of the building is in the Early English style of the 13th century. Unusual graffiti in the upper S window of the S aisle record, in early Arabic, the produce from various vines growing around the church. The church leaflet tells more. The cheerful painted organ was given "in token of loving friendship between the American and English people in 1968."

89

Weston Colville

WESTON COLVILLE *St. Mary* [G7]

A neat looking church with grey brick framing the flint work, and a tidy outline to tower and chancel; the result of rebuilding about 1825. The porch is late medieval and some evidence of the 14th century interior remains, notably the chancel arch. Two good brasses: Abraham Gates with his wife (1636); also Robert Leverer (1427), who stands in a field of cheerful flowers, with his wife beside him, and their son, a priest. All watched over by angels high in the E windows, each with a musical instrument.

WEST WICKHAM *St. Mary* [G8]

Set in a picturesque churchyard almost on the Suffolk border. The interior is painted a cheerful pink throughout, which particularly enhances the early 14th century chancel and the very tall chancel arch. Above the arch hangs the Royal Coat of Arms of Queen Anne dated 1708. Notice the medieval timber roof, and the delicate carving on one massive beam. Several medieval benches survive and a sturdy parish chest.

WEST WRATTING *St. Andrew* [G7]

The 14th century building was 'modernized' in 1746 and then again in 1896. The elegant iron screen is a more recent addition of 1922; beside it notice the doorway to the original rood loft which must have been quite massive and well forward of the chancel arch. Lovely high timber roof with elegant bosses. The 18th century font, used as a flower holder, now stands upside down near the north wall of the chancel. Beside it read the complicated memorial to Annie Walker (d. 1610) "both she and her mother saw her daughter's daughter's daughter ..." Stained glass (1910) by Morris & Co.

Whaddon

WHADDON *St. Mary* [D8]

Handsome flint and pebble church with battlements all around. The chancel dates to about 1300; notice the dogtooth moulding on the E side of the arch. Large two-tiered aisle windows lighten the nave, and the tall arcades are *c.*1375. The E window is later and restored. Note the altar tomb for John d'Eschallers (1469). The family were Lords of the Manor for 400 years and their arms are also on the font. Read of the history of the Hatchment of the 3rd Earl Hardwicke. The organ with its mighty angel with gilded trumpet was installed in 1832.

90

Whittlesey-St. Mary

WHITTLESEY *St. Andrew* [C3]

Not as grand as St. Mary's on the other side of town, but this is a fine church surrounded on three sides by a park-like churchyard. Tower and porch are both early 16th century; notice the Tudor rose on the W door. There are chapels to N and S of the chancel, all with original roofs. Look at the piers in the nave, lozenge-shaped N to S, typical of the Perpendicular building of the 15th century. Lovely tracery in the chancel E window. A tall wooden angel holds the lectern and there is good 20th century carving on the pulpit. Interesting memorial (1703) to the rector of both Whittlesey churches.

WHITTLESEY *St. Mary* [C3]

One of the very best Perpendicular spires in the country dates from *c.*1450, probably based on Northamptonshire designs. Stand back in the great churchyard and admire the large window an elaborate doorway. No expense was spared with the building of the tower and the crocketed spire, the four flying buttresses and elegant corner pinnacles. Inside, the N arcade and chancel arch are 13th century, the Early English period. The S aisle and chapel are in the more flamboyant Decorated style. The raised part of the chapel once had an altar but only the piscina remains; the crypt below was the charnel-house. In the chancel read the memorial to Elizabeth Kentish. Underneath is an empty monument to the Hake family (1590), supporters of the Royalist cause; the kneeling figures were probably destroyed during the Common-wealth.

WHITTLESFORD *St. Mary and St. Andrew* [E8]

A lovely little church with 12th century nave and central tower. In the S aisle there is a pictorial history of the building. Alabaster fragments from a medieval altar were found only 100 years ago. Many benches with medieval carving. The wall-paintings

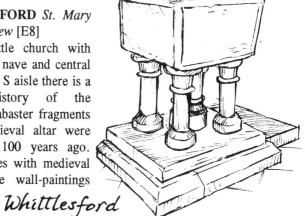

Whittlesford

Porch rafters.

'Sheela-na-gig' lintol.

Whittlesford

were discovered in 1905 and are thought to be part of a Doom, the shield of the Scaler family and a pattern of pomegranates. There is also fine 13th century ornament on the N side of the chancel. The four pillared font also dates from the Early English period. Graffiti of an archer on the pillar next to the pulpit. Outside, notice the strange 12th century carving of a sheila-na-gig built decorously high on the tower below the clock. Also see the tomb of the Hollicks family, who, as Nonconformists, were buried just outside the churchyard; but they made sure that the handsome stone urn would draw attention to their high standing in the community.

WICKEN *St. Laurence* [F5]

A quiet unpretentious village church built surprisingly close to the fen, perhaps to take advantage of the convenience of transportation of the building materials. The simple interior is largely 14th century and the nave is quite broad; six sturdy heads support the medieval roof. Three generations of Oliver Cromwell's family are buried here. Two small but elegant brasses to Margaret Peyton (d. 1414) and John Peyton (d. 1520).

WILBURTON *St. Peter* [D5]

There are two porches and the N porch has two storeys. A dignified interior with fine large 15th century windows outlined by blind arcading in nave and chancel. A cockerel hangs high in the nave roof and this emblem is continued elsewhere in the roof and rood screen, showing the patronage here of Bishop Alcock of Ely. Thomas Alcock, related to the Bishop, was rector here in 1496 and was probably responsible for part of the rebuilding of the nave roof. Very fine brasses now hang on the walls. Faded 15th century wall-paintings show two Bishops - one may be St. Blaise, who with St. Leger is a patron saint of woolcombers; St. Christopher can only be seen very faintly. The N transept has various monuments to the Pell family. Note the 20th century "Gothic" monument.

92 *Wilburton*

WILLINGHAM St. Mary and All Saints [D5]

You are greeted by cheerful gargoyles outside and marvellous wall-paintings throughout the interior; also a quite spectacular nave roof, almost bursting with angels. The stone porch is early 14th century, as is much of this handsome church. The building and land surrounding were given to Ely before the Conquest and this may account for the extravagance of some of the later building. The church was used for large ordination services in the 14th century. In the chancel are triple sedilia and a piscina, the typically Decorated ogee arch over the

Willingham

Willingham

Easter Sepulchre and again over a tomb recess in the N parclose. The screens, still colourful, stretch across nave and aisles. The very unusual stone vaulted sacristy to the NE of the chancel may have been a treasury as well as a chapel. It has very small windows which were originally protected by iron bars and the stone ribs are built as imitation wooden trusses. The church was in a ruinous state in the last century. In 1890 the Revd. John Watkins undertook

a major restoration and the wall-paintings were discovered at this time. Pamela Tudor-Craig suggests that the figure of St. Etheldreda (c.1300) may be the earliest surviving wall-painting representation of the saint. The splendid St. Christopher was painted at least a century later. Notice particularly the Visitation scene (perhaps 15th century), high in the SE corner or the nave. Both Mary and Elizabeth are highly pregnant and are wearing maternity dresses with expandable cross laced fronts.

WIMBLINGTON St. Peter [E3]

This was the first church in the village and was designed in 1874 by Thomas Henry Wyatt, replacing an earlier chapel. A sturdy cruciform building with low tower and spire. Elegant ironwork for the screen and communion rail and a fine W window as a memorial for villagers who died in World War I. Several interesting 19th and 20th century headstones in the churchyard.

WIMPOLE St. Andrew [D8]

The church was the centre of the medieval village of which nothing survives; the whole village was moved out of sight during the 18th century landscaping of the park. The interior is perhaps not what you expect to find in a country church; all that remains of the medieval building is the 14th century N chapel, now a treasure-house of monuments and memorials. Sir Thomas Chicheley, an ardent Royalist (d.1616), his wife and their six children surround the large alabaster table-tomb. There are several monuments to the Earls of Hardwicke, owners of the Hall in the 18th and 19th

Wimpole

centuries; many devoted their lives to public office. One spectacular window is filled with 14th century heraldic glass. The 19th century W window of the N chapel shows what appears to be Prince Albert. Nave and chancel were rebuilt in 1749 by Flitcroft, the architect who had also largely rebuilt the Hall. However, a late Victorian restoration took place, and Pevsner says "little survives inside of the good manners of the 18th century, and the West gallery of 1887 ... leaves one bewildered."

WINWICK *All Saints* [B4]

Another handsome Huntingdonshire tower. It has an unusual little S door with heavy moulding which then continues around the tower. The main S doorway has been here since the 12th century and the chancel, with two lancet windows, is a century later. A lovely window of the Decorated period at the E end of the N transept, but the windows beside it to the N are later. Several interesting contemporary wall-paintings: Christ the Sower and others by Hamish Moyle; in the S transept the Creation by Elizabeth Tudor-Craig is flooded with light from the tall Perpendicular window.

WISBECH *St. Augustine* [E2]

A fine Victorian church designed by W. Basset-Smith in 1867 and consecrated in 1869. Basset-Smith had earlier been involved with the restoration of St. Peter and St. Paul in Wisbech. Light and welcoming interior with whitewashed walls and stripped pine pews. In 1953 a simple reredos, by David Roberts of Cambridge, as a memorial to those who died in World War II, was erected in front of the more ornate original. Traces of 19th century painted panels of St. Augustine and St. Monica can just be seen on either side of the large E window.

WISBECH *St. Peter and St. Paul* [E2]

A curious building indeed. The rather grand tower with battlements and pinnacles is set apart from the main building. It dates from about 1525 when the Norman tower collapsed. The interior becomes more complicated still, with two naves and two aisles. The Norman arcade remains from the 12th century church.

There have been many additions and rebuildings over the centuries resulting in windows and arches being off-centre, and what is known as the "crank" between the chancel arch and the Norman arcade. A very fine brass (1401) lies in the chancel floor; there are also several elaborate 17th century monuments here which may draw your attention to the fact that the chancel walls slope to the outside. For all that, it is a fine place with much of interest.

WISBECH ST. MARY *St. Mary* [E2]

Late 14th century, extended later when the characteristic 15th century clerestory was added. Beside the font, a very rare 20th century brass commemorates Canon Mowbray Smith, shown as a young man in Mass vestments. He was vicar here from 1914 until 1951. The church is filled with statues, carvings and medieval glass all collected by the indefatigable Mowbray Smith. He found the lectern in Suffolk, said to have been part of the figurehead of a 16th century Spanish ship, but probably of later, Low Countries' origin. He saved the Sanctus bell, which was being used as a gas alarm, from a ruined church in World War I. The helmet which saved his own life has a place of honour here too. Don't miss the corbels in the S aisle. Allow yourself time to enjoy this very lovely church and to admire what has been described as all its "Bon Dieuserie."

WISTOW *St. John the Baptist* [C4]

Don't let the gargoyles deter you from enjoying this interesting church. Its mid-16th century tower may have been completed after the Reformation. The stone-masons were given free rein here: there are gargoyles all round the exterior and a lion lies curled around the SW corner. Inside too there are faces or animals on corbels on the arcades, in the aisles; no suitable place has been left empty. Detailed craftsmanship everywhere: early 14th century ironwork on the S door; dark carved figures of saints almost hidden in the nave roof. In the chancel roof the angels are more easily visible, supported on stone corbels; here also the ogee arch, used to such great effect by masons during the Decorated period, over the sedilia and low side window. The medieval rood screen

largely 13th century, as can be seen by the Y-tracery in the lancet windows in the W tower and chancel. Much brickwork patching has been used over the years. Rebuilding of the tower was completed in 1691 and the date is carved in the W wall. Inside, notice the outline of an earlier and much larger arch. Good corbels in the nave roof, especially the bearded man with

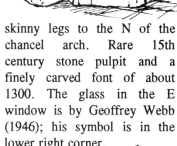

skinny legs to the N of the chancel arch. Rare 15th century stone pulpit and a finely carved font of about 1300. The glass in the E window is by Geoffrey Webb (1946); his symbol is in the lower right corner.

Wistow

now stands in the S aisle. Fragments of carving by Norman masons have been set in the S wall. The highlight is surely the 15th century window in the S aisle; it was once part of the E window, but has somehow survived several periods of destruction and was lovingly restored in the last century. It shows the Annunciation; also the Resurrection scene where, unusually, Christ is shown stepping onto the near prostrate centurion as he leaves the tomb. This scene was taken from a text used in several medieval Mystery plays.

WITCHAM *St. Martin* [E4]
The unusual dedication to this 4th century apostle of Touraine usually indicates a pre-Conquest church. The present building is

Witcham

WITCHFORD *St. Andrew* [F5]
An alarming lean to the short tower, but it has been here since the 13th century. Three stone faces, perhaps from an earlier building, are let into the outside walls. The Witchford Lion is a fine piece of Norman sculpture and looks down from above the lancet window to the W of the porch. A primitive bearded face can be found on the chancel S wall, and a happier cherub

Witchford

below the E window. The consecration date of the church is known to be 1376. In the chancel the delicate colours can still be seen around the piscina. A modern window shows St. Joseph teaching carpentry to the Boy Jesus, a fitting memorial to a past carpenter-churchwarden. High in a N window a foundering ship is an equally suitable memorial to John Townsend, lost at sea in 1872.

Wittering

WITTERING *All Saints* [A2]

The short rather upright building, with 13th century tower, does not prepare you for the splendour of the interior. The nave and

chancel are still much as they were when built in the 11th century. The awesome proportions of the massive but simple chancel arch dominate this small pre-Conquest parish church; the arch may have been built after the Conquest but in the Saxon tradition. The 12th century Norman arcades seem almost over-decorated in comparison. On the outside of the chancel E wall there is a good example of the long-and-short work used by the Saxon masons. The Royal Air Force Commemorative Chapel was dedicated in 1968. The window above, by H. W. Harvey of York, shows St. Michael, the patron saint of the RAF. The candlesticks and crucifix were made in the station workshops, using metal from propeller blades. The chancel E window is by Kempe, complete with his wheatsheaf mark.

WOODHURST *St. John the Baptist* [D5]

A compact little church standing under silver birch trees. The N doorway remains from the Norman building, though it is blocked now and the octagonal font must be almost as old. The S arcade is 13th century. The sallow brick chancel was added in the 19th century but the more attractively coloured brick floor is a recent addition. On a wall at the W end of the churchyard, a 13th century coffin lid is used as coping. A lovely village with thatched houses and duck pond; the daffodils in the spring are dazzling.

WOOD DITTON *St. Mary* [G7]

Large flint church, mainly 16th century. The massive tower could certainly support a much larger belfry and steeple than the octagon it carries. The older nave roofline can be seen on the W face. The porch roof holds interesting figures and bosses and inside are some medieval alabaster fragments Medieval carving on some of the benches to the W of the nave, including a priest at prayer and a lamb. Fragments of wall-painting and faded colours of flowers and leaves still decorate the

Wood Ditton

Wood Ditton

The dedication to St. Augustine may well relate to a very early Christian settlement. Much of what you see dates to the Victorian restoration, but in the W tower are fragments of Anglo-Saxon masonry and a small window of the same period. Two Saxon cemeteries were found nearby as well as evidence of Roman occupation. Several fine 17th and 18th century monuments hang in the aisles.

Woodston

Wood Walton

WOOD WALTON *St. Andrew* [C4]

Looking from a distance like a child's drawing of a church, it stands on a hill some way from the village. Peter Bigmore suggests that it may have been sited centrally to serve several hamlets and possibly the situation was determined by the site being a much earlier heathen temple. Nowadays it is quite a landmark for travellers on the many trains that pass close by on

rood screen. Brasses in the S aisle to Henry English (1393) and his wife; he has a lion tucked under his spurs and her feet rest on a little dog with bells on its collar. A churchwarden of 1632 was remembered by his American descendants who placed a window in the chancel in his name in 1905. In the churchyard there is an epitaph for William Simmons, who "loved a sup in the dripping pan... but could not eat"; he died in 1753 and his dripping pan is embedded in the headstone.

the London Scotland line. It is largely a 14th century building though the S arcade is Early English. In the 16th century the clerestory was added. A major rebuilding took place in 1859/60 when the aisles and tower were sympathetically rebuilt using much of the original materials. The church was declared redundant and since 1979 has been in the care of the Friends of Friendless Churches who have retiled the roof and installed vandal-proof glass. The medieval glass has been moved to the museum at Ely.

Yaxley

YAXLEY *St. Peter* [B3]
Wonderful late Perpendicular tower with airy flying buttresses supporting the recessed spire. Walk round the church and notice the different styles of tracery in the windows: plain Y-tracery of the 13th century; the E windows of S aisle and chancel, though restored, are full-blown Decorated (*c.*1330). The Perpendicular windows of clerestory and tower are more straightforward. The churchyard has risen so much over the centuries that you now walk down into the church itself; there is much of interest. Glass

in the chancel window by Sir Ninian Comper (1947, his strawberry symbol in one corner); you can read a detailed description of the window in the W end of the nave; the reredos and High Altar also by Comper. Fine medieval rood screen; remains of wall paintings; details of a curious **Heart Burial** of 1293 in N transept and nearby a memorial to a "humane" Prison Commander paid for by French prisoners from the prison camp at Norman Cross during the Napoleonic Wars. The memorial on the site of the camp is on the west of the A1 just north of the Norman Cross roundabout.

YELLING *Holy Cross*
The dedication may remain from a pre-Conquest church, as the Saxons particularly venerated the Holy Cross. There was certainly a church here in 1086, a simple building of nave and chancel only. Stand in the nave and see the distinctive arcades in the N aisle (*c.*1180) with rounded piers and scalloped capitals. Compare with the S arcade of *c.*1300 when the usually severe Early English windows were given trefoil decoration. The 14th century saw a major building programme, including the tower, clerestory and enlargement of the chancel. Henry Venn, father of the founder of the Church Missionary Society, was rector here 1770-97. Early in the 19th century the spire was removed when it appeared to be in a state of imminent collapse on to the rectory.

Yaxley

GLOSSARY

AISLE see CHURCH PLAN

APSE A semi-circular or polygonal end.

ARCADE Range of arches supported on PIERS or columns. A blind-arcade, same attached to a wall.

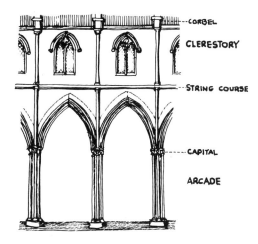

AUMBRY A recessed cupboard for the sacred vessels for Mass or Communion, usually on N wall of CHANCEL. Also used in some churches for the purpose of housing the reserved Sacrament.

BALLFLOWER Globular flower of three petals enclosing a small ball. Decoration used in the first quarter of the 14th century (DECORATED period).

BATTLEMENT a parapet with gaps at regular intervals (*see* drawing for QUOINS).

BOSS An ornamental projection, generally carved with foliage or figures, used to conceal the crossing of the ribs in a vaulted roof.

BROACH SPIRE *see* SPIRE.

CAPITAL Top or head of a column. (*see* drawing for **ARCADE**)

CHANCEL *see* CHURCH PLAN.

CHAPEL OF EASE A small building for worship other than the parish church.

CHANTRY CHAPEL Chapel attached to or inside a church, endowed for saying of Masses for the soul of the founder or another individual.

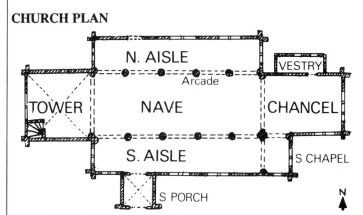

CHURCH PLAN

AISLE The side part of a church

CHANCEL The eastern compartment of the church beyond the nave, and housing the altar or communion table.

NAVE The main body of a church.

VESTRY A room in which robing takes place.

CHARNEL HOUSE A room, often below ground level, where the bones of the dead are deposited.

CHEVRON A zigzag ornamentation typical of the NORMAN period (*see* drawing for TYMPANUM).

CHRISMATORY Vessel for holding consecrated oil used in baptism, or cupboard for holding the vessel.

CLERESTORY The upper part of the NAVE and CHANCEL walls, containing a series of windows (*see* drawing for ARCADE).

CLUNCH a soft, chalky stone quarried in the SE of the county.

CORBEL Block of stone projecting just below the roof eaves externally or internally. Often adorned with carving (*see* drawing for ARCADE).

CROCKETS Decorative projections placed on sloping sides of SPIRES, pinnacles, gables (*see* drawing for SPIRE).

DECORATED ('DEC') Stylistic division of English GOTHIC architecture from *c.*1290 to *c.*1350 (*see* drawing for OGEE and TRACERY).

DOG-TOOTH Typical EARLY ENGLISH ornament, consisting of a series of raised four-cornered stars.

DRIP MOULDING *See* HOOD-MOULD.

EARLY ENGLISH Stylistic division of English GOTHIC architecture roughly covering the 13th century.

EASTER SEPULCHRE Recess to hold the consecrated Host prior to the Easter celebration. Usually in N CHANCEL wall.

ENTASIS The swelling of a column or SPIRE to prevent optical distortion.

FLUSHWORK Decorative use of flint to form patterns, monograms, inscriptions etc.

GOTHIC English architectural term covering 1200 to 1539, and including EARLY ENGLISH, DECORATED and PERPENDICULAR styles.

GREEN MAN A foliate face, often with leaves coming from its mouth. Seen on fonts, CORBELS etc.

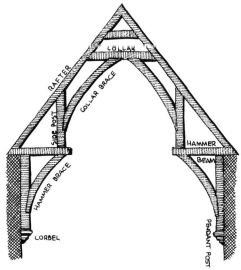

HAMMER BEAM ROOF

HAMMER-BEAMS Beams projecting at right angles, to provide support for vertical members or braces of a wooden roof.

HOOD-MOULD Projecting moulding above an arch or LINTEL to throw off water.

INDENT Matrix for brass.

INDULGENCE See Papal Indulgence.

JESSE (WINDOW) Visual genealogy of Christ's descent from Jesse. Jesse is portrayed at the base of a tree trunk with Christ's other forebears depicted in loops of braches.

LANCET Narrow windows which terminate in a sharp point; characteristic of the EARLY ENGLISH period.

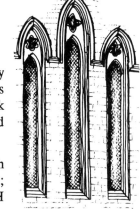

EARLY ENGLISH LANCETS *c.*1220

LECTERN Free standing reading desk.

LEDGER A flat stone covering a grave; often forms part of a church floor.

LINTEL Load-bearing support over door or window.

LONG AND SHORT WORK Alternate vertical and horizontal stonework, used as corner quoins in SAXON churches (*see* drawing for QUOINS).

LOW-SIDE WINDOW A small window low down in the CHANCEL wall, just E of the arch. They were not originally glazed. It is generally thought that a handbell would be rung through the opening at the elevation of the Host during Mass, so that those who heard it could thus share in the Celebration. Their exact purpose is not known for certain.

LUCARNE A vertical opening in the tapering surface of a SPIRE, never glazed (*see* drawings for SPIRE).

LYCH-GATE Roofed gate at entrance to churchyard where coffin was traditionally rested.

MASS DIAL A sun dial showing the times of Mass, usually close by porch or entrance. Also referred to as a Scratch Dial.

MINSTER CHURCH The church of a monastery.

MISERICORD Bracket, often richly carved, on the underside of a hinged choir stall seat which when turned up provided the occupant of the seat with a support during a long period of standing.

NAIL-HEAD EARLY ENGLISH ornamentation, consisting of small nail-like pyramids, regularly repeated.

NAVE *See* CHURCH PLAN.

NORMAN Style of architecture, typified by rounded arches and massive

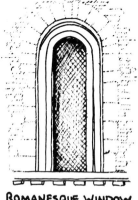

ROMANESQUE WINDOW
c. 1150

piers, from 1066 to *c.*1200. *See also* ROMANESQUE.

OGEE A double curved arch, very characteristic of the DECORATED period.

PAPAL INDULGENCE Pardon from punishment for sin, granted for an act of devotion.

PARAPET SPIRE *See* SPIRE

PARCLOSE A screen separating a chapel or aisle from the body of the church.

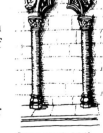

BLIND OGEE ARCH

PERPENDICULAR (PERP) Stylistic division of English GOTHIC architecture *c.*1335-50 to *c.*1530 (*see* drawing for TRACERY).

PIER A strong solid support, pillar or column.

PISCINA A stone basin, with a drain, for washing the sacred vessels, usually to the S of an altar.

POPPY-HEAD The carved ornament on top of bench-ends or pew-ends.

QUATREFOIL Four-lobed decorative opening or window.

QUOINS Stones at the angles or corners of a building.

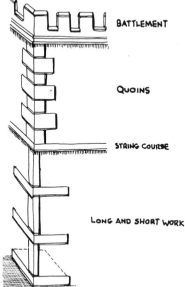

BATTLEMENT

QUOINS

STRING COURSE

LONG AND SHORT WORK

101

REBUS Pun, representing a name or word by the use of symbol, e.g. Bishop Alcock, represented by a cockerel.

REREDOS Painted or carved screen behind altar.

RETABLE Painted or carved panels behind altar.

ROMANESQUE Architectural style from 9th to 12th centuries. In England known as SAXON and NORMAN. In Britain synonymous with the NORMAN style. On the continent from which it was introduced, the term goes back earlier.

ROOD A cross or crucifix.

ROOD LOFT Gallery on top of ROOD SCREEN, to contain the ROOD and also for use by singers and musicians.

ROOD SCREEN A screen at the entry of the CHANCEL, occasionally in stone, usually in wood; on which was erected the ROOD LOFT or rood beam.

SARSEN STONE Stone traditionally marking meeting place of the Hundred.

SAXON Style of architecture linked with period before Norman Conquest.

SEDILIA Seats for clergy usually on S side of CHANCEL.

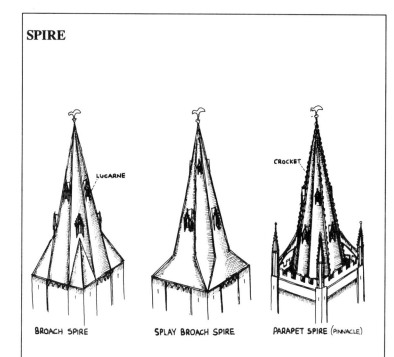

SPIRE

BROACH SPIRE — LUCARNE

SPLAY BROACH SPIRE

PARAPET SPIRE (PINNACLE) — CROCKET

BROACH SPIRE Spire rising directly from the tower with no intervening parapet. The corner junctions between the octagon and the square are covered by triangular spurs, or broaches.

PARAPET SPIRE Spire rising behind the parapet, sometimes supported by flying-buttresses. Also called pinnacle spire.

SHEILA-NA-GIG Female (or male) figure displaying genitalia.

SQUINT A hole cut in a wall or through a PIER to allow a view of the main altar of a church.

STEEPLE Tower together with SPIRE, cupola etc.

STIFF LEAF EARLY ENGLISH, 13th century, type of foliage.

STOUP Vessel for the holy water, usually placed by a door.

102

TRACERY Open pattern of stonework in upper part of GOTHIC windows. Also, can be of wood in screens, etc. or on a solid background to be blind.

EARLY ENGLISH c. 1240

LATE C13 TRANSITIONAL

DECORATED TRACERY

PERPENDICULAR TRACERY

STRING-COURSE A projecting horizontal band set in the surface of a wall. It acts as a division (*see* drawing for QUOINS).

TRANSEPT An arm of a cross-shaped church.

CHEVRON

CAPITAL

ROMANESQUE TYMPANUM

TYMPANUM Area between lintel and arch of a doorway, often filled with a relief sculpture.

VESTRY See CHURCH PLAN

BIBLIOGRAPHY

ANDERSON, M.D., *Looking for History in British Churches* (John Murray, London, 1951)

BETJEMAN, Sir John (ed.), *Parish Churches of England & Wales* (Collins, London, 1980)

BIGMORE, Peter, *The Bedfordshire and Huntingdonshire Landscape* (Hodder and Stoughton, London, 1979)

CLIFTON-TAYLOR, Alec, *English Parish Churches as Works of Art* (B.T. Batsford, London, 1986)

COCKE, T; FINDLAY, D; HALSEY, R; WILLIAMSON, E., *Recording a Church: an illustrated glossary* (Council for British Archaeology, London, 1982)

CONYBEARE E., *Highways & Byways in Cambridge and Ely* (MacMillan and Co., London, 1923)

COOK, G.H., *English Medieval Parish Churches* (Phoenix House, London, 1954)

COWEN, Painton, *A Guide to Stained Glass in Britain* (Michael Joseph, London, 1985)

COX, J. Charles, *Pulpits, Lecterns & Organs* (Oxford University Press, 1915)

HALL, James, *Dictionary of Subjects and Symbols in Art* (John Murray, London, 1987)

MEE, Arthur, *The King's England Cambridgeshire* (Hodder & Stoughton, London, 1965)

MEE, Arthur, *The King's England, Bedfordshire & Huntingdonshire* (Hodder & Stoughton, London, 1973)

MESSENT, Claude J.W. Messent, *Lych-gates and their Churches in Eastern England* (The Author, Blofield, 1970)

PEVSNER, Nikolaus, *Bedfordshire, & the County of Huntingdon and Peterborough* (Penguin Books, Harmondsworth, 1968)

PEVSNER, Nikolaus, *Cambridgeshire* (Penguin Books, Harmondsworth, 1986)

PRITCHARD, V., *English Medieval Graffiti* (Cambridge University Press, Cambridge, 1967)

RAVENSDALE, Jack, *The Domesday Inheritance* (Souvenir Press, London, 1986)

R.C.H.M. *North-East Cambridgeshire* (H.M. Stationery Office, London 1972)

R.C.H.M. *West Cambridgeshire* (H.M. Stationery Office, London, 1968)

RUSSELL, Ronald, *Cambridgeshire and Cambridge* (Shire Publications, Aylesbury, 1988)

SCARFE, Norman, *Cambridgeshire, A Shell Guide*, (Faber & Faber, London, 1983)

TAYLOR, H.M. & J., *Anglo-Saxon Architecture, Vols. I & II* (Cambridge University Press, Cambridge, 1965)

TAYLOR, H.M., *Anglo-Saxon Architecture, Vol.III* (Cambridge University Press, Cambridge, 1978)

RESILIENT GARDEN

RESILIENT GARDEN

SUSTAINABLE GARDENING
FOR A CHANGING CLIMATE

TOM MASSEY

CHAPTER 4
CLIMATE RESILIENT GARDEN DESIGN
092

CHAPTER 5
RESILIENT PLANT GUIDE
156

CHAPTER 6
SUSTAINABLE MATERIALS
206

WWW.DK.COM/RESILIENT-GARDEN

CHAPTER ONE

RESPONDING TO CLIMATE CHANGE

[Above] My mother gave me a small area of our garden to experiment with when I was a child, and my fascination with gardening rapidly developed.
[Left] Thirty years later, I am pictured on my garden for Yeo Valley Organic at the RHS Chelsea Flower Show 2021.

THE MAKING OF A GARDEN DESIGNER

A question I am often asked is, "What inspired you to become a garden designer?" It's a hard question to answer succinctly, because the answer is so multifaceted; there are many factors that influenced my decision to pursue this career.

Starting at the beginning, I grew up in Richmond upon Thames, a leafy suburb in southwest London. We had a small back garden, typical of a London terraced house, and my mother – a keen gardener – gave me an area to call my own. I was allowed to experiment, choosing a variety of plants on exciting trips to the garden centre to try out in combination. I remember being fascinated by the huge array of colour, form, texture, habit, scent, and all the other attributes plants could display. I was moved by the change of the seasons, seeing green shoots emerge, followed by flowers, fruit, and berries, then bare winter stems. The plants changed the look, atmosphere, and character of the space and they could even affect my mood. At the time I didn't know it, but on looking back I can see this was an early foray into the world of garden design, with my successes and failures acting as an important learning experience.

We also had a small allotment, and understanding that we could grow plants to eat was a revelation. My mother was a fervent believer in the importance of good-quality organic food. We always had fresh organic fruit and vegetables in the house, some home-grown, some shop-bought. Seeing produce

> I felt elation when successes were achieved: seeing a flower open and develop into a fruit, then plucking and eating that fruit, savouring the succulent and sweet flesh.

grow and ripen, to be harvested when ready to eat, gave me a new-found respect for plants. I learned that they could provide for us, nourishing both the body and the soul.

When plants died, I felt devastated. How could I have failed the plant? How could I have let it die? On the flip-side of the coin, I felt elation when successes were achieved: seeing a flower open and develop into a fruit, then plucking and eating that fruit, savouring the succulent and sweet flesh. I felt an overwhelming sense of achievement that this was something that had been produced by my hard work and patience.

Looking back, gardening and growing plants was a formative experience, and my successes and failures were important in learning about both the frailties and the resilience of life. It was a process in which I could escape the mundanity of daily existence, and it was the start of a deep love of, and connection to, the natural world. I am eternally grateful for that introduction at a young age.

FORMATIVE LANDSCAPES

My two younger brothers and I were regularly forced to undertake long walks. Every day, come rain or shine, whether we wanted to or not, we were marched up to Richmond Park and encouraged to run wild. This was a ploy to get us to expend some energy, three lively small boys being a bit of a handful – but that early connection to a landscape forged a deep and profound love of it that persists to this day.

Richmond Park is an amazing place, a site of both national and international importance for wildlife conservation. It has been designated as a Site of Special Scientific Interest (SSSI), a National Nature Reserve (NNR), and a Special Area of Conservation (SAC). The park is full of veteran oaks that are hundreds of years old, rich with complex detail, character, and incredible ecosystems. They also make dynamic climbing frames!

Invertebrate life is particularly abundant: billions of yellow meadow ants have sculpted the landscape of acidic grassland, and their relationship with the green woodpeckers that feed on them is of particular scientific interest. As a child jumping from mound to mound, I had no idea about the complex ecosystems and interconnected life forms co-existing beneath my feet in the soil, as well as on the trees and in the air. From the micro (ants and insects) to the macro (trees, birds, and the wild deer that roam the park) that early connection to nature led me to want to study, observe, and interact with it in deeper and more meaningful ways as I grew older.

[Above] A scene typical of Richmond Park, which contains an estimated 1,300 veteran oak trees, of which 320 are classed as ancient.
[Left] There are an estimated 3 billion yellow meadow ants residing in the richly biodiverse landscape of Richmond Park. Together they weigh about the same as 125 of their fellow residents, the fallow deer. Some of the 400,000 anthills have been found to be more than 150 years old.

[Above] In Cornwall, the coastal cliff face has always fascinated me. How can plants grow out of a sheer rock face, battered by wild salt and spray, frozen in winter and scorched in summer, surviving rock falls and landslides, recolonizing quickly after devastating events? There is so much to be inspired by and so much to learn from.

[Right] Coastal plants can thrive in extremely harsh environments. Here, *Carpobrotus edulis* (pigface) and *Crithmum maritimum* (rock samphire) are growing out of an almost vertical rock face on the Lizard Peninsula, the southernmost point in Cornwall.

Another landscape that exerted a profound effect on me was the rugged beauty of the Roseland Peninsula in Cornwall. Every summer, my family would decamp to a tiny hamlet near Portscatho on the south coast. The azure waters, gnarled coastal woodlands, wildflower-filled pastures, and rocky coastal landscapes provided an amazing adventure ground. My grandparents had a friend in the hamlet, wonderfully named Dick Twist, who owned a beautiful, crumbling, and ancient house where we used to stay. He would spend the summer holidays studying Stonehenge, and we would occupy his house with cousins and family friends. The house was cold and damp, filled with mice, voles, spiders, and other insects. The beds were stiff and hard and it definitely wasn't comfortable, but it had an incredible atmosphere. A hushed and reverent magic emanated from the fabric of the building, and the garden in particular was a place of wonder and excitement.

I can still vividly remember the scent of lavender on a hot summer day, and getting lost among wild flowers and weeds that hummed with grasshoppers and bees. The garden was full of forgotten wonders; greenhouses that were covered in climbers, filled with triffid-like tomato plants, filling the air inside with their pungent perfume; summerhouses with stunning sea views hidden behind overgrown hedges; apple orchards lost to seas of savage stinging nettles. The garden was gradually being reclaimed by nature, slowly being lost to the wild, while still retaining an imprint and memory of its man-made self.

It was a magical thing to witness, this yearly degradation of a garden into an increasingly natural space as the rugged Cornish landscape, fervent and fertile, slowly reclaimed it. My connection with this space was, and still is, profound. It lives on vividly in memories, and I still return there in dreams. But, as with most beautiful and fragile things, it came to an end. Dick died and the house was sold. Both the house and garden were sterilized, modernized, and re-landscaped, Cornish nature banished to the boundaries. Worse still, it sat empty for years, with the only signs of life being regular gardening to keep out the wild; manicured lawns, pristine paving, and clipped hedges were all perfectly maintained.

This made a deep impression on me and forced me to question what constitutes a garden. How is it different from a landscape? Can the two co-exist, and could we not work with nature to achieve a more profound and harmonious result? I was a teenager when I first formed these thoughts, and although at that point I had other ambitions – I was keen on drawing and went on to do a BA honours degree in animation – they returned to me constantly, and still do. How can we embrace the wild force of nature and not fight it? How can we be inspired by it, utilize it, and engage with it to create successful, harmonious, and magical spaces? Landscape or garden – do we need a distinction?

RADICAL GARDENS

RADICAL AND RESILIENT GARDEN DESIGN HAS BEEN EMPLOYED THROUGHOUT HISTORY AND IN EXTREME SITUATIONS TO PURSUE SURVIVAL AND PROVIDE HOPE. WE NEED TO LEARN FROM THE INSPIRING PIONEERS OF THESE GARDENS SO THAT WE CAN BECOME THE RADICALS OF THE FUTURE.

I have always been excited and inspired by all things radical. My first show garden at RHS Hampton Court Palace Flower Show in 2016 was inspired by the resilience of refugees. Entitled "Border Control", it was sponsored by the UN Refugee Agency (UNHCR) and designed in collaboration with a friend, John Ward. The garden used British native and non-native plants as a metaphor to represent British residents and refugees. A central, seemingly British, wildflower meadow thrived on an island surrounded by a wide moat and a razor-wire fence, while non-native plants struggled to survive in rubble and desolation outside. Amid the rubble, some plants bloomed: colourful jewels of hope and resilience in the harsh environment, small displays of strength in the face of adversity.

To enter the central meadow, visitors first had to pass through a turnstile and show a border guard a pass, adding to the theatrical experience. Once inside, the British meadow could be viewed in closer proximity. Woven among the British native plants was an array of non-native species from the outer rubble zone. These plants had made

Woven among the British native plants was an array of non-native species from the outer rubble zone. These plants had made the leap and were adding to the beauty, biodiversity, and harmony of the planting; they were a simple metaphor for the benefits of inclusion.

the leap and were adding to the beauty, biodiversity, and harmony of the planting; they were a simple metaphor for the benefits of inclusion and integration. I remember many of the conversations that arose at the show. So many people were moved, some to tears – including the RHS judges – by the stories woven into the garden.

Strewn amid the rubble were toys, life jackets, and items of clothing that had washed up on Greek beaches – lost possessions from people making a perilous journey. A journey which, for many, would have been their last. Other visitors questioned, "How could this be called a 'garden'?" I remember the almost incandescent rage that emanated from some people: "There is rubble and waste! It's not beautiful!"

[01] This view of the "Border Control" garden from beyond the razor-wire fence and heavy-duty turnstile gives visitors a sense of how it feels to be unwelcome. [02] *Salvia nemorosa* 'Ostfriesland' thriving in the rubble just outside the razor-wire fence. [03] A bright poppy growing out of the rubble: a glimmer of hope representing resilience and determination emerging from destruction.

Even then, in my early career, I was questioning whether a garden needs to be beautiful. What is beauty? Is it only the traditional picture-postcard version of it that should be applauded and revered? Is there not also beauty in resilience, decay, and destruction?

THE LEMON TREE TRUST

This show garden led to me being introduced to the Lemon Tree Trust, with a view to designing a show garden at the RHS Chelsea Flower Show to promote its work. This is a charity that engages with refugees, encouraging gardening in harsh camp environments. One of the most profound and inspiring trips of my life was a visit to Domiz 1, a refugee camp where staff from the Trust were working, near the Syrian border in Northern Kurdish Iraq. The research trip was an opportunity to speak to people in the camp, one gardener to another. I wanted to understand why they were gardening, and what benefits it brought them while they lived in the difficult situation of forced migration and displacement. I had some incredible conversations, and heard stories of people who had the presence of mind to take a cutting of a favourite rose, or a selection of seeds, before fleeing for their lives. These plants were so important that they could not be left behind. But what was it that the gardens brought to the harsh, dry, and dusty camp environment, where water, such a precious resource, was so scarce? It was a sense of home, a small reminder of better times, a glimmer of hope, and a sense of order; the very process of sowing, growing, and gardening restored some normality to broken and devastated lives.

01

03

[01] Even in limited space, and with scarce resources, ornamentals and edibles can be grown together. [02] The Azadi Community garden in Domiz 1 camp in Northern Kurdish Iraq is a green space within the camp for gardeners to come together and build a sense of community. It provides some respite from the harsh environment.

02

04

[03] The Trust pilots agricultural businesses and gardening initiatives in refugee communities, creating employment opportunities and restoring cultural identity, dignity, and purpose.
[04] Resilient plants are common in the camp, like this drought-tolerant *Gazania*. The dry, dusty environment requires creative and resilient planting solutions.

I was awed by the way these people were using landscaping and garden design for human benefit, creating shade from the searing heat by growing tough, drought-tolerant, and fast-growing trees and plants; producing food where food was scarce; and designing hushed, sheltered, and calm courtyards to escape to. These gardens were wide-ranging and beautiful. The plants were growing in almost impossibly difficult conditions, but the gardeners were skilfully using all the resources available to them: waste materials were turned into shelters, structures, and planters; grey water was diverted and collected in containers; rills and channels were used for irrigation. The gardeners learnt from friends and neighbours, sharing knowledge and skills across the community. It was a profound learning experience for me. This truly was radical gardening, designing for the environment in which these people were forced to live. They were resilient gardeners by necessity. This forced change was unwelcome and unavoidable, enacted by powers outside of their control. What was so inspiring was their willingness, ingenuity, and determination to adapt, to survive, and to thrive.

Yet we are all going to have to become more radical and flexible as the planet we live on is threatened. Dramatic and rapid changes to the world we live in are happening before our eyes. Global powers have been criticized for sleepwalking into an emergency, and now the changes that were predicted by scientists and science fiction writers are here: warming climates, increasingly unpredictable weather, droughts, floods, and rising sea levels.

Fortunately, human beings have been capable of adapting since the dawn of time. It is our modus operandi. Our large brains are an evolutionary advantage that make us ingenious. Now is the time for ingenuity, experimentation, grit, and determination. We should look to teachings of the past for inspiration, to the radicals of previous eras who dared to try something different. We should also pay heed to the radicals of the present, the pioneers flouting the rigid teachings of textbooks that will soon be outdated as the rules have to change. We need to become the radicals of the future. We are the pioneer gardeners, growers, designers, architects, engineers, botanists, farmers, horticulturists, planners, and global leaders who can and must adapt. Our very existence is threatened. Just like the inspiring people living in the Domiz camp, we have no choice.

[Above] Drought-resilient Mediterranean-inspired planting in the Lemon Tree Trust Garden at Chelsea Flower Show in 2018; the planting scheme, tough and hardy but also colourful and uplifting, was inspired by the gardens of Domiz 1 camp and what people there were growing. [Left] I used a palette of resilient and drought-tolerant planting for the Lemon Tree Trust Garden at Chelsea Flower Show, inspired by what I saw in the Domiz 1 Camp gardens.

[Top] In the Ruin Garden by Tanja Lincke, a dilapidated building has been transformed into a real ruin, artfully capturing the romantic atmosphere of a disused industrial site.
[Right] The rawness of the hard material is contrasted with seemingly wild planting, characterized by loose perennials, grasses, and trees such as birch, pine, and staghorn sumac (*Rhus typhina*).

RESILIENT LANDSCAPES

THE POWER OF NATURE TO SURVIVE IN CHALLENGING CONDITIONS
IS TRULY INSPIRING, WHETHER YOU SEE A SINGLE PLANT EMERGING
FROM A CRACK IN A CONCRETE PAVEMENT OR A CONTAMINATED
BROWNFIELD SITE FULL OF BIODIVERSITY. NATURE WILL ADAPT
TO CLIMATE CHANGE – BUT THE BIG QUESTION IS, HOW WILL WE?

Harsh landscapes define resilience, and offer us lessons that are far more profound than the quick fix offered by chemical fertilizers, pesticides, and watering-intensive maintenance regimes. Resources worldwide will become scarcer as populations increase and the climate changes. We need to learn to be less wasteful. Being inspired by nature, and by resilient landscapes, is key to the success of resilient garden design, as we plan for the changing climate. By looking at nature and how it deals with extreme conditions or events, we can find the answers we need.

This thinking can be applied to general landscape and garden design. There are so many books, resources, talks, and lectures on the subject that sometimes the information can be overwhelming. Learning from the past is important, of course, but so is experimentation. If everyone always followed the rules, did as others have done before them, then nothing would ever progress. It is the radicals, the innovators, the forward-thinking practitioners and designers willing to try something new who may enact meaningful change. Often these people have been inspired by radical landscapes or experiences that set their world alight, sparked an interest, or triggered an idea. Climate change is one such experience to which we are all going to have to adapt.

CHAPTER TWO

WHAT IS RESILIENT GARDENING?

A CALL TO ACTION

WE ARE IN THE MIDST OF A CLIMATE EMERGENCY, FACING THE REALITY OF A SUBSTANTIAL LOSS OF BIODIVERSITY, WITH THREATS TO OUR LOCAL FLORA AND FAUNA BY INVASIVE SPECIES AND A STEADILY WARMING PLANET.

This is on top of mounting societal crises as we see ever-rising levels of mental, physical, and social health issues, all of which were magnified by the Covid-19 pandemic. However, while world events can seem to be daunting and relentless, leaving us feeling impotent, our gardens and outdoor spaces are places where we can enact visible change. They also offer us a respite from the pressures of daily life; tending to them gives us something meaningful to focus on.

HUMAN EFFECTS

As custodians of this planet – the dominant sentient beings – we have to acknowledge that our own actions have caused the crises that loom. We have sleepwalked into a series of environmental disasters that are slowly unfolding before our eyes. Over the past few years, I am sure we can all think of ways in which we have experienced the effects first-hand: more extreme weather; yearly temperature records eclipsed; plastic pollution everywhere, from the remotest beaches to the highest mountains; loss of habitat due to urbanization; and free-falling biodiversity decline.

This translates to our garden spaces, too, where you may have observed flowers blooming weeks earlier than usual. Higher rainfall and extreme weather events lead to flooding, swamped plants, and winds that can bring down trees, blow away sheds, or tear down walls. You may have also experienced drought and relied heavily on irrigation to avoid your plants dying. Wildlife is disappearing from our gardens, too. With the overuse of harmful chemicals, too much hard landscaping, and artificial plants and lawns, it is no wonder that these spaces can be hostile, offering wildlife no natural habitat.

01

[01] Workers in the Philippines sorting through mountains of plastic waste. [02] Flooded houses in the Windsor suburb near Sydney, Australia, where the Hawkesbury River burst its banks due to torrential rain in 2022. [03] Wildfires in Australia: in 2020 more than 10 million hectares were burnt. Peoples lives, homes, and an estimated 3 billion wild animals were detrimentally affected.

02

03

"DELAY IN CONCERTED
GLOBAL ACTION WILL MISS
A BRIEF AND RAPIDLY
CLOSING WINDOW TO SECURE
A LIVEABLE FUTURE."

PROFESSOR HANS-OTTO PÖRTNER,
IPCC WORKING GROUP II CO-CHAIR

In February 2022, the Royal Society in London published a report that looked at the first flowering times of plants, using more than 400,000 studies and starting as far back as 1753. It found that flowering timings varied year on year based on fluctuating temperatures, but ultimately, a 1.2°C (2.2°F) temperature rise has advanced flowering times, and therefore spring, by a full month. Between 1987 and 2019, plants in the UK were flowering a month earlier than they did before this period.

But a rapidly changing climate means early-blooming flowers are not the only indication of a dramatic shift in the natural order of things. There have been earlier sightings of migrating wildlife, birds nesting ahead of schedule, and insects premature to the party before flowers have emerged. All of these shifting timetables could become even more wildly out of sync if we stay on our current course, throwing the delicate ecosystem into dysfunction and having drastic knock-on effects. For example, pollinators may emerge to find that the blooms they rely on have come and gone. This could then affect bird populations that rely on those insects for food.

Ulf Büntgen, lead author of the Royal Society report and professor of environmental systems analysis at the University of Cambridge, warns that "ecological mismatch" could have a damaging impact. "If the trends continue like this, that could have more profound effects, severe effects, on the functioning and productivity of ecosystems, because things that depend on each other in terms of timing – insects, plants, other animals – get disrupted."

How can we gardeners help? The answer is to grow a range of adaptable plants that cover a long period of flowering, extending the season during which food is available to pollinating insects.

SOLASTALGIA

Solastalgia is a word coined by Glenn Albrecht, an environmental philosopher and an honorary associate in the School of Geosciences, the University of Sydney, New South Wales, Australia. It first appeared in print in an essay written by Albrecht entitled "Solastalgia: A New Concept in Human Health and Identity", published in 2005. Using the concept of "nostalgia" as a starting point, solastalgia is an amalgamation of the Latin word sōlācium, meaning comfort, or solace, and the suffix -algia, from Greek, indicating pain in specified parts of the body. It describes the solace of home and the pain of its loss: it is the feeling when one's sense of place and belonging are threatened by climate change. In other words, it is homesickness while you are still home, and distress at your home being destroyed while you are still living there.

SHIFTING SEASONS

DUE TO RISING TEMPERATURES, SPRING FLOWERS ARE BLOOMING A MONTH EARLIER IN THE UK. THIS IS NOT THE ONLY INDICATION THAT OUR DELICATE ECOSYSTEM IS BEING THROWN OUT OF BALANCE, WHICH MAY LEAD TO CATASTROPHIC CONSEQUENCES.

This apple tree blossomed early before being hit with low temperatures and snow, which caused the plant damage from the cold and limited its harvest.

MAKING A DIFFERENCE

A LACK OF COMMITMENT FROM GOVERNMENTS AND A SLOW-TO-ACT ETHOS CAN MAKE THE FUTURE LOOK DAUNTING, BUT THERE ARE MANY THINGS THAT WE, AS GARDENERS, CAN CONTRIBUTE. WE CAN CHANNEL OUR ANXIETY INTO ACTION; NEGATIVE EMOTIONS CAN BE THE DRIVERS OF CHANGE.

We have probably all questioned what difference our individual actions could make in the face of such a monumental threat – but if we all commit to making small changes, it can lead to a huge net effect. A simple example from an RHS study is that if every UK gardener planted a medium-sized tree – such as a cherry tree, crabapple tree, or birch – in their community, school, workplace, or garden and nurtured it to maturity, these trees would store carbon the equivalent of driving 11.4 million times around the planet. Trees have so many positive effects, from supporting wildlife with habitats and food sources, to human benefits such as providing shade, cooling hot summer temperatures, increasing wellbeing, and removing pollutants from the air we breathe. Even dead trees are beneficial to the environment, as degrading wood provides habitats and food sources for many species of insects, plants, fungi, and animals.

CONNECTING WITH NATURE

When we as a society feel more connected to nature and the world around us, our desire to protect it is cultivated. With a growing urban population, and pandemics a real threat, the presence of gardens and attractive green public spaces as places for respite is increasingly vital for our health and wellbeing. Despite all the portents of disaster, and the destruction of the planet's fragile ecosystems that have already occurred, we are living in a time of opportunity for radical change. Landscape design professionals and gardeners have suddenly risen in stock; planners, architects, developers, government ministers, and the heads of corporate businesses realize that a deeper connection to the natural world is not just increasingly desirable but vital and can lead to increased productivity, wellbeing, and prosperity for society.

[Top] Here, I used *Betula utilis* var. *jacquemontii* in the foreground, and a multistemmed *Amelanchier lamarckii* in the background, to evoke the feel of a woodland edge.
[Right] Our gardens and green spaces provide us with an essential connection to nature. This garden, which I designed for a client, provides an immersive view to draw the inhabitants outside.

GARDENS IN THE LANDSCAPE

We must all reconsider our perspective on what our gardens should look like and how they function. We need to move away from gardens that are designed only to provide aesthetic perfection, and instead see our personal outside space as part of a vast landscape. Although individual gardens may be small, they are often adjacent to others, which makes them a valuable environmental resource. We, as custodians of these spaces, can enact change to benefit not only us individually, but also the wider environment, and society in general.

We can start to plan now for the changes that we will need to introduce to our gardens. We must design spaces that have the ability to thrive in present conditions, and recover from adverse events predicted for the future: that is the definition of a resilient landscape.

Technological advancements mean that climate scientists can map out our future weather, modelling with increasing accuracy what the local conditions will be like in five, ten, and even fifty years' time. That means that we can start to plan now for the changes that we will need to introduce to our gardens. We must design spaces that have the ability to thrive in present conditions, and recover from adverse events predicted for the future: that is the definition of a resilient landscape. Rather than seeing the climate emergency as catastrophic for our gardens, we can embrace the opportunities that a changing climate provides.

Through resilient design and the avoidance of products and materials that are unsustainable, reduce biodiversity, or have a high carbon footprint, gardeners and the horticultural industry can help. There are more than 30 million people involved in gardening in the UK alone, and we all have the potential to grow beneficial plants at our homes or in allotments and community spaces.

THE FOOTPRINT OF GARDENS

The total area of gardens in the UK is estimated at approximately 433,000 hectares (1,670 square miles). That's slightly more than a fifth the size of Wales, or approximately the same size as the Cape Verde Islands.

As can be seen here, gardens are not isolated landscapes. They connect to form larger landscapes and green corridors. It is important to allow wildlife to move though and between our gardens to protect local wildlife and promote biodiversity.

01

03

[01] The "Garden of Eden", a community garden in Manhattan constructed over five years by Adam Purple. In 1973, a building behind Purple's home on Eldridge Street was flattened. He decided to start a garden in the resulting space with his companion, Eve. [02] The resulting garden was 1,494 sq m (15,000 sq ft), featuring 45 trees, including eight black walnuts, and a wide range of produce, including corn, cherry tomatoes, asparagus, and raspberries. He regularly cycled to Central Park to collect horse manure to use as fertilizer, and volunteers helped with upkeep. [03] Purple, as an activist and urban Edenist, became famous in New York for taking "guerrilla gardening" to new extremes.

GUIDING PRINCIPLES

WORKING TOGETHER, SHARING KNOWLEDGE, AND EMBRACING SUSTAINABLE PRACTICES ARE MEANINGFUL ACTIONS WE CAN TAKE - IMPERATIVE CONTRIBUTIONS TO THE RESCUE MISSION FOR OUR PLANET.

In the push to mitigate climate change, let's come together, share ideas, be honest about the challenges, and disseminate knowledge and insights from inspiring books, talks, or events we have attended. Let's encourage a community, connecting with other gardeners either over the fence or across the world on social media. Gardeners need to talk to those in areas with a warmer climate to study what grows well there and adjust their ideas about a garden that will flourish in the long term.

We can combine all our efforts to make a meaningful contribution, providing joined-up, global thinking. We need to be radical, resilient, and willing to change. For this is what humans have always done – we adapt, we survive, we overcome problems by designing solutions to them. We are at a critical point in human history, as the actions we take today will determine the outlook for the planet we inhabit. It's not too late – we gardeners can do our bit, no matter how small it seems, to help save the planet. Let's embrace sustainable and resilient gardens, designed for the present day, as well as for the uncertain future. If we can come together as a global gardening community, we are capable of enacting big change. We can edge one step closer to securing the outlook for future gardeners, for the health of our planet, and for the life of future generations.

DESIGN FOR THE ENVIRONMENT

Gardens can be positive for human health: they provide aesthetic beauty, increase wellbeing, reduce the impact of climatic conditions such as heat and wind, and can reduce the effects of pollution. But gardens can also support wildlife, increase biodiversity, and be naturally resilient to the effects of climate change, drought, flooding, and wind. Creative thinking can produce both aesthetically beautiful and environmentally sustainable gardens.

REDUCE RESOURCES

You can design your garden to need less water, and to avoid reliance upon the use of chemical pesticides and synthetic fertilizers. Circular thinking, zero-waste strategies, rainwater harvesting, and resilience can be built in at the outset.

SOURCE SUSTAINABLE MATERIALS

From responsibly sourced and sustainably produced timber to ethically sourced stone, peat-free compost, and biodegradable pots, be mindful of all the materials and resources you use. Research where your proposed materials come from and question suppliers about production. Make decisions driven not only by aesthetics, durability, and function, but also by sustainability. Can it be maintained long-term? If not, are there sustainable alternatives?

CONSIDER THE SUSTAINABILITY OF THE CONSTRUCTION

Are there products or practices that could reduce the need for concrete? Does a tree really need to be felled? Can you work with the site as it is, rather than removing everything and starting from scratch? How can the carbon footprint be reduced? Can waste be recycled or repurposed? If there are better methods that can be used, assess and implement them.

DESIGN WITH TIME IN MIND

The desire for instant gratification – for gardens that "look good all year round" – needs to be abandoned, along with plastic grass and fake plants. Replace harmful chemical pesticides, herbicides, and fertilizers with the growing range of organic and eco-friendly alternatives. A garden is a living, fragile ecosystem, encompassing a complex web of interlinked species and processes. We need to respect nature and understand the web of life so that we co-exist with it instead of trying to master it.

INTRODUCE RESILIENT DESIGN

Consider the site and its conditions in the past and present so you can determine the characteristics of the site and work with them, not against them. Be mindful of previous land usage, potential contamination, and average rainfall, as well as present conditions such as soil geology and exposure to the elements – wind, rain, and sun; and today's gardeners must also design for future conditions, climatic changes, and unpredictable weather events.

[Above] This show garden by Sam Ovens at RHS Tatton Park Flower Show celebrated light-touch landscaping: open timber structures floated over a dense matrix of plants.
[Right] On the Yeo Valley Organic show garden, I designed the planting scheme to show that seasonality can be beautiful. The garden was at the first-ever Autumn Chelsea Flower Show (postponed from May due to Covid 19 lockdowns in 2021), so I chose late-season colour and plants "going over" to celebrate the colours of the time of year and the ephemeral beauty of flowers in bloom.

GARDENING FOR EVERYONE

TAYSHAN HAYDEN-SMITH is a social activist, guerrilla gardener, and RHS ambassador. He founded Grow2know in 2019 with the aim of making horticulture accessible to all.

Tayshan in Hope Gardens, previously named the Grenfell Garden of Peace. Created with no plan, the garden provided a place for the community to gather and unify in what was a barren space.

"

WHY DO YOU THINK COMMUNITY GARDENS ARE SO IMPORTANT?

Community gardens are where the seeds of change will be sown – a space where people and plants coexist to create social and environmental impact.

I grew up in the shadow of Grenfell Tower in North Kensington, London, where the fire of 2017 took 72 lives and left a legacy of trauma, anger, and shock. The response to the tragedy demonstrated the importance of community; with no particular plan, people turned to nature, reclaiming a barren and unloved space. A transformation occurred as the community came together to dig, plant, and talk, and the space became known as the Grenfell Garden of Peace. It was a symbol of hope to many, as community members would walk past to share a smile, a conversation or to offer their time – often, five minutes would turn into ten, which would turn into an hour, which would turn into days.

THIS EXPERIENCE WAS THE BIRTH OF GROW2KNOW, A GRASS-ROOTS NON-PROFIT ORGANIZATION THAT YOU FOUNDED IN 2019. WHAT ARE THE MAIN AIMS OF GROW2KNOW?

The heart of the organization lies in reclaiming space and reconnecting people with nature and each other. Putting community at the forefront in the creation of public, outdoor spaces, we focus on consultation, collaboration, and place-making. We are committed to inspiring a culture change to implement more sustainable systems that promote biodiversity, circular economies, and regenerative practices. We are on a mission to inspire, heal, and educate through horticulture.

HOW IMPORTANT DO YOU THINK IT IS THAT WE MAKE HORTICULTURE ACCESSIBLE TO ALL?

Gardening should be a core skill, as it is through plants that we will start to understand how we can solve both environmental and societal issues. Without education, understanding, or points of access, we are becoming further disconnected from nature. The environment must be a priority, but it can't be unless we make more of an effort to bring the younger generations with us to explore a truly sustainable future.

WHAT IS CLIMATE CHANGE?

CLIMATE CHANGE REFERS TO A FLUCTUATION IN LONGSTANDING RECORDED AVERAGES OF WEATHER PATTERNS. THESE CHANGES ARE ESCALATED BY GREENHOUSE GASES, OF WHICH HUMAN ACTIVITY PRODUCES SUBSTANTIAL EMISSIONS.

The climate is generally defined as the prevailing weather conditions over a specific region, or globally, looking at factors such as temperature, rainfall, and wind. Typically, average readings are taken over a 30-year period to assess the climate. "Climate change" refers to instances where this average alters, and generally when the changes continue over decades, centuries, or even longer, while "weather" is defined by conditions in a particular area, over a shorter term of days and weeks. Climate change is accelerated by emissions of greenhouse gases, which become trapped in the Earth's atmosphere, absorbing and generating heat, and warming the planet. These gases consist mainly of naturally occurring carbon dioxide, methane, nitrous oxide, and water vapour, as well as synthetic fluorinated gases. While most of the gases occur naturally on Earth, they are also produced in large quantities through human activities.

A report that was issued in 2021 by the IPCC (Intergovernmental Panel on Climate Change) attested to the fact that we are in a state of climate catastrophe, with a dramatic increase in the kind of events indicative of the early consequences of an increasingly unpredictable and altering climate. Soaring temperatures, destructive flooding, and ferocious forest fires are events that will continue to escalate unless we intervene rapidly. Though the Covid-19 pandemic saw a dip in emissions in 2020 to 2021, as the world stood still, this was not enough to decelerate our course for climate disaster. The report demonstrates how we need to employ momentum, innovation, and global cooperation to use our ever-narrowing window of opportunity to avoid a catastrophic global temperature increase of up to 3°C (5.4°F) in the next 50 years.

THE INTERGOVERNMENTAL PANEL ON CLIMATE CHANGE

The Intergovernmental Panel on Climate Change (IPCC) was established by the World Meteorological Organization and the United Nations Environment Program in 1988 to assess scientific information on climate change and to publish reports that summarize the science. In IPCC reports, climate change is referred to as a combination of both natural and human-induced factors. In other documentation, the term "climate change" is sometimes used to refer specifically to change caused by human activity.

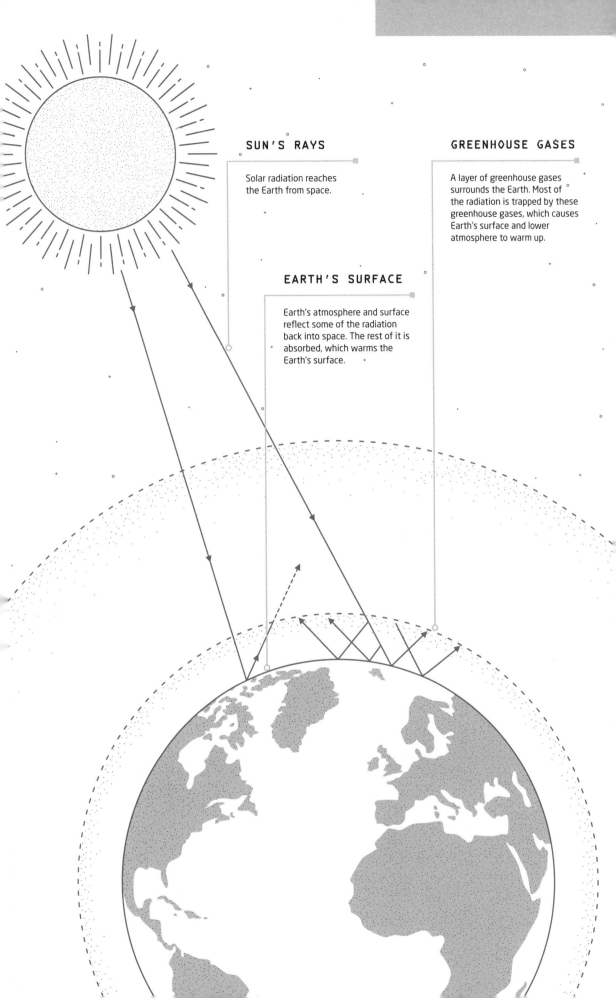

SUN'S RAYS

Solar radiation reaches the Earth from space.

GREENHOUSE GASES

A layer of greenhouse gases surrounds the Earth. Most of the radiation is trapped by these greenhouse gases, which causes Earth's surface and lower atmosphere to warm up.

EARTH'S SURFACE

Earth's atmosphere and surface reflect some of the radiation back into space. The rest of it is absorbed, which warms the Earth's surface.

Effects on the planet at 1.5 and 2°C
In 2022, the global warming level of approximately 1°C (1.8°F) was already causing damage, such as global heatwaves, ferocious wildfires, and devastating hurricanes. This graphic shows that for temperature increases of 1.5 and 2°C, the effects would become more widespread and extreme worldwide.

RISING TEMPERATURES

There have been natural shifts in Earth's climate since the birth of the planet. Over millennia, conditions have fluctuated substantially between colder glacial and warmer interglacial periods. There is irrefutable evidence to support the claim that human output directly affects the current global changes in our climate, largely due to the burning of fossil fuels that leach carbon dioxide into the atmosphere.

Temperatures in the atmosphere, greenhouse gas concentrations, and sea levels have all risen, while sea ice and snow levels have been steadily decreasing. There is now more than enough evidence to indicate that the climate has been warming since the arrival of the Industrial Revolution, in ways unparalleled to those seen even when looking back over millennia. Temperatures will continue to rise, bringing problematic consequences, with the outpouring of greenhouse gases.

It is estimated that if we continue to emit these gases at the present rate, there could be a temperature rise of 2.5–5°C (4.5–9°F) by the end

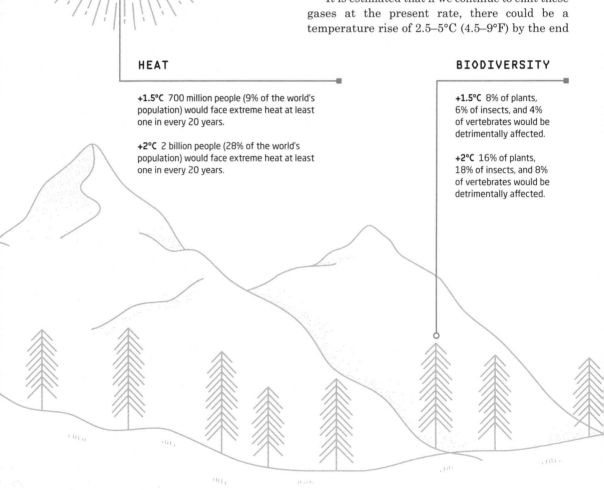

HEAT

+1.5°C 700 million people (9% of the world's population) would face extreme heat at least one in every 20 years.

+2°C 2 billion people (28% of the world's population) would face extreme heat at least one in every 20 years.

BIODIVERSITY

+1.5°C 8% of plants, 6% of insects, and 4% of vertebrates would be detrimentally affected.

+2°C 16% of plants, 18% of insects, and 8% of vertebrates would be detrimentally affected.

There is now more than enough recorded evidence to indicate that the climate has been warming since the arrival of the Industrial Revolution, in ways unparalleled to those seen even when looking back over millennia.

of the century. With a turn towards sustainable energy, this could drop to a rise of 0.25–1.75°C (0.4–3.1°F), but to achieve this, a considerable global effort will need to be adopted. Even with our best efforts, we are at a point now where we cannot completely alleviate the effects of climate change. We will need to adapt, finding new ways to build resilience and cope with threatening prospects worldwide.

CLIMATE EMERGENCY

In 2019, the Oxford Dictionary word of the year was "climate emergency". Data showed that use of the phrase had increased by over 10,000 per cent during the course of the year. The definition of "climate emergency" as given by the Oxford Dictionary is: "a situation in which urgent action is required to reduce or halt climate change and avoid potentially irreversible environmental damage resulting from it."

EXTREME WEATHER

+1.5°C The risk of flooding would increase by 100%.

+2°C The risk of flooding would increase by 170%.

WATER AVAILABILITY

+1.5°C 350 million urban dwellers would experience severe drought conditions by 2100.

+2°C 410 million urban dwellers would experience severe drought conditions by 2100.

SEA-LEVEL RISE

+1.5°C A sea-level rise of 48cm (19in) by 2100 would impact 46 million people.

+2°C A sea-level rise of 56cm (22in) by 2100 would impact 49 million people.

GLOBAL CLIMATE CHANGE

WE ARE AT A CROSSROADS: IF A GLOBAL EFFORT IS MADE NOW TO SUBSTANTIALLY MINIMIZE GREENHOUSE GASES, THE RISE IN TEMPERATURES COULD BE ONLY TEMPORARY.

An interactive map is available that details the future climates of 530 cities across the world and links them to those that have their anticipated 2050 climate in the present day. London's climate could resemble that of Barcelona, a city 1,140km (708 miles) closer to the Equator, which would mean a 2.1°C (3.8°F) increase in the city's annual temperature forecast. Paris would probably resemble Canberra, while Milan could have the climate of present-day Dallas by 2050.

MITIGATION OF CLIMATE CHANGE

The IPCC's third report instalment, which was issued on 4 April 2022, states that without immediate and deep reductions of emissions across all sectors, limiting global warming to 1.5°C (2.7°F) is beyond reach; but if the world's nations endeavour to substantially minimize greenhouse gases in the 2020s, then the overreach could be temporary, and temperatures would have the potential to revert by 1.5°C (2.7°F) by the end of the century.

To lower and restrict carbon dioxide accumulation in the atmosphere, it is expected that technologies such as carbon dioxide removal will need to be utilized, and the world must achieve net zero emissions by 2050.

"We are at a crossroads. The decisions we make now can secure a liveable future. We have the tools and know-how required to limit warming," said IPCC Chair Hoesung Lee. "I am encouraged by climate action being taken in many countries. There are policies, regulations, and market instruments that are proving effective. If these are scaled up and applied more widely and equitably, they can support deep emissions reductions and stimulate innovation."

Key
- City with annual temperature rise
- Future city climate

SEATTLE
Annual temperature rise: **2.6°C (4.7°F)**
Future climate: **San Francisco**

WASHINGTON
Annual temperature rise: **3°C (5.4°F)**
Future climate: **Nashville**

SANTIAGO
Annual temperature rise: **1.1°C (2°F)**
Future climate: **Nicosia**

SAO PAULO
Annual temperature rise: **1.4°C (2.5°F)**
Future climate: **Miami**

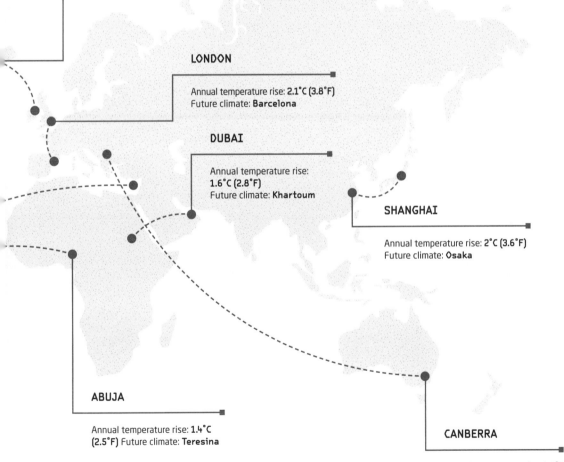

REYKJAVIK

Annual temperature rise: **2.2°C (3.9°F)**
Future climate: **Belfast**

LONDON

Annual temperature rise: **2.1°C (3.8°F)**
Future climate: **Barcelona**

DUBAI

Annual temperature rise: **1.6°C (2.8°F)**
Future climate: **Khartoum**

SHANGHAI

Annual temperature rise: **2°C (3.6°F)**
Future climate: **Osaka**

ABUJA

Annual temperature rise: **1.4°C (2.5°F)** Future climate: **Teresina**

CANBERRA

Annual temperature rise: **1.6°C (2.8°F)** Future climate: **Skopje**

The ability to grow warm-climate fruits outdoors
in the UK, such as *Citrus lumia*, the lemon pear
shown here, may sound like a bonus, but certain
plants – both native and non-native – may not
grow as well in our new climate, causing losses
to the ecosystem.

WHAT DOES THIS MEAN FOR GARDENING?

GLOBAL WARMING WILL AFFECT OUR LIVES IN MANY WAYS, SOME OF WHICH WE CANNOT INFLUENCE. BUT HERE, WE SHALL EXPLORE WHAT THE CONSEQUENCES ARE FOR GARDENERS, LANDSCAPE DESIGNERS, AND THE HORTICULTURE INDUSTRY, AND HOW GARDENS CAN BE DESIGNED SO THEY ARE RESILIENT TO THE PREDICTED EFFECTS.

The world is made up of varied landscapes and habitats, for example polar regions, tundra, evergreen forests, seasonal forests, grasslands, deserts, tropical rainforests, oceans, and the built environment, meaning towns, cities, and other human architecture. Climate change is expected to affect every country across the globe, but the impact will not be equal, due to social, political, geographic, and climatic conditions. This book cannot provide specific information for gardening in worldwide environments; however, it offers guidelines, principles, ideas, and inspiration that can be adapted to a number of different contexts to help mitigate the negative impacts of climate change and make the most of the opportunities a warming climate presents.

LOCAL CHANGES

I live in the UK, which is in a temperate region, where climate scientists predict that we can expect to experience warmer, wetter winters and hotter, drier summers, with frost potentially being a thing of the past. In some ways, this doesn't sound too bad, as it presents the opportunity of cultivating a wider array of exotic and unusual plants. The idea of being able to grow avocados, pomegranates, mangoes, and citrus fruits in our gardens and allotments probably sounds enticing to most British gardeners. However, the planet's ecosystems are in fine balance, and as climate change takes effect, we need to consider the risks and the loss of plants that we might mourn alongside the opportunities.

RESTORING ECOSYSTEMS

"Healthy ecosystems are more resilient to climate change and provide life-critical services such as food and clean water," said IPCC Working Group II co-chair professor Hans-Otto Pörtner in February 2022. "By restoring degraded ecosystems and effectively and equitably conserving 30 to 50 per cent of Earth's land, freshwater, and ocean habitats, society can benefit from nature's capacity to absorb and store carbon, and we can accelerate progress towards sustainable development, but adequate finance and political support are essential."

HOTHOUSE PROJECT

The Hothouse, a collaboration between myself and Je,
was commissioned by developer Lendlease as a landmark
project for the London Design Festival 2020.

JE AHN is an architect and founder of design practice Studio Weave in London. The Hackney-based studio creates pioneering designs for pubic and private clients with a focus on building community, championing sustainable practice, and initiating collaborations across disciplines.

"

WHAT INSPIRED THE DESIGN FOR THE HOTHOUSE? IT'S A BEAUTIFUL STRUCTURE WITH AN ELEMENT OF PLAYFULNESS IN THE DESIGN.

I feel architecture should offer delight, and garden design is similar – something that gives us comfort and joy, seeing ourselves as not separate from nature but a part of it.

The Hothouse design comes from the context of the site, Lee Valley, where the landscape has been used for food production for generations. The controlled environment of the hothouse building gives the opportunity to cultivate plants that won't necessarily grow or be productive in the current climate in this country.

I love the idea of having a more Mediterranean climate in the UK, but on the flip side, it is a scary thought that the climate is changing so rapidly that scientists predict that we may see avocado and citrus trees as common plants in London in the near future. I thought this was an interesting way to transmit a message on the changing climate.

HOW IMPORTANT DO YOU THINK THE LANDSCAPE IS IN THE PUBLIC REALM, AND HOW CAN WE IMPROVE THE DIALOGUE BETWEEN LANDSCAPE AND THE BUILT ENVIRONMENT?

I don't see a distinction between designing buildings and designing for land around them. Some rebalancing is needed – we went through an era where design was too human-centric, and we need to change to nature first, with humans and nature in harmony.

HOW ARE YOU DESIGNING CLIMATE RESILIENCE INTO YOUR WORK, AND HAS THIS CHANGED IN THE TIME YOU HAVE BEEN PRACTISING?

My attitude has always been that a building is something we create to protect ourselves from certain environments, but while we're doing that we also have to protect our habitat, the planet itself. On the practical side, it was a lot harder ten years ago to find information or products seeking to reduce carbon footprint. While this is increasingly easy, there are still regulations that need to be adapted to encourage sustainable use of materials, how labour is organized, and how we transport materials.

RISKS AND OPPORTUNITIES

There are several main climate issues facing gardeners and landscape designers in the UK and other temperate regions. Flooding and heavy rainfall causes waterlogged soil and damages plants; it can also cause or worsen soil erosion, as can strong winds, which have the capacity to bring down mature trees, too. Warmer winters could spell an increase in diseases and pests, without the cold to eliminate them. Unpredictable frosts may kill off plants blooming earlier in milder winters, while hotter, drier summers will bring heat stress and parched soil, meaning that the need for water will escalate.

KEY OPPORTUNITIES

These issues can also create opportunities, with the possibility of cultivating a more diverse range of species over a longer growing season. Floodwater can be accommodated within green spaces and retained for irrigation during the drier months, while green infrastructure offers cooling potential, and planting schemes can be designed to be adaptable and less reliant on input of resources.

BIOPHILIC DESIGN

Psychoanalyst Erich Fromm first introduced the word "biophilia" in his 1973 book *The Anatomy of Human Destructiveness*. He described it as the "passionate love of life and of all that is alive . . . whether in a person, a plant, an idea, or a social group".

Biophilic design is employed by architects and designers to increase connectivity to the natural world in built environments at both residential and city scale. It is argued that biophilic design and an increased connection to nature has health, environmental, and economic benefits. Initiatives can be as small as bringing cut flowers into the home, or as large as mass tree plantings or urban greening plans.

[Above] Nigel Dunnett, professor of landscape architecture at Sheffield University and landscape designer, uses logs as sculptural wave forms in his own garden, providing habitats as well as aesthetic structures.

[Left] Charred logs sweep through the landscape in the Yeo Valley Organic Garden at RHS Chelsea Flower Show 2021. Such logs eventually break down, adding charcoal to the soil to hold nutrients and water.

01

[01] In the Perennial Sanctuary Garden, exhibited at RHS Hampton Court Flower Show in 2017, I used minimal hard landscaping and championed swathes of uplifting planting to create an immersive, peaceful escape. [02] Small multistem trees, such as this *Amelanchier lamarckii*, are a good option for small gardens, as their light canopy allows dappled light to filter through. [03] *Crataegus monogyna* is a typical hedgerow plant in the UK, but "pruned up" to reveal the multistem form, it can be a beautiful specimen tree. [04] Timber composting bays, with a roof designed to be covered in climbing plants, create an aesthetically pleasing compost area.

02

03

KEY ACTIONS FOR GARDENERS

CONSIDERING HOW WE OPTIMIZE OUR OUTSIDE SPACE AND MAKING SUSTAINABLE CHOICES CAN HAVE A HUGE IMPACT IN SUPPORTING OUR ECOSYSTEMS AND INCREASING THE SUSTAINABILITY OF OUR GARDENS.

INCLUDE TREES

There is nearly always a suitable tree for any garden; choose species that are able to deal with local climatic conditions and will cope with the future changes to the climate, too. Mitigate the loss of any trees with at least one, preferably multiple, replacements, as they draw carbon out of the air. As it is an important habitat for many species, including rare invertebrates, dead wood is best left in the landscape – with a bit of creative thinking, it can be aesthetically pleasing, too.

REDUCE HARD LANDSCAPING

While gardens need hard surfaces for practical accessibility, areas of hard materials such as paving don't need to be impermeable deserts. For example, leaving planted channels between slabs or using permeable materials such as gravel can add to the aesthetic interest of the space as well as reducing the risk of flooding.

PRODUCE COMPOST

Every 1kg (2¼lb) of site-made compost typically saves 100g (3½ oz) of carbon dioxide emissions, which could add up to more than 5.1kg (11¼lb) carbon saved per gardener every year. Although it doesn't usually represent the most beautiful space, compost production is key to a sustainable, circular approach where the aim is that nothing is sent to landfill. With forethought, the composting area can be screened creatively. There are also discreet and compact "off-the-shelf" composting units for small spaces. These take up little room and can compost at accelerated rates due to their innovative designs.

04

[01] Solar panels on a green roof provide renewable energy. [02] Pioneering green architect Emilio Ambasz transposed a 100,000sq m (120,000sq yd) park in the city centre onto 15 stepped terraces of the ACROS Fukuoka Prefectural International Hall, creating a stunning roof park and utilizing roof space that would otherwise lie empty. [03] Productive beds can be incorporated in many different spaces, and growing food can bring us closer to nature. Here, an allotment on the roof of the Queen Elizabeth Hall, South Bank, London, provides food for the centre's cafés and restaurants.

[04] At Stylus, 116 Old Street, London, landscape designer John Davies' primary aim was to maximize the biodiversity of the roof area to increase the ecological impact on the local environment. An intensive green roof system supports a mix of trees, shrubs, perennials, and grasses, combined with 40sq m (48sq yd) of green walls designed in collaboration with Tapestry Vertical Gardens, a green wall specialist. [05] Seedheads and grasses provide beautiful interest in the autumn and winter months, as demonstrated here by Nigel Dunnett's planting at the Barbican Centre, London.

USE RENEWABLE TECHNOLOGIES

Reduce your reliance on fossil fuels and incorporate renewable technologies where climatic conditions allow, for example solar panels, solar lighting, wind power, and hydroelectric, ground- and air-sourced heating technologies.

THINK ABOUT GREENING ON ALL PLANES

Vertical surfaces such as fences and walls can be greened with climbing plants or green wall technologies, offering a range of benefits that include habitats, food, and shelter for animals and invertebrates. They can also provide insulation for buildings.

ADD GREEN ROOFS

Green roof systems can be incorporated into any structures – sheds, garages, bin stores – with forethought and planning. This will increase biodiversity and can sequester up to 0.375kg carbon per sq m (¾lb per 1¼sq yd) per year. They also insulate the internal spaces beneath them and increase the life of the roof membranes. For retro-fitting projects, ensure that the structure is capable of taking the increased weight; consult a structural engineer if you are in doubt.

INCLUDE PRODUCTIVE PLANTS

You could opt for a formal productive area, with raised beds; a more integrated approach, with edimentals (ornamental edibles) incorporated into the wider planting; or a "food forest" approach, where interlinked species of productive plants and trees sustainably co-exist. Planning for food production can be educational, particularly for children, and deepens our connection with nature. It is rewarding and the end result is delicious, too!

DESIGN SEASONAL PLANTING AREAS

Successional planting design, where different species of plants flower throughout the year and succeed each other, can mean that cut flowers, foliage, and seedheads are available for use year-round. Cut flowers and foliage bring nature inside, and can save up to 7.9kg (17 ½lb) carbon per bunch compared with buying imported or commercially produced bunches.

05

THE BIODIVERSITY CRISIS

ALONGSIDE THE CLIMATE EMERGENCY IS THE BIODIVERSITY CRISIS, WHICH IS EQUALLY URGENT. WE ARE SEEING A DECLINE IN, AND EXTINCTIONS OF, WILD AND CULTIVATED SPECIES WORLDWIDE.

The depletion of pollinators and declining soil health has a devastating effect on the food chain and delicate global ecosystems. Sir Robert Watson, who is chair of the Intergovernmental Science-Policy Platform on Biodiversity and Ecosystem Services (IPBES), states that there is overwhelming evidence that "the health of ecosystems on which we and all other species depend is deteriorating more rapidly than ever. We are eroding the very foundations of our economies, livelihoods, food security, health, and quality of life worldwide." Urgent and sustained action is required to remedy the biodiversity crisis across all activities of the economy.

MAP LOCAL BIODIVERSITY

If you live in the UK, you can help to map the biodiversity of garden plants by adding the plants in your garden to RHS My Garden online (rhs.org.uk/my-garden). The RHS has information and resources that will help you to grow and conserve this important biodiversity for future generations to enjoy. Species identification apps are also available worldwide that enable anyone with a smartphone to identify and learn about the plants in their garden or local area.

INSECT ARMAGEDDON

Entomologists are warning us of the disastrous effect environmental pressures are having on the essential insect population. A warming planet, overzealous usage of pesticides, pollution (of light, soil, and air), and loss of habitat are some of the factors in a dangerous concoction threatening insect life. The crucial role insects play within our ecosystem cannot be overestimated: they are the tiny workers holding the rest of us up. Without them we would be plunged into ecological pandemonium.

Professor Dave Goulson of Sussex University in the UK states: "Insects make up about two-thirds of all life on Earth [but] there has been some kind of horrific decline. We appear to be making vast tracts of land inhospitable to most forms of life, and are currently on course for ecological Armageddon. If we lose the insects, then everything is going to collapse."

As gardeners, we can support insects in many ways, providing habitats, food sources, cover, and protection, and avoiding the use of harmful and indiscriminate chemical pesticides.

[Top] You may have noticed that there are not nearly as many insects splattered on your car after driving as there used to be. **[Left]** Bees killed by the use of agricultural pesticides.

INCLUDE INSECT HABITATS

Invertebrate and insect decline is a global crisis driven by unsustainable practices. We need to consider insects in our planning, designing their habitats into the gardens. A garden designed for diverse invertebrate life will also be full of biodiverse plant life: one sustains the other.

DESIGN FOR WILDLIFE

Larger wild animals, such as birds and mammals, also need our help. Habitat loss is an increasing global problem due to urbanization: local wildlife is being forced out. We can provide food and shelter in our gardens and share these spaces with wild species. Our gardens are not just for us.

GARDEN WITHOUT TOXIC CHEMICALS

Pesticides, fungicides, and weedkillers are not specific to the pests, pathogens, and weeds that users are targeting. Beneficial pollinating insects can be killed by pesticides, and poisoned slugs can be eaten by wild animals and pets, unintentionally killing them. Adopting good practice in cultivation, cultivar selection, and garden hygiene – and encouraging natural enemies – reduces pest, disease, and weed problems and helps biodiversity. Using sustainably produced fertilizers such as organic seaweed feed, homemade comfrey tea, or organic farmyard manure further avoids environmental damage.

PLANT SUSTAINABLE SCHEMES

"Right plant, right place", the adage coined by visionary gardener Beth Chatto, is increasingly important. Today it refers not only to current conditions, but to future conditions and unpredictable weather events. Well-designed plant communities can adapt to local climate events, such as flooding or drought, needing little human intervention. Victorian-style bedding plantings, expansive lawns, and regularly mown roundabouts and roadside verges need to be relegated to history.

INCLUDE NATURAL WATER

Natural ponds and small water features provide an extra habitat in gardens, significantly enhancing biodiversity. These need to be free of harmful chemicals such as chlorine and bromine, and should ideally include planting as shelter for wildlife, which also oxygenates the water, keeping it healthy.

CONSIDER ALTERNATIVES TO LAWNS

Traditional mown green lawns, which are limited to a few species of turf grasses, could be described as "green deserts" with little ecological value. By mowing less, you will allow flowering species to provide food for pollinators. Consider alternatives to a lawn where it is not possible to keep it in good condition without constant input of resources, such as water and fertilizers.

01

BUILDING IN BIODIVERSITY

PLACING BIODIVERSITY AT THE FOREFRONT OF OUR GARDENING CHOICES WILL HELP TO PROTECT AND SUPPORT AN ESSENTIAL PART OF OUR ECOSYSTEM, AS WELL AS CREATING A BEAUTIFUL, THRIVING GARDEN FULL OF LIFE.

[01] Including insect habitats will help to support our dwindling and essential invertebrate and insect populations. [02] Natural ponds and small water features provide an extra habitat for biodiversity, and frogs and toads are a natural form of pest control. [03] Using non-toxic ways to manage your garden means a safe environment for wildlife, and will encourage natural pest control. Comfrey (*Symphytum officinale*) can be used to make an organic fertilizer.

02

03

04

05

06

[04] Sustainable planting schemes with a mix of native and non-native plants provide a beautiful, diverse habitat, as demonstrated here by Professor James Hitchmough at RHS Garden Wisley, UK. [05] Natural water features provide peaceful sounds and can be chemical free, with natural filtration systems.
[06] Meadow planting is a great alternative to a lawn and requires less maintenance. There are meadow mat products that are laid like turf, yielding quick, reliable results.

Thousands of ancient olive trees in Italy,
destroyed by *Xylella fastidiosa*.

BIOSECURITY THREATS

THE INTRODUCTION OF PESTS AND DISEASES CAN SPELL DISASTER FOR NATIVE PLANTS, COMPOUNDED BY UNSUSTAINABLE HORTICULTURAL PRACTICES AND CLIMATE CHANGE.

Threats to plants can come in the form of pests, diseases, and invasive non-native plants. The introduction of plants for aesthetic or commercial reasons can sometimes spell disaster for native species. This issue can be compounded by the effects of climate change, which can act in favour of aggressive, adaptable, non-native plants, and unfavourably for sensitive native species. Horticulture is often regarded as the main entry point for these non-native species, which have usually been introduced for their ornamental properties. Legislative developments around the world now recognize this, with the introduction of programmes aimed at managing non-native invasive plant species such as Japanese knotweed and giant hogweed, pests such as Asian hornets and American bullfrogs, and diseases such as Dutch elm disease and horse chestnut bleeding canker.

The shift in horticultural rhythms is one way in which gardeners can see a noticeable effect, especially at the turn of the seasons, noting a change in the emergence of new leaves, the early appearance of flowers, or tree foliage beginning to change hue. The timing of these occurrences is unequivocally related to the changing climate and can affect biosecurity too – for example, pests may no longer be killed off by cold weather, and invasive species may be able to thrive in warmer, wetter, or dryer climates. A resilient garden is one that is resilient to pests and diseases, as well as to climate change.

> The introduction of plants for aesthetic or commercial reasons can spell disaster for native species. This can be compounded by the effects of climate change, which can act in favour of aggressive, adaptable, non-native plants and unfavourably for sensitive native species.

XYLELLA FASTIDIOSA

An example of a bacterial disease that has damaging effects on a wide range of plants is *Xylella fastidiosa*, which is spread solely by xylem sap-feeding insects. There have been outbreaks of this disease in many parts of Europe, with the decimation of thousands of olive trees in Italy, including ancient groves. As the disease causes afflictions such as leaf scorch, wilting, dieback, and plant death, the UK government and horticultural industry have understandable anxieties over the risk of it being introduced to the environment by means of imported contaminated plants. Stringent measures are being executed in an attempt to keep *Xylella* from entering the UK. A scheme has been initiated by Natural England (NE) to prevent and manage invasive non-native species such as this.

CHAPTER THREE

ANALYSING YOUR SITE

061

SITE ANALYSIS

IT IS ESSENTIAL TO UNDERSTAND THE SPECIFIC CONDITIONS OF YOUR GARDEN IN ORDER TO DESIGN A RESILIENT AND SUSTAINABLE LANDSCAPE.

When designing a resilient and sustainable garden, it is important that you acquire a good understanding of the climatic conditions of your site and how they will affect it in both the short term and the future. Planning for adaptability at the outset is important to ensure resilience long term. This ethos needs to run through the entire design, from what happens on and beneath the ground (topsoils, subsoils, drainage, and even subbase materials) through to the surface finishes (paving, decking, cladding, and mulches) and into planting and tree selection, ensuring that all plants are suitable for the site long term. Ultimately, the aim is to provide multiple benefits for our gardens, ourselves, and the wider environments around us.

Understanding soil conditions is integral to designing a planting scheme that will thrive. A trial pit reveals the below-ground conditions, showing the soil profile (see pages 66–67).

LOCATION

WHERE IS YOUR SITE LOCATED AND WHAT ARE THE ASSOCIATED CLIMATIC CONDITIONS THAT WILL AFFECT WHAT YOU CAN GROW?

The location can dramatically affect the suitability and sustainability of your garden's plants and materials. For example, a coastal garden will often have to cope with high winds, and may be exposed to high levels of salt, which can be corrosive and damaging to plants that aren't adapted to these conditions. City gardens may be affected by contaminated soils, pollution, raised temperatures from an urban heat island, and wind tunnels caused by tall buildings. Gardens may also be located in floodplains (or potential floodplains in the future), deserts, mountainous regions, or forests. Each type of location will have unique characteristics and a microclimate that will need to be assessed.

[Top] My design for the Yard House city garden is situated within a courtyard, so it is very sheltered. This garden is close to a busy high street, so it has to contend with high pollution levels and urban temperatures.
[Above] Coastal gardens can get battered by strong winds and high levels of salt from the sea, so hardy shrubs and trees are good choices. Look at what is growing well locally for inspiration.

URBAN HEAT ISLANDS

Cities and other built-up urban sprawls can considerably affect the environment as human intervention creates distinctive changes in both weather and climate. The combination of an intense concentration of towering buildings, networks of roads, and concrete and glass structures can create complex temperature, rain, wind, and atmosphere formations. The siting of tall buildings can cause wind tunnels, while impermeable surfaces channel water and increase the risk of flooding. Air quality is compromised by pollution from invisible particles expelled by traffic and industry. The urban heat island effect can cause temperatures in cities to rise by up to 5°C (9°F), which heightens the intensity of heatwaves.

MICROCLIMATE

This term refers to the climate of a small area, especially one that differs from the climate of the surrounding area, for example, an urban light-well or a walled garden.

SUBURBS

Areas with more built structures will absorb more heat, and reradiate it back into the atmosphere, increasing the temperature.

RURAL AREAS

The plants and trees in rural areas absorb far less heat than the dark, man-made materials that are more prevalent in urban environments.

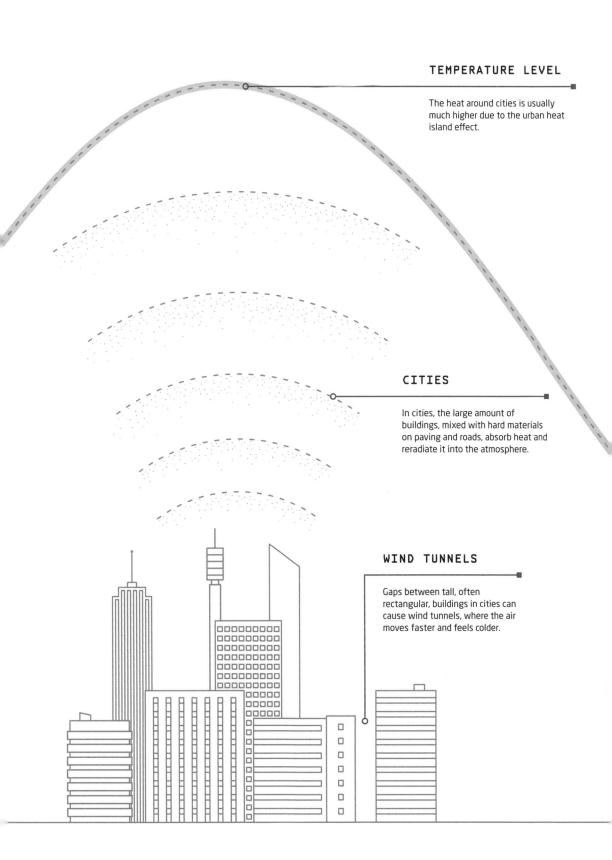

TEMPERATURE LEVEL

The heat around cities is usually much higher due to the urban heat island effect.

CITIES

In cities, the large amount of buildings, mixed with hard materials on paving and roads, absorb heat and reradiate it into the atmosphere.

WIND TUNNELS

Gaps between tall, often rectangular, buildings in cities can cause wind tunnels, where the air moves faster and feels colder.

065

SOIL AND GEOLOGY

WHAT IS THE MAKE-UP OF THE EXISTING SOIL IN YOUR GARDEN? DO YOU HAVE A SUFFICIENT DEPTH OF TOPSOIL, AND WILL IT BE AFFECTED BY EROSION?

Understanding your soil is key to knowing what will grow successfully on the site; while some plants are tolerant of a range of conditions, others are not, so you need to know whether yours is light and sandy, heavy clay, or loamy soil (see pages 68–69). You may have a deep layer of topsoil, or it may be scarce or even non-existent. Soil erosion is a risk on exposed sites on steep slopes, and it may be worsened by the effects of climate change, such as heavy rainfall, flash flooding, or baking heat.

Existing soils can be improved by adding organic matter, such as homemade compost. If the condition is really poor, or the soil is contaminated, you can import topsoil – but bear in mind that this isn't always the most sustainable practice. Check that the soil supplier complies with local laws and standards for sustainability, and that the soil has been properly screened for contaminants. If this information is vague, you may prefer to look for a more reputable supplier who is transparent about their sources and processes of production.

SOIL MAPS

Consulting soil maps is a good way to learn about the conditions of your site. Geographical maps that break down the soil type and geology of an area are available online, often provided as free resources from universities. You can investigate further by digging trial pits, testing by hand, or engaging a soil expert to analyse the makeup, pH, and condition of the soil. In the UK, the RHS offers a

> Existing soils can be improved by adding organic matter, such as homemade compost. If the condition is really poor, or the soil is contaminated, you can import topsoil - but bear in mind that this isn't always the most sustainable practice.

soil analysis service, which examines soil texture, pH, organic matter content and the presence of three major plant nutrients: potassium, phosphorus, and magnesium.

TOPSOIL

The type of topsoil you buy is also important to consider. A fertile, moisture-retentive, humus-rich loam would not be suitable for a planting of drought-tolerant species inspired by Mediterranean landscapes, for example: most plants from that region will not tolerate damp soils and need a more free-draining medium. A good starting point is to research where the plants you have in mind grow in the wild, and what type of soil conditions they thrive in. Telling topsoil suppliers about the planting you hope to achieve will allow them to recommend suitable soil blends for your garden.

Soil is formed in layers, and individual layers are referred to as soil horizons. These make up the soil profile. In order to discover the soil profile of a site, a pit is dug to reveal a vertical cross-section.

ORGANIC LAYER

This layer is dark black-brown, undecomposed at the top and more decomposed at the bottom. The organic layer can be deep, shallow, or even absent in some soils.

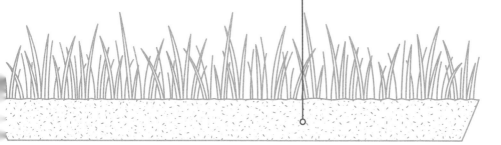

TOPSOIL

The topsoil is made up of decayed organic matter (humus) and a combination of sand, silt, and clay. It is dark brown in colour, as it contains organic matter with some minerals.

SUBSOIL

Subsoil is lighter than topsoil due to lower humus and higher mineral content. It is more rigid and compact than the topsoil. Substances move down from the topsoil layer and accumulate in the subsoil.

PARENT ROCK

The parent rock layer is made of broken-up bedrock, making it hard and stony. It is devoid of organic matter. Plant roots do not extend into this layer. This is the transition between the inner rock layer of the earth and the upper layers of soil.

BEDROCK

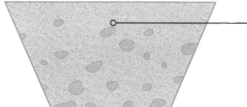

The bedrock is hard, compact, and consists of unweathered igneous, sedimentary, and metamorphic rocks. This largely comprises continuous masses rather than smaller rocks.

SOIL COMPOSITION

Soil is made up of varying proportions of inorganic particles of many different sizes. The combination of size and proportion determines some of the properties of the soil.

Permeable soils allow water to move freely through their structures, as the spaces between the particles are large and well connected. Sandy and silty soils display these characteristics and are often referred to as "light". They hold less water and don't become waterlogged or "heavy", as soils with a high clay content do.

Other soils have numerous small spaces that retain water. Clay, for example, is made up of numerous small particles, and this makes the soil "heavier", meaning it has a denser structure that compacts easily.

A mixture of grain sizes is referred to as a "loam". Measuring the percentage of sand, silt, and clay allows soil scientists to describe the soil type.

CHALKY SOIL

Soil with particles larger than 2mm (1/16in) is classified as stony. Chalky soils are often very stony, and are also made up of calcium carbonate, or lime, making them alkaline and difficult to keep fertile.

CLAY SOIL

Also known as heavy soils, clay soils have particles of less than 0.002mm, and they are composed of more than 25 per cent clay. Nutrients bind to the clay minerals in the soil, which makes this soil type very fertile. However, the spaces between the clay particles are tiny, so clay soil holds water, drains slowly, and is easily compacted if it is trodden on when wet. It also takes a while to warm up during the hotter months, but once it has done so, it can then bake to a hard consistency with visible cracks.

LOAM

A loamy soil combines different soil types, which avoids the extreme characteristics of each. Made up of clay, sand, and silt, loams are fertile, free-draining, and easy to work. You can buy loam that is predominantly clay or sand, depending on your planting scheme.

SANDY SOIL

The particles of sand are defined as 0.05 to 2mm. Also known as light soils, sandy soils have a high proportion of sand and very little clay, meaning water drains through them easily, and they warm up more quickly than soils with a higher proportion of clay. However, the water washing through the particles can remove nutrients, leaving sandy soils dry, low in nutrients, and acidic.

SILT SOIL

This type of soil has particles from 0.002 to 0.05mm in size. It is fertile, drains well, and also holds moisture well, but a disadvantage is that it is easily compacted in wet weather.

SOIL MICROORGANISMS

All soil teems with microorganisms, such as fungi, algae, and bacteria. They help to supply plants with the minerals and nutrients that are crucial for keeping them healthy, as well as enriching the soil.

SOIL TYPES

YOUR GARDEN MAY HAVE A MIXTURE OF SOIL TYPES. EACH TYPE HAS DIFFERENT CHARACTERISTICS, WHICH PARTLY DEPEND ON THE SIZE OF THE PARTICLES WITHIN IT. SOIL CAN BE DIFFICULT TO ANALYSE WITHOUT PROFESSIONAL ASSESSMENT, BUT HERE IS SOME GUIDANCE.

[01] Chalky soil is very alkaline and supports plants that are drought tolerant and like nutrient-poor soil. [02] Clay soils are very moisture retentive and often rich in nutrients.

[03] Loam is a mixture of clay, sand, and silt that avoids the extremes of other soils. Loam is generally well drained, fertile, and easy to work with. [04] Sandy soils are often very acidic, quick to drain, and quick to dry out. [05] Silt soils are fairly rare to find in a garden. They are usually fertile, fairly well drained, and they hold more moisture than sandy soils but are easily compacted. Silt soils are prone to washing away and being eroded by wind if they are left exposed without plant cover or a surface mulch.

TESTING YOUR SOIL

IT'S USEFUL TO KNOW WHERE THE SOIL IN YOUR GARDEN SITS ON THE PH SCALE OF ACIDITY/ALKALINITY AS THIS WILL INDICATE THE TYPES OF PLANTS THAT WILL STRUGGLE OR THRIVE.

It is a good idea to test the soil before you start designing your plot so that you don't waste money on plants that won't grow well. If you already have an established garden but have had a run of failed crops and yellowing leaves, testing your soil might determine the cause.

The pH scale runs from 1 to 14. If the pH level of your soil is below 7, it is acidic; above 7, it is alkaline (rich in lime and chalk). A pH level of 7 is neutral, which is best for most plants. A basic way of checking the lime levels of your soil at home is to add vinegar to a sample of soil; if it fizzes, this indicates the presence of calcium carbonate (chalk). You can buy inexpensive kits for testing pH levels at most garden centres, but for more specific results, send a sample of your soil to a laboratory for analysis. Bear in mind that if you have added lime, fertilizer, or organic matter to your soil within the last three months, this will affect the results.

If your soil is acidic, you can add lime to balance out the pH levels. Alternatively, if it is alkaline, you can balance it by adding acidifying materials to neutralize the pH, such as sulphur dust or granules. However, it takes a lot of additives to cause a significant change in pH. This has sustainability implications and the soil will soon revert to type, so it's best to plant species that are suited to your existing soil.

HOW TO PREVENT SOIL EROSION

The effects of climate change can lead to soil erosion, which is where the structure of the soil is degraded; it may be washed away by flooding, displaced by high winds, and dehydrated by high temperatures. By encouraging the health of microorganisms in the soil, gardeners help it to build resilience against these challenges. Here are some tips:

• Maintain a healthy level of plant cover in the soil all year round.
• Mulch to cover and protect the soil. Types of mulch used worldwide can include stone aggregate, woodchips, or bark mulch.
• In heavily trafficked areas, and where planting is difficult to establish and maintain - such as under the canopy of evergreen trees or shrubs - use mulches to cover and protect the soil.
• Use products such as geotextile materials and meshes to help retain the soil. Planting can be done through the mesh - if it is made of biodegradable material such as coir or jute, it will degrade as the plants become established.
• Address areas vulnerable to stormwater runoff with solutions such as swales (see p. 136), which can settle and dissipate water, preventing erosion.

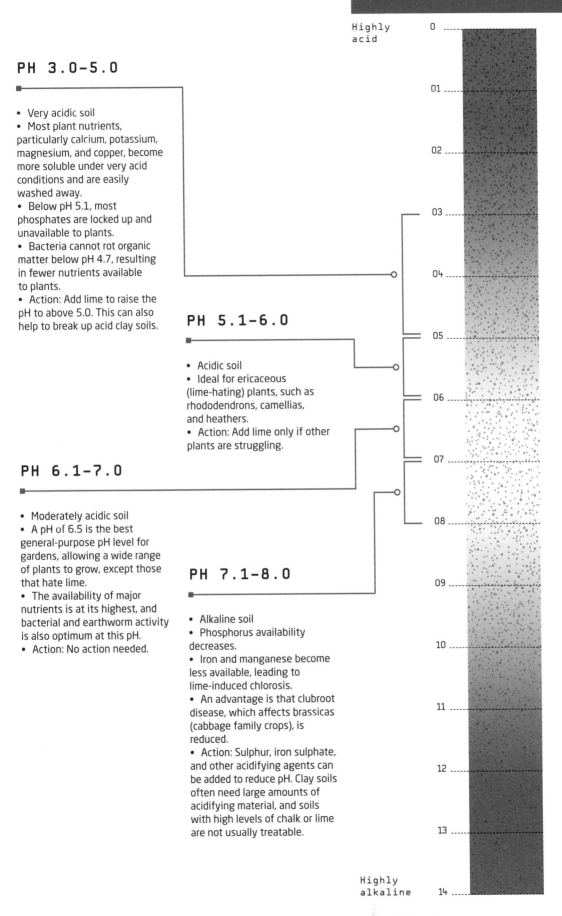

PH 3.0-5.0

- Very acidic soil
- Most plant nutrients, particularly calcium, potassium, magnesium, and copper, become more soluble under very acid conditions and are easily washed away.
- Below pH 5.1, most phosphates are locked up and unavailable to plants.
- Bacteria cannot rot organic matter below pH 4.7, resulting in fewer nutrients available to plants.
- Action: Add lime to raise the pH to above 5.0. This can also help to break up acid clay soils.

PH 5.1-6.0

- Acidic soil
- Ideal for ericaceous (lime-hating) plants, such as rhododendrons, camellias, and heathers.
- Action: Add lime only if other plants are struggling.

PH 6.1-7.0

- Moderately acidic soil
- A pH of 6.5 is the best general-purpose pH level for gardens, allowing a wide range of plants to grow, except those that hate lime.
- The availability of major nutrients is at its highest, and bacterial and earthworm activity is also optimum at this pH.
- Action: No action needed.

PH 7.1-8.0

- Alkaline soil
- Phosphorus availability decreases.
- Iron and manganese become less available, leading to lime-induced chlorosis.
- An advantage is that clubroot disease, which affects brassicas (cabbage family crops), is reduced.
- Action: Sulphur, iron sulphate, and other acidifying agents can be added to reduce pH. Clay soils often need large amounts of acidifying material, and soils with high levels of chalk or lime are not usually treatable.

Highly acid 0

01

02

03

04

05

06

07

08

09

10

11

12

13

Highly alkaline 14

PLANTS

TO DETERMINE WHICH PLANTS WILL GROW SUCCESSFULLY IN YOUR GARDEN, LOOK AT THE WIDER NATURAL ENVIRONMENT TO DISCOVER SPECIES THAT ARE THRIVING NEARBY.

One of the best ways of analysing what will grow successfully in a garden is to look at what else is thriving locally. Spend time gathering photographs, articles, and scientific reports on local nature reserves, parks, or botanic gardens; you can then use this data to guide your planting process. This approach is particularly important when you're designing and maintaining sustainable planting schemes. Forcing plants to grow where they won't thrive is never going to be sustainable, as huge amounts of time and resources will be needed to keep them going in conditions to which they aren't naturally suited.

In the wild, plants thrive in sustainable communities without any human input such as watering, pruning, mowing, or tidying. However, it is worth noting that natural processes, such as wildfires or grazing by deer, often replicate these processes. Many wild species can also work well in a garden setting. Consider the site's existing conditions, and those it is expected to experience in the future, and add adaptable plants that will be able to deal with those conditions, increasing the resilience of your garden.

[Top] Warm temperatures and steady rains lead to an explosion of colour in the Anza-Borrego desert: a super bloom of California poppies and other wildflowers blankets the hills.
[Right] The stunning colours of the super bloom of spring flowers on the Temblor Mountain range in California draws visitors from miles around.

072

"A SITE CAN BE CHANGED TO FIT A PLANT;
BUT ONLY WHEN A PLANT FITS A SITE WILL
YOUR PLANTING TRULY BE SELF-SUSTAINING."

THOMAS RAINER, PLANTING IN A POST-WILD WORLD

073

NATIVE OR NON-NATIVE PLANTS?

A CONSIDERED MIX OF NATIVE AND NON-NATIVE PLANTING COULD BE THE ANSWER TO MITIGATING THE ISSUES CAUSED BY CLIMATE CHANGE, PROVIDING A RESILIENT, RICH, AND DIVERSE ECOSYSTEM.

Exotic, non-native landscapes are often alluring. Botanic gardens and glasshouses are popular places to visit, but the non-native plants that grow within bring with them issues of culture, context, and potentially invasive species, pests that have no local predators, and devastating diseases.

Native-only planting schemes are also an attractive idea, but they often don't provide the hit of colour or sustained interest that non-native or cultivated varieties can bring. Native plants may also have shorter flowering seasons, and, in a changing climate, non-native varieties may be better suited to their new conditions. Perhaps the answer is that we should plant a mix: cultivated "wild" environments.

Both private gardens and public parks can demonstrate the role that non-native plants play alongside native species, dramatically extending the flowering season. Non-native plants can also offer food for pollinators where native species affected by climate change are flowering too early or declining in heat or drought. Careful and sensitive design, combining native and non-native species, can ensure that biodiverse ecosystems are provided.

WILD VS CULTIVATED PLANTS

The word "cultivar" is derived from the description "cultivated variety". Cultivar names are assigned to plants that are a variant within a species, or that have been formed via hybridization, where two botanically distinct plants are cross-bred to produce something new. The names are denoted using single quotation marks and are not presented in italics, which differentiates them from botanical names.

Cultivars are bred to encourage desirable qualities, such as the size and colour of blooms, or a longer flowering period. An amalgamation of wild species with cultivated variants can create a richer and more enduring plant display than either alone.

[Right] The planting at the Queen Elizabeth Olympic Park in London subtly mixes natives and non-natives, and was designed by James Hitchmough, Nigel Dunnett, and Sarah Price. [Below] The famous High-Line planting in New York, designed by Piet Oudolf, mixes native and non-native species to dramatic effect.

[Top] In urban spaces, permeable surfaces, such as areas of planting, mitigate flash flooding. The Grey to Green scheme in Sheffield is the UK's largest retro-fit SuDS project (see pages 78–79), and the UK's largest inner-city "Green Street". Designed by Nigel Dunnett, Zac Tudor, and Robert Bray Associates, the scheme offers a calm refuge in an urban environment and a green space that encourages cycling and walking.
[Left] A sealed rainwater storage tank collects water from the adjacent roof.

GREY WATER

Waste water from domestic settings - runoff from sinks, baths, and showers - can be used to irrigate plants, as long as it has no faecal contamination. Test grey water on a sample area or on specific plants before using it for large-scale irrigation, and remember that certain cleaning products can have detrimental results, damaging soil or even killing plants.

WATER

ANALYSING YOUR SITE AND EXPLORING WATER FLOW
AND STORAGE OPTIONS CAN INFORM YOU HOW TO USE
THIS PRECIOUS RESOURCE MOST EFFICIENTLY.

To make the most of rainfall, whether it is scarce or plentiful, it is essential to understand how the water will move through and over the different surfaces of your garden, including roof structures, paving, soil, and plantings.

You can analyse this by paying attention to the way your site retains water: are certain areas boggy? Does the ground feel soft underfoot? If so, this indicates poor drainage, which may need rectifying. On the other hand, cracked and degraded soil or dead plants can be signs that the site is prone to drought.

It's also worth considering whether any part of the site will be under water for a prolonged period of time – for example, a seasonal pond, swale, or stream. If so, what kind of plants and landscaping will be suitable for these areas?

Next, ask yourself how climate change will affect your garden. Will it be subject to increasingly heavy rainfall and freak weather events? Or will water be steadily more scarce, leading to periods of drought? You can assess this by referring to climate maps that predict the future climate in a given area (see page 42).

Once you have a clear idea of how water affects your plot, you can choose plants that will not only withstand the existing conditions, but will remedy them where needed. For example, in a plot that is too wet, consider plant species that will dry it out (see Chapter 5). In urban areas in particular, permeable surfaces, such as lawns or areas of planting, help to prevent flash flooding.

WATER STORAGE

You can collect and store water using underground or surface tanks and containers, then use these reserves to irrigate planting through passive wicking systems, or filling your watering cans from the taps on a water butt. Storing rainwater in urban areas reduces water reaching mains sewers, which in turn works to prevent raw sewage being discharged into waterways and oceans. Rainwater will usually become contaminated with algae which will block light from reaching plant leaves after about one week, but you can prolong its lifetime indefinitely by keeping it out of the light and away from animal and insect contact.

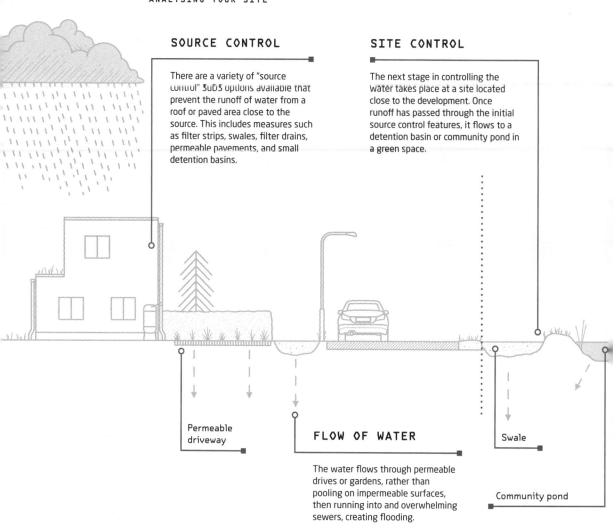

SOURCE CONTROL

There are a variety of "source control" SuDS options available that prevent the runoff of water from a roof or paved area close to the source. This includes measures such as filter strips, swales, filter drains, permeable pavements, and small detention basins.

SITE CONTROL

The next stage in controlling the water takes place at a site located close to the development. Once runoff has passed through the initial source control features, it flows to a detention basin or community pond in a green space.

Permeable driveway

FLOW OF WATER

The water flows through permeable drives or gardens, rather than pooling on impermeable surfaces, then running into and overwhelming sewers, creating flooding.

Swale

Community pond

SUDS: SUSTAINABLE DRAINAGE STRATEGIES

SUSTAINABLE DRAINAGE SYSTEMS (REFERRED TO AS SUDS) RECREATE THE FORMATION OF WATER SYSTEMS THAT OCCUR NATURALLY. BY DOING THIS, THEY TEMPER THE NEGATIVE EFFECTS THAT MAN-MADE DEVELOPMENTS CAN HAVE ON THE FLOW OF WATER.

REGIONAL CONTROL

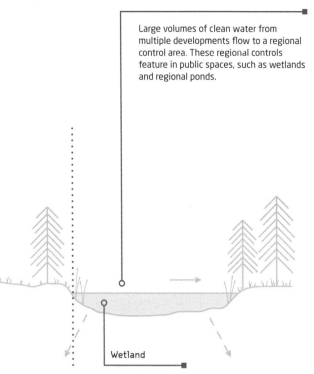

Large volumes of clean water from multiple developments flow to a regional control area. These regional controls feature in public spaces, such as wetlands and regional ponds.

Wetland

WATER SECURITY

In some parts of the world, it would already be thought shocking that drinking water is used to irrigate plants. By 2050, 5 billion people could be affected by water shortages, according to a UN report. Currently, more than 2 billion of the world's population do not have safe drinking water available in their homes, and it is predicted that by 2025, more than 50 per cent of the world's population will live in places suffering from water stress. These figures have the potential to escalate if rates of climate change and the multiplying population follow, or surpass, predictions. The reduction in quality of water, and decreasing levels of groundwater, will restrict access to water for drinking and for growing food, which will lead to a host of political and socioeconomic difficulties. There will undoubtedly be societal damage unless urgent measures are taken to alleviate the stress on rivers, lakes, and other bodies of water.

SuDS imitate a flow of water similar to that of a non-developed site, expelling water into the surrounding environment in a regulated way. This minimizes the effect on the environment when it comes to collecting, storing, and cleaning water. It is also economically effective.

When thinking about sustainable drainage systems, it is imperative for gardeners and garden designers to consider the long-term impacts. For outdoor spaces on a large scale, this includes paying attention to the social needs of the area, as well as examining the volume of water that will drain away, considering the quality of the water, and the potential for it to be directed for use elsewhere. Reusing water could help to maintain local green spaces. These systems address the issues of climate change and urbanization, and set out a solution to water drainage problems (such as flooding) and the effects of pollution from runoff. SuDS can also be incorporated in gardens on a much smaller scale by including swales in the design (see page 136).

SUDS AND SEWAGE

Unfortunately, rivers and oceans are plagued by sewage and agricultural pollution. For example, in the UK in 2020, there were more than 400,000 discharges of untreated sewage into rivers and almost 5,500 discharges into UK coastal bathing waters. This is one of the several reasons why it is important to slow the flow of water through the landscape, and SuDS contribute to that.

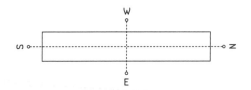

GARDEN AT 9AM

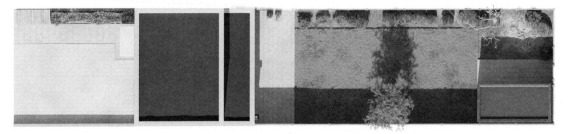

These three shadow plans show areas of shade in a garden in midsummer. This plan shows which areas of a will be in shade at 9am.

GARDEN AT 12 NOON

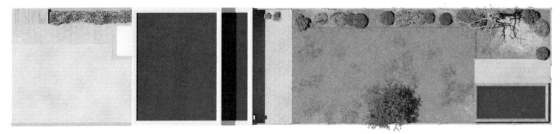

In the same garden at noon, there is only a minimal amount of shade being provided, by the house and two trees.

GARDEN AT 4PM

At 4pm, more of the garden falls into shade, but a large area in the middle and at the west-facing boundary remains exposed to the sun's glare.

SUN AND LIGHT

THE DIRECTION YOUR GARDEN FACES, AND THE AMOUNT OF LIGHT AND SHADE IT EXPERIENCES, ARE CRUCIAL TO THE CHOICES YOU MAKE ABOUT THE PLANTS YOU GROW.

The amount of sun that a garden receives is key to knowing what kind of conditions it will experience. Light is essential for plant growth and survival, and it can differ from one part of the site to another; for example, there will be a difference in light and heat levels on walls facing north, south, east, and west. Understanding the way that light moves through a space informs you how different areas will feel in terms of light, shade, and warmth, and how plants will perform in each of them.

You can analyse the light conditions in your garden by simply observing how sunlight moves over it throughout the day, year-round. Buildings, trees, fences, hedges, and structures can all block light, increasing shade, so factor this into your design decisions; bear in mind that future tall plantings in a garden can affect the light in neighbouring spaces, too. If you would prefer a more detailed analysis, you can ask a professional garden designer to generate a 3D model of your plot using Computer Aided Design (CAD) software, showing the way light will fall on it.

SHADE LEVELS

The levels of shade need careful consideration when you are designing your garden, as plants need varying levels of sunlight. Planting sun-loving species in the shade, or vice versa, will mean they won't thrive, and may even die. Sun and light also affect the way a garden will feel for people; shade-giving structures, or plants such as trees, climbers, and large shrubs, can offer respite in spaces exposed to the sun. Fast-growing species of climber, shrub, or tree can be cost-effective and environmentally friendly alternatives to building hard structures, such as covered pergolas.

TYPES OF SUN AND SHADE

Full sun More than six hours of direct sunlight each day during the summer.
Light shade The site is open to the sky, but an obstacle such as a group of trees screens it from direct sunlight.
Partial/semi-shade A plot that sees three to six hours of direct sun per day
Dappled shade Light diffused through fairly open tree canopies.
Moderate shade A site receives sunlight for two or three hours per day.
Deep/heavy shade An area that receives less than two hours of sun per day, perhaps shaded by trees or buildings.

WIND

HIGH WINDS CAN CAUSE DAMAGE IN A GARDEN, BUT WINDBREAKS AND DESIGNED FEATURES CAN CREATE SHELTER

Wind is an often overlooked factor in the garden, but it can have a serious impact on plants and our enjoyment of them. High winds can scorch leaves, damage plants, and, in some cases, kill them, if they are tender or in need of a sheltered site. You can analyse the amount of wind that affects your plot by looking for signs of damage or stress such as stunted growth on existing plants.

To protect a site from prevailing winds, make use of windbreaks and shelterbelts. These are semi-permeable masses of wind-resistant plants and trees that form a protective barrier. Designed elements, such as planters, walls, and screens, can also reduce windspeed and create shelter, resulting in a more comfortable space in which to enjoy your garden.

WHAT CAUSES WIND?

Wind can be a capricious element of our weather system, from a welcome gentle breeze on a sunny day to a ravaging force capable of ripping mature trees from their ancient standing. Although it's such a familiar presence, many of us aren't aware of what causes wind and dictates its behaviour. The simple answer is temperature and, more specifically, the inconsistencies in temperature between different areas, such as land and sea. This creates contrasting atmospheric areas of low and high pressure, and when air moves between these areas, it results in a range of wind speeds and forces.

[Left] Windbreaks can be created using semi-permeable masses of wind-resistant plants.
[Below] Winds can damage even well-established trees, from ripping branches off to felling an entire tree.

A hedge, a fence, or just a row of trees can create a windbreak in any garden. For a larger plot, a shelterbelt – a staggered planting of three or four rows of tall trees and shrubs, more than 4.5m (15ft) high – may be more suitable. All types must be semi-permeable, to avoid them being blown over or creating wind tunnels, when the wind is funnelled along a valley between a line of trees or structures, potentially harming plants.

Trees, shrubs, and hedges are attractive and long-lasting, but they take a while to establish. If you're looking for a quick fix, you can buy screens and mix them with shrubs that will take longer to grow. Solid surfaces, including fences, won't be effective as the wind will buffet up and over the top; instead, try woven fences of willow or hazel that will still allow some of the wind through. Ideally, a windbreak should filter 50–60 per cent of the wind blowing towards it. Ensure that it is wider than the particular area that you're looking to protect; it will reduce the wind speed over a distance of ten times its height.

WINDBREAKS AND SHELTERBELTS

WINDBREAKS AND SHELTERBELTS ARE SEMI-PERMEABLE BARRIERS THAT REDUCE WIND SPEED AND PROVIDE SHELTER FOR PLANTS THAT STAND THROUGHOUT WINTER. THEY ALSO LESSEN THE RISK OF DAMAGE TO BUILDINGS AND PROVIDE SHELTER FOR WILDLIFE.

[Top] I designed these louvred timber screens to provide a windbreak for a productive area, while also bringing a beautiful element of design and zoning into the garden.

[Right] This artful woven screen by willow artisan Jay Davey flows through the garden. Its semi-permeable surface reduces wind speed.

DROUGHT-TOLERANT PLANTING

In their experimental Mediterranean garden, Olivier and
Clara Filippi have developed drought-resilient planting
methods that are increasingly relevant worldwide.

OLIVIER FILIPPI is a pioneer of drought-tolerant planting, experimenting with plants in his nursery Le Jardin Sec in Southern France, and exploring resilient schemes as a necessary adaptation in the face of climate change and warmer, drier conditions.

WHAT KIND OF CHALLENGES ARE YOU FACING IN THE CHANGING MEDITERRANEAN CLIMATE?

Traditionally, many gardeners thought they had to choose mainly local species for a drought-tolerant garden, but there is a new view of this. If an invasive weed is the only plant able to survive in increasingly difficult conditions, that might be considered positive, because its interactions with birds and insects might lead to a hybrid range of native and non-native species. The garden becomes like an experimental lab of what could be the landscape of the future.

We have about 2,000 species and some express their beauty through their drought-tolerance strategy – for example, *Phlomis* shed their leaves and produce new shoots covered in golden-brown hairs, giving a striking appearance. So drought is not a problem for design, it can mean more structure, volume, and texture in summer.

HOW IMPORTANT IS SUBSTRATE?

Very important, because we have summer drought and intense winter rainfall. Most of our plants are from eroded, rocky landscapes, so they would never face excessive water naturally. Their ability to survive such conditions is due to symbiosis [a mutually beneficial relationship] with bacteria or mycorrhiza, and these organisms need oxygen, which is not present in waterlogged soil.

HAVE YOU SEEN ANY ARCHETYPAL CHARACTERISTICS IN DROUGHT-TOLERANT PLANTS, AND HOW DO YOU SUCCESSFULLY ESTABLISH A DROUGHT-TOLERANT PLANTING SCHEME?

There are many and varied strategies available to plants in the wild, but grown in nursery conditions drought-tolerant plants behave differently as their root systems are limited by pot size. We use anti-spin forestry pots to prevent roots from circling in the pots, which enables the plants to develop their proper double root system when they are planted in the garden. On the nursery we employ hardening techniques, watering and fertilizing as infrequently as possible, irrigating with salty brackish water so that the plants face an artificial drought, and inoculating with fungus for symbiosis.

When planting out, we never irrigate with a drip system as this encourages shallow rooting. During the first summer we water deeply once every three weeks, filling a watering basin around each plant to guide the roots deep down. The choice of species is key, but we must also prepare poor, well-oxygenated soil, plant in autumn before the rainfall, and select plants that have a similar volume of vegetation above ground and root system below.

AIR QUALITY

IS THE AIR IN YOUR GARDEN HEALTHY ENOUGH FOR PEOPLE AND PLANTS? IF NOT, THIS CAN BE IMPROVED WITH CONSIDERED PLANTING CHOICES.

Air quality will be affected by the location of your plot, whether it is near a busy road or airport, or in an urban environment that traps pollution. The quality can be assessed in simple terms by using your nose: does the air smell fresh or polluted? Another method is to look at the amount of particulate matter captured on hard surfaces as black grime. The finer details of pollution can be assessed with air-quality monitors: small devices that analyze pollutants in the air and highlight potential risks to human health are now widely available.

Where gardens look on to busy roads, the types of plants you select can assist in cleaning the air by trapping particulates (see Chapter 5). In urban areas, parks and gardens act as green lungs, filtering and purifying air, removing gaseous and particulate pollutants. However, plants are the third line of defence, after reducing emissions and increasing the distance between us and the source of pollution.

DO GREEN WALLS FILTER AIR POLLUTION?

Green walls in urban areas offer many benefits, including the capacity to reduce air pollution and provide a habitat for small animals and insects. I collaborated with Tapestry Vertical Gardens to design this backdrop wall for a residential dining area. The landscapers building the garden nicknamed it the RHS Television!

Pollution accumulates within enclosed street valleys as it lacks an escape route. Based on a study conducted by Professor Rob MacKenzie of the University of Birmingham, UK, "green walls" - vertical swathes of grasses, ivy, and other plants - have the capacity to reduce pollution by more than ten times the 1-2 per cent originally thought.

Singapore's air-quality initiatives include the "supertrees", which consist of 18 vertical gardens that generate solar power, collect rainwater, provide shade, and act as air venting ducts for nearby conservatories, using plants to filter the air.

[Top] Toads can help organically control slug and snail populations as they predate on them. Including a water feature or pond in your garden will help attract amphibians, such as frogs and toads.   [Right] A biodiverse planting scheme full of colourful perennials provides aesthetic interest as well as food sources for pollinators.

WILDLIFE

DOES WILDLIFE THRIVE IN YOUR GARDEN? LOOK FOR CLUES
TO DISCOVER WHICH ANIMALS AND INVERTEBRATES MIGHT BE
THERE AND HOW YOUR GARDENING STYLE CAN SUPPORT THEM.

Urbanization and increasing human populations mean that wildlife habitats are disappearing at an alarming rate. We are in the midst of a biodiversity crisis, with many species declining rapidly across the globe. Designing our garden spaces in a way that means we can share them with wildlife is not difficult – it just takes a little forethought, and potentially a shift in our expectations of what makes a garden beautiful and functional.

To discover the wildlife in your garden, look for tracks, faeces, damage to plants – such as nibbled leaves and scraped bark – and holes in structures or the ground. Then consider the potential for wildlife: are you near a forest, a coast, or a road? What forms of wildlife are you likely to find in your area and how can you attract those species to your own space? Certain species, such as rabbits, deer, and some insects, can cause significant damage, but there are non-destructive methods that keep them out, such as fencing, caging, and covering, or organic and biological controls.

Designing our garden spaces in a way that means we can share them with wildlife is not difficult - it just takes a little forethought, and potentially a shift in our expectations of what makes a garden beautiful and functional.

INSECTS

Insects – often overlooked and underappreciated – are a key part of the food chain, providing sustenance for birds and mammals. Pollinating insects are key to global food security as we rely on them for the pollination of vital crops. Their decline will cause immeasurable problems for humans and lead to global food shortages, but gardeners can go some way towards offsetting the damage that is caused by pesticides.

Creating a garden that functions as an ecosystem, and supports wildlife all the way up the food chain, is key to climate resilience. Think creatively – for example, add a pond to attract toads and frogs that eat slugs, and put bird feeders next to plants that suffer from caterpillar damage. This can create a balanced, self-sustaining garden that doesn't need constant – and potentially harmful – human intervention.

CHAPTER FOUR

CLIMATE RESILIENT GARDEN DESIGN

093

RESILIENT GARDEN DESIGN

THIS CHAPTER DEMONSTRATES HOW SOME OF THE IDEAS
THAT HAVE BEEN DISCUSSED IN THE BOOK SO FAR CAN BE
PUT INTO PRACTICE IN EVEN A RELATIVELY SMALL SPACE
THAT IS TYPICAL OF MANY URBAN GARDENS.

Do we need to heavily control our gardens, or is a light touch more sustainable? The answer is that by aiming for a looser, more "wild" aesthetic, we can reduce the need for intervention. Abandoning the idea that "neatness" is attainable or even desirable in a garden or landscape allows us to aim instead for a resilient and wildlife-friendly area that is created with sustainable materials. By using ecological design principles, we can encourage plenty of biodiversity in a garden that flourishes naturally, rather than one that needs constant human intervention to keep it looking attractive.

VIRTUAL REALITY

We have worked with graphic visualization company AVA to create a virtual front and rear garden inspired by the principles discussed in this book. The images of the resilient garden throughout the book are computer generated. To enrich the experience of understanding the garden design, you can explore it via the QR code here, using a smartphone, tablet, computer, or VR headset.

WWW.DK.COM/RESILIENT-GARDEN

A timber boardwalk floats through the
resilient garden, crossing a water feature
and passing through a forest garden planting
full of edible delights.

FRONT GARDEN
SITE ANALYSIS

The original site is an end-of-terrace house in a built-up urban environment, with a busy road running adjacent to the property (to the right of this image). Not only is the front garden space dull, it is not environmentally friendly, and nor does it provide much benefit to wildlife or to those living in the house.

DEGRADED SOIL

The soil is poor quality – dry, degraded, and full of rubble. Hard landscaping has created a harsh, sterile environment.

HARD SURFACES AND COOLING PLANTS

Heat islands in cities are caused partly by the lack of natural landscapes and the materials used in urban developments. Traditional fabricated materials - those used for roofing, pavements, roads, and vehicles - absorb and release more heat from the sun's rays than vegetation does. These solid, hard, dark surfaces are less efficient at deflecting solar energy, with the result that there is less shade and less moisture in the air, causing the temperature to rise. In urban settings, heat builds and is stored over the course of the day; as the sun sets and the temperature drops, the heat is then radiated out into the environment.

Areas of vegetation and water are naturally effective at cooling the air and keeping temperatures down. Trees offer shade; plant leaves exude moisture; and rivers and ponds evaporate surface water, cooling the atmosphere with water vapour.

POOR PLANT CHOICES

The box hedge (*Buxus sempervirens*) is in poor condition. Box is susceptible to pests and diseases, in particular box-moth caterpillar and box blight. It needs time-consuming maintenance, and often harmful chemical treatments, to keep it looking pristine.

EXPOSED PLOT

The front garden is exposed and suffers from drying winds. Air quality in the space is poor: a busy road runs to the east and there is no barrier between the garden and the road, so the traffic is in full view and there is no protection from air and noise pollution. Excessive hard landscaping has created a harsh and sterile environment.

HOSTILE HABITATS

The garden has very few signs of wildlife, apart from the caterpillars that have been eating the box hedge. No provision has been made for any habitats, nor has the planting been designed to support biodiversity and encourage wildlife.

HEAT TRAP

The south-facing aspect of the garden and lack of planting means this space is very hot. It offers no shading for the house nor to cool the space.

IMPERMEABLE SURFACE

Water runs over the impermeable paving straight into the mains sewers, wasting a valuable resource and contributing to flooding when rainfall is excessive.

097

FRONT GARDEN
RESILIENT DESIGN

The front garden design offers a solution that is focused on improving the local environment, benefitting wildlife, and improving the wellbeing of those using the garden.

RECLAIMED MATERIALS
pages 148-51

Waste materials have been used in the paving - a terrazzo-like material using site rubble as an aggregate. This shows how rubbish can be made into treasure if it is treated and processed in creative ways (see page 224-25).

BIODIVERSE HABITATS
pages 140-43

A biodiverse mix of plants for pollinators provides food for insects, drawing them to the garden. Several wildlife habitat panels have also been built in the garden, providing shelter for insects and other invertebrates.

MINERAL MULCH
pages 128-29

The recycled aggregate gravel acts as a mineral mulch while bringing a Mediterranean feel to the garden. The gravel areas and channels between paving slabs have been populated with colourful, drought-tolerant, scented plants that are able to deal with the polluted site, poor soil, and hot conditions. Rugged and tough species, such as thyme, spill out onto the drive.

PROTECTIVE BOUNDARIES
pages 138-39

Hedges and trees cool the air, reduce the impact of the wind, and provide food and shelter for wildlife. Dense hedges provide a barrier from the busy road, with species that have been selected for their ability to capture pollutants (see pages 170-71).

PASSIVE IRRIGATION
pages 134-35

The paving has been replaced by permeable recycled aggregate gravel. A rainwater harvesting system stops surface water running off the drive into mains drains, and this passively irrigates the plants.

099

REAR GARDEN SITE ANALYSIS

The original rear garden is as dull as the front garden. The garden offers little benefit to wildlife, with limited biodiversity, but a rowan tree (*Sorbus aucuparia*) is thriving. Valuable water is wasted, as there is no means of storing rainwater.

WASTED WATER

Water that falls on the roof of the garden office is diverted into the strip of soil behind the building, wasting a resource on an area of the garden in which very little will grow.

DULL VIEW

The view from the garden office is of the dead ash tree, which is depressing. The glazed façade faces west, with little cover from the sun now that the tree has no foliage, which creates a hot internal environment.

STARK BOUNDARIES

The boundaries are softwood timber fences in good condition. They offer some shelter to the site, so the rear garden does not suffer from the same drying winds as the front. However, nothing is growing on them, so they feel stark and imposing, boxing in the space rather than creating a feeling of sanctuary.

LACK OF BIODIVERSITY

The rear garden is a little more wildlife-friendly than the front, but it lacks biodiversity in the planting; there are few flowering plants for pollinating insects to visit.

100

UNHEALTHY LAWN

The downpipe from the roof discharges into a blocked gully pot, which floods onto the impermeable terrace outside the extension, creating boggy conditions on the lawn and wasting water. The owners apply chemical feed and mow the lawn, but it never looks pristine because the area is too shady and damp.

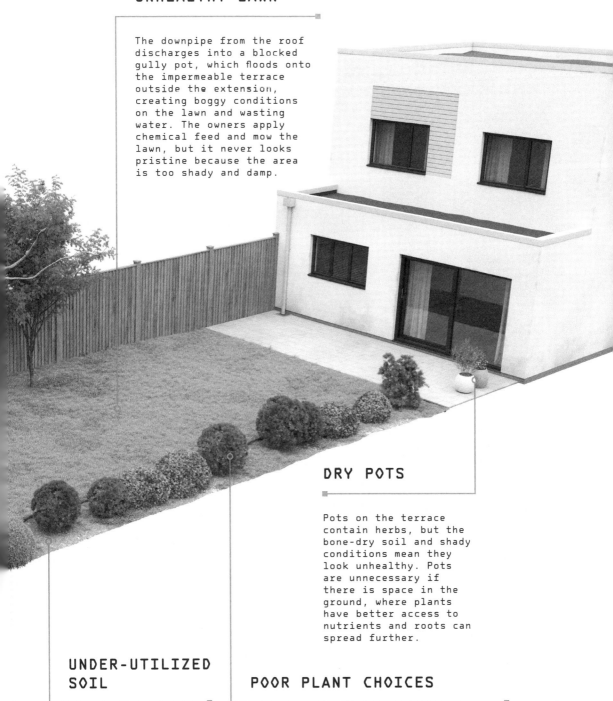

DRY POTS

Pots on the terrace contain herbs, but the bone-dry soil and shady conditions mean they look unhealthy. Pots are unnecessary if there is space in the ground, where plants have better access to nutrients and roots can spread further.

UNDER-UTILIZED SOIL

The soil is not of bad quality; a soil test shows it to be a pH-neutral natural loam. This is a good general-purpose soil that could be improved by adding organic matter. Some builders' rubble exists at the back, around the tree.

POOR PLANT CHOICES

The planting to the side of the lawn is dull and mainly evergreen – a mix of clipped topiary balls and drab shrubs. At the rear, a large ash tree (*Fraxinus excelsior*) has succumbed to ash dieback.

REAR GARDEN RESILIENT DESIGN

The rear garden has been transformed into a biodiverse area full of life, texture, colour, and interest, with multiple new trees and an understorey planting beneficial to local wildlife, and attractive to those using the garden.

FOOD FOREST
pages 114–15

The lawn is gone; it was in poor condition and offered little visual or wildlife benefit. The planting follows a "food forest" concept (see page 53), where edible plants co-exist with ornamental species in a layered understorey. This kind of planting uses species known as "edimentals"(see pages 180-97 for a list of edimental plants).

RECLAIMED MATERIALS
pages 148–51

A reclaimed timber boardwalk "floats" over the garden, creating a dynamic and immersive walkway. Plants and wildlife are able to occupy space beneath it, lowering the impact of the hardscape. It could be removed with little damage to the garden, and the environmental impact of its disposal would be minimal, as timber is a biodegradable material.

COMPOST AREA
pages 122–25

A compost area allows green garden waste to be utilized. Compost can be applied to the planting, enriching the soil and creating a healthy and circular ecosystem.

CONNECTING WITH NATURE
pages 154-55

The layout brings planting close to the house. From inside, a framed view of a tree increases the connection with nature even when the inhabitants are indoors.

BIODIVERSE HABITATS
pages 140-43

Five new multistemmed trees evoke a woodland edge atmosphere, and associate with the rowan, which has been pruned to allow light to the plants beneath it. As well as providing protection from sun and wind, the trees are a mix of fruiting and flowering species that offer food for humans, animals, and insects.

RECLAIMED MATERIALS
pages 148-51

The use of hard paving has been minimized to increase permeability; paved areas have been limited to providing hard standing for the dining table and access to the doors into the house. Channels for planting and gravel break up the hard surface, making it permeable and less hard and sterile than the previous mortar-jointed paving. The paving is the same recycled terrazzo that is used at the front.

WILDLIFE POND
pages 144-45

The garden includes a pond that fills with rainwater runoff from the roof during the wetter seasons, which provides a habitat for wildlife and encourages beneficial predators into the garden, such as toads and frogs.

GREEN ROOF
pages 108-09

A green roof has been laid on the roof of both the house and the rear extension, providing insulating properties, added wildlife benefit, and reducing stormwater runoff.

REWILDED AREA
pages 116-17

The main area of the garden has essentially been rewilded. This informal design approach embraces a wild aesthetic and provides vital habitats for wildlife including insect species that are in decline, due in large part to habitat loss. The boundaries and the garden office have been covered in climbing plants and wildlife habitat panels.

SUDS PLANTER
pages 136-37

The downpipe from the roof now discharges into a SuDS planter, with plants that tolerate both dry conditions and occasional waterlogging. In heavy rainfall, the water discharges into a swale, which collects runoff water from the roof of the house and hard surfaces in the garden, and fills the wildlife pond.

ORGANIC MULCH
pages 126-27

All of the planted areas in the resilient garden design have been mulched. A protective layer of material covers the soil, emulating natural landscapes where bare earth is rarely found.

HUGELKULTUR MOUNDS
pages 146-47

Wood from the dead ash tree and other organic waste, such as the removed turf, has been piled into a hugel mound. These contoured mounds provide interesting landscape features as well as nutrients and moisture for plants.

MUSHROOM LOGS
pages 152-53

The dead ash tree has been reused in multiple ways, including as informal seats, both sawn and natural, and as logs to grow mushrooms.

RAINWATER HARVESTING
pages 132-33

A SuDS water butt planter has been added to capture water from the roof of the garden office. This can be used to water the garden by hand when needed.

BIODIVERSE ROOF
pages 110-11

The garden office now has a biodiverse roof that is a mix of waste materials, including dead wood and crushed concrete from the build. It has been seeded with native wildflowers and designed to provide visual impact and habitats for insects.

105

SIDE-BY-SIDE COMPARISON

The plan views of the original and resilient garden show a stark comparison. There are many changes we can make to improve the sustainability and resilience of our gardens.

ORIGINAL FRONT GARDEN

This is a stark and sterile space with abundant hard landscaping and very little room for planting. Hot and south-facing, it feels stark, exposed and lacking in life and atmosphere.

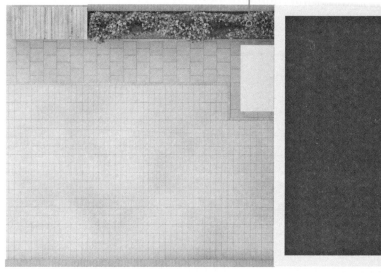

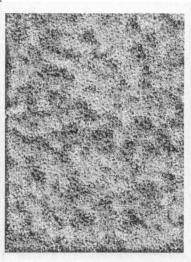

RESILIENT FRONT GARDEN

The parking space is retained but the hard paving is replaced with permeable gravel. New trees and gravel-garden planting cool the space and provide atmosphere and interest as well as food and habitat for visiting wildlife.

ORIGINAL REAR GARDEN

A large area of lawn and wide
expanses of paving mean the garden
is very open and lacking in interest.
Planting is limited and struggling,
while a dead tree offers a depressing
view from the garden studio.

RESILIENT REAR GARDEN

The lawn and paving have been replaced
by landscape features that sustain
wildlife. The planting creates a dynamic
space offering visual interest and
forageable treats. Rainwater is slowed
and collected for sustainable use.

107

GREEN ROOF

A GREEN ROOF CONSISTS OF A LAYER OF PLANTING AND GROWING MEDIUM (SUBSTRATE) SET OVER A WATERPROOF MEMBRANE ON EITHER A FLAT OR PITCHED ROOF. PRE-GROWN GREEN ROOF SYSTEMS ARE AVAILABLE AND GENERALLY EASY TO INSTALL.

A green roof can be considered for a pitched roof, but if your roof has a slope more severe than 9.5 degrees, take extra measures to secure the substrate and consider a solution for water retention, since water will run off the steeper pitch. Have your roof checked by a structural engineer first to make sure it can take the added weight, and consult local planning laws. Green roofs can generally be placed into three categories: extensive, intensive, and semi-intensive.

EXTENSIVE

This type of roof (see right) has a shallow growing substrate, usually less than 150mm (6in). It weighs only moderately on the roof and has a limited range of plants, for example a mix of sedum species. It is usually inaccessible and low maintenance, able to thrive with minimal watering or none at all in wet climates or with suitable planting mixes.

INTENSIVE

With a deeper substrate, up to 1m (3¼ft) or more, intensive green roofs make a heavier load on the structure. They can bear a wider variety of plants and even small trees, and will usually require maintenance and frequent watering. They often take the form of roof gardens.

SEMI-INTENSIVE

A semi-intensive roof shares qualities with both extensive and intensive green roofs. The depth of the substrate, and so the plants you are able to include, is dependent on the structure and integrity of the roof, the level of annual rainfall, and any water harvesting capacity such as passive irrigation (see pages 134–35) included in the design.

On the bio-diverse roof of the garden office,
a substrate of crushed construction waste
has been allowed to self-seed with local
species blown in by the wind or deposited
by animals. Dead wood provides habitat.

BIODIVERSE ROOF

THE ROOF OF THE GARDEN OFFICE HAS BEEN TRANSFORMED
INTO A BIODIVERSE ROOF. BOTH BROWN AND BIODIVERSE ROOFS
ARE AN EFFECTIVE WAY TO RECREATE THE UNCULTIVATED URBAN
AREAS FOUND AT GROUND LEVEL, WITH PLANTS OF THE SAME
KIND ABLE TO POPULATE THE ROOF SPACE.

On a biodiverse roof, the substrate medium is seeded or planted at the time of construction. Such roofs are considered by many urban planning bodies to be a natural extension of the landscape that provides further habitats for insect life and a variety of plant species.

An alternative to a biodiverse roof is a brown roof. Here the substrate medium is left to self-seed via airborne dispersal and other natural means, such as bird droppings. However, biodiverse roofs achieve a more instant and designed impact as a result of purposeful planting and seeding.

INSTALLATION

Brown and biodiverse roofs typically do not require any irrigation and are naturally low maintenance. The depth of the substrate tends to be up to 150mm (6in), with a medium weight pressure, in general no more than 120kg per m² (2½ cwt per 1¼ sq yd). This can support stones, rocks, and decaying timber, which attracts insects and other wildlife. Brown and biodiverse roofs can also insulate a building, helping to regulate the temperature as well as improving acoustics.

You can incorporate sustainable materials by using recycled aggregate in the substrate, such as construction waste material and rubble that has been washed – but, when using waste from a building site, make sure that the material does not contain contaminated matter or sharp fragments that might damage the waterproof membrane below. Once it has become established, a brown roof will mature into a green roof as wind-borne seeds settle and develop into colonies of plants.

BIODIVERSE HABITATS

John has experimented with substrates ranging from
rubble and sand to chalk and crushed ceramics, yielding
exciting results for biodiversity in the garden.

JOHN LITTLE is a living roof and brownfield gardening expert and the founder of the Grass Roof Company. He plants inspiring biodiverse habitats, including his own garden, where he experiments with an array of waste materials for habitat provision and as a growing medium for resilient plants.

WHY ARE BROWNFIELD LANDSCAPES SO INSPIRING TO YOU?

The combination of substrates and materials creates places for biodiversity to thrive, and their complexity makes them great for wildlife. They are harsh environments, so nettles, brambles, and docks have less chance to establish, and the species that like less competition, such as wildflowers that grow on poor or chalky soils, can thrive. If we can be inspired by brownfield sites and bring some of this chaos into our gardens using waste materials destined for landfill, so much the better.

HOW IMPORTANT DO YOU THINK IT IS THAT WE INCLUDE HABITAT IN OUR LANDSCAPES AND GARDENS?

The Great Dixter Biodiversity Audit of 2017–2019, from a garden in Sussex, showed that a garden is not just a mass of plants as a food source for pollinators – it's also about buildings, dry-stone walls, dead wood, and compost heaps, which are great for biodiversity. In the yard where we build our products, thousands of invertebrates live in the piles of waste materials that we generate, which encourages biodiversity. You can place waste materials in your garden in an ordered fashion to improve its biodiversity by creating much-needed habitat and shelter.

HOW DO YOU DESIGN A RESILIENT GREEN OR BROWN ROOF THAT WILL STAND THE TEST OF TIME?

First, you must ensure the roof will take the added weight. As you would on the ground, integrate a mix of materials – structural elements such as log piles are key to creating a roof that is beneficial for biodiversity. A harsh substrate is important to stop competition and slow succession – you don't want a rich and fertile environment as it won't survive the conditions of the roof-top setting, where the plants need to be resilient.

Lawns often contain limited or monoculture plant species, so they have low biodiversity and negligible wildlife value. Many people see a lawn as an essential element for children to play on, but alternative types of garden offer a sensory treasure trove where children can explore and really engage with the natural environment. Lawns can be replaced with many different types of planting to create a richer, more atmospheric, and biodiverse environment.

EDIMENTAL PLANTING

A fusion of the words "ornamental" and "edible", often used to describe plants, "edimental" is a term coined to describe those that provide both of these qualities. Edimentals are a great way to increase the productivity of a garden while also keeping it looking aesthetically pleasing. Some edimentals have leaves and shoots that can be eaten, while others have edible flowers, roots, or tubers – but do check before consuming as only certain parts of the plant may be edible. Always ensure that you know what is safe to eat, since certain plants and fungi are poisonous and even deadly.

GREEN CARPETS

It is not only grass that can tolerate foot traffic. Many plants are low-growing and hug the ground to form green carpets, including creeping thyme (*Thymus praecox*) and mind-your-own-business (*Soleirolia soleirolii*). A mixture of ground-covering plants requires less maintenance than a single-species carpet and also provides more resilience and biodiversity.

SPECIES-RICH LAWNS

A grass lawn will try to revert to a mixed grassland if it is not regularly mowed and weeded. A lawn richer in species is easier to maintain and sustain than a single-species monoculture. Allowing some dandelions, clover, and other wild flowering species into your lawn provides food for popular pollinators such as bees and butterflies.

FOOD FOREST

LUSH GREEN LAWNS USUALLY REQUIRE HUGE AMOUNTS OF FERTILIZER, WATER, AND MAINTENANCE TO KEEP THE DESIRED GREEN AESTHETIC YEAR-ROUND, SO CONSIDER A FOOD FOREST FULL OF VARIED EDIMENTAL PLANTS INSTEAD.

LAYERS OF THE FOOD FOREST

The planting of the food forest, or forest garden, takes inspiration from the layers found in a natural woodland:
1 Canopy: The highest layer of trees, spaced to allow light to permeate through to the lower layers.
2 Small trees: Beneath the canopy of taller trees.
3 Shrubs: Tolerant of partial shade.
4 Herbaceous perennials: Die back in winter and return in the spring, opening up space for autumn- and spring-flowering bulbs.
5 Ground cover: Creeping and carpeting plants that suppress weeds and cover and protect the soil.
6 Climbers: Scrambling upwards, towards light, they generally require trees or structures for support.
7 The soil, roots and fungi.

[Left] Large swathes of monoculture lawn are high maintenance and of low value to wildlife. [Below] Replacing a lawn with a biodiverse mix of plants creates a haven for wildlife as well as an uplifting and immersive aesthetic display.

[Right] The contrast of before and after is quite stark when seen side by side, the flat lawn and drab shrubs look dull and lifeless in contrast to the abundant and biodiverse planting.
[Below] Planting in a randomized matrix rather than formal blocks will give a natural and wild feel. Some "weeds" can remain if they are not invasive and provide benefit, such as food for pollinators or nitrogen-fixing properties.

REWILDED AREA

REWILDING IS DEFINED AS "RESTORATION OF ECOSYSTEMS TO THE POINT WHERE NATURE IS ALLOWED TO TAKE CARE OF ITSELF". THIS MEANS REINSTATING NATURAL PROCESSES AND REINTRODUCING SPECIES THAT HAVE DECLINED OR DISAPPEARED, THEN ALLOWING THEM TO SHAPE THE LANDSCAPE AND HABITATS.

CULTIVATED WILD

Rewilding encourages people to reconnect with nature, and this can be implemented even in a small garden. The resilient garden aims to be a "cultivated wild" – an augmented version of a natural landscape. The design achieves this with loose and informal planting, including a biodiverse mix of plants in naturalistic groupings; habitats added to encourage predators into the garden to feed on pests, including bird feeders, insect habitats, and a wildlife pond; an absence of harmful chemicals for fertilizers, sterilizing, or pest and weed control; and garden waste composted on site, with the compost utilized to improve the soils for growing.

The wild aesthetic should be included wherever possible. Allowing a less visible area of the garden to go wild – such as the boundaries, where the garden bleeds into the wider landscape – could be a good compromise to gain the benefits without losing a "tidy" aesthetic in more visible areas.

WILD NATURE IN THE GARDEN

One way of storing carbon in your soil is to cover it with plants. Incorporating organic matter into your soil beforehand helps to lock in carbon and adds nutrients to the soil to help plants flourish. Growing deep-rooting plants will then capture carbon through photosynthesis and feed it to the soil. In simple terms, the more plants the better.

HOW PLANTS ABSORB CARBON DIOXIDE

In the same way that humans need oxygen to survive, plants take up carbon dioxide, and by using photosynthesis, they transform it into glucose, a vital energy source the plant needs to grow. They also release oxygen as a byproduct of photosynthesis. By increasing the number of plants and reducing hard landscaping, you can make your garden more effective at absorbing carbon, acting as a living, breathing lung, expelling oxygen and purifying the air. This is a great excuse for any green-fingered enthusiast to indulge in more plants.

PROTECTING YOUR SOIL

Healthy soil acts as a carbon sink by drawing carbon into it. Plants capture carbon dioxide in their leaves through photosynthesis, then pump the carbon underground through their roots. Simply leaving soil undisturbed will allow it to store the carbon.

THE STATE OF THE SOIL

Soil degradation is a global problem, affecting a third of the world's arable soils. While soil takes thousands of years to form, an area the size of 30 football pitches is destroyed worldwide every minute through erosion, which means we lose fertile soil for growing food, and the carbon stored within it is released. However, by gardening sustainably, composting, mulching, protecting, and organically improving soils in our own plots, we gardeners can help.

NO-DIG GARDENING

Disturbing the soil as little as possible prevents the soil structure being damaged, and stops carbon from being released into the atmosphere. British organic gardener Charles Dowding is a pioneer of the no-dig approach. The main benefits of it are:
- When left undisturbed, soil has less need to recover, so grows fewer weeds.
- Undisturbed soil is full of organisms and microbes that help plants find the nutrients and moisture they need. Eating vegetables grown in this type of soil is beneficial to your own health by improving your gut microbiome.

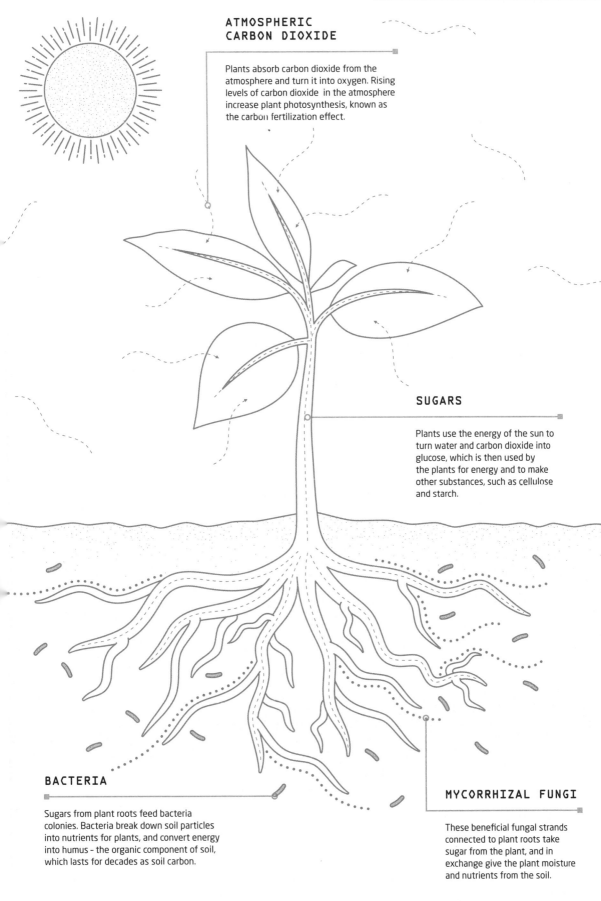

ATMOSPHERIC CARBON DIOXIDE

Plants absorb carbon dioxide from the atmosphere and turn it into oxygen. Rising levels of carbon dioxide in the atmosphere increase plant photosynthesis, known as the carbon fertilization effect.

SUGARS

Plants use the energy of the sun to turn water and carbon dioxide into glucose, which is then used by the plants for energy and to make other substances, such as cellulose and starch.

BACTERIA

Sugars from plant roots feed bacteria colonies. Bacteria break down soil particles into nutrients for plants, and convert energy into humus - the organic component of soil, which lasts for decades as soil carbon.

MYCORRHIZAL FUNGI

These beneficial fungal strands connected to plant roots take sugar from the plant, and in exchange give the plant moisture and nutrients from the soil.

WILDING URBAN SPACES

Thomas founded Phyto Studio with Melissa Rainer and
Claudia West to create artistic, technically driven design
solutions for resilient and beautiful planting schemes.

THOMAS RAINER is a landscape architect and a leading voice in ecological landscape design. A specialist in using pioneering planting concepts to design ecologically functional landscapes, he is influenced by wild landscapes in his designs for planting schemes that thrive in the urban environment.

HOW DO YOU DEFINE A RESILIENT PLANTING SCHEME?

Resilient planting means an alignment of site conditions, plant palette, and human management. For a new site, we try to understand what its natural ecological trajectory would be; which invasive species are in the seed bank or likely to migrate in? Which stresses (drought, disturbance, herbivory) will shape its future?

Next, we select plants that can survive with minimal input. If drought and low-productivity soils are the driving factors, can we build a plant palette with stress-tolerating species? If we have a rain garden with excess moisture and fertility, can we use well-behaved competitors to absorb excess nutrients and water?

Finally, we consider the management of a scheme. Will it be high or low maintenance? Will it be cut back with a mower or strimmer? Then the palette is simplified to species that are suited to that management regime. Next we eliminate those that are prone to dominate.

HOW IMPORTANT IS SOIL OR SUBSTRATE IN A SCHEME?

Our entire palette is based on specific soil conditions. On urban sites, we may create stressful soils so we can use short, floriferous planting schemes that thrive in such conditions. Shorter plantings often require low-fertility soils; highly productive soils often produce competitive vegetation that flops. Using gravel or coarse sand in the top 15–20cm (6–8in) can help to reduce fertility and weed growth.

HOW DO YOU APPROACH PLANTING DESIGN FOR A SPECIFIC SITE?

We use naturally occurring plant communities so the entire community will be stable over time. The dynamic qualities of species should balance each other; for example, if some taller species are winter-dormant, the ground layer beneath will be winter-green. If one species blooms in early summer, another will bloom in midsummer. By selecting plants with distinct shapes and behaviours, we can cover the soil with vegetation to protect it.

121

COMPOSTING IN A SMALL SPACE

In any garden, even a small one, composting is beneficial. If you are short of space, consider worm composting or an off-the-shelf compost bin, many of which are designed to heat the compost to high temperatures, speeding up the composting process and making it more efficient. Fairly new to the market are electric composters that function like kitchen appliances and turn food waste into usable compost in a matter of hours. They can provide a handy way to deal with food and kitchen waste, leaving the outdoor heap or bin for composting garden waste only.

COMPOSTING TIPS

The microorganisms (bacteria and fungi) that transform waste material into compost work most effectively when they are kept at consistent levels of temperature and moisture, so make use of a shady corner of the garden, perhaps behind a shed or somewhere else out of sight. A bin placed on an earth base provides easy drainage and allows access to the organisms in the soil. If your bin is on a hard surface, you can add a layer of garden soil to the compost bin to introduce those organisms.

Most home compost bins on the market should produce usable compost, provided they keep out most of the rain, let in air, permit drainage, and maintain some warmth, though small bins (less than 1cu m/1¼cu yd) are less effective than larger ones. As bins reserve heat and moisture they speed up the composting process, but a traditional open heap in the garden will compost down with time.

PLANT NUTRIENTS

To mature and flourish, all plants need a blend of different nutrients, though the quantities of these depend on the species of plant and its stage of growth. Plants extract carbon, oxygen, and hydrogen from the air; the three primary nutrients they derive from the soil are nitrogen, phosphorus, and potassium, with magnesium, calcium, and sulphur in lesser quantities. In areas where these nutrients are absent, or if you want your plants to produce maximum flowers and fruit, you can add nutrients with natural fertilizers, including homemade compost.

COMPOST AREA

COMPOSTING YOUR KITCHEN AND GARDEN WASTE AT HOME IS ENVIRONMENTALLY FRIENDLY AND HAS THE ADDED BENEFIT OF PROVIDING MATERIAL THAT CAN IMPROVE YOUR SOIL. WHILE LOCAL AUTHORITIES OFTEN PROVIDE COLLECTIONS FOR GREEN WASTE, COMPOSTING AT HOME HAS A LOWER CARBON FOOTPRINT.

A timber composting bin is unobtrusive and fits in with the natural aesthetic of the garden. Tucked away in a shady corner, a bin deals with garden waste, reduces the carbon footprint associated with transporting it off site, and saves money and waste associated with bought-in bagged soil improvers.

GREEN MATERIALS

Aim for between 25 and 50 per cent soft green materials (grass clippings, annual weeds, uncooked fruit and vegetables, kitchen waste) to feed the microorganisms. Do not have one material dominating the heap, especially grass clippings, as these can become a slimy mess.

BROWN MATERIALS

The remainder of the heap should be brown woody material, such as prunings, wood chippings, paper, cardboard, straw, dead leaves, and plant stems.

Examples of brown compost materials: [1] Dead leaves **[2]** Uncoated cardboard and paper **[3]** Wood ash.

124

Examples of green compost materials:
[1] Uncooked plant-based food waste; [2] Garden prunings; [3] Grass clippings from mowing the lawn.

TURNING THE HEAP

Air is essential for composting to happen – if the heap becomes too condensed or waterlogged, the composting process slows down. Turning the heap incorporates air, and neglecting to do this is probably the main reason why composting might not work. Ideally, turn it about once a month. This also gives you an opportunity to gauge the moisture level in the heap – be especially vigilant during drier months.

WHEN IS THE COMPOST READY?

Garden compost is usually ready to use in six months to two years, depending on the amount of heat and moisture it receives. Ripe compost should have a dark brown hue and smell like a damp forest floor, with a texture resembling soil. There will probably be some material that has not rotted down sufficiently, but that can be incorporated into the next heap to be re-composted.

TROUBLESHOOTING

- **Sodden, slimy, smelly compost** This is usually a result of too much moisture, perhaps caused by poor drainage and not enough air. Shield the heap with a cover and add extra brown waste.
- **Dry and fibrous compost that hasn't rotted** This is caused by the heap being too dry, with too much brown material. Add more green waste, or fresh manure (1 bucket per 15cm/6in layer of compost).
- **Flies** A well-managed compost heap should not attract flies, but if they become a problem, cover any kitchen waste with a layer of garden waste. Check that there isn't too much moisture in the heap, restricting the air.

ORGANIC MULCH

MULCH IS THE MATERIAL LAID OVER THE SURFACE OF BARE SOIL, OR ON TOP OF COMPOST IN CONTAINERS. ALL OF THE PLANTED AREAS IN THE RESILIENT GARDEN DESIGN ARE MULCHED. AN ORGANIC MULCH IS GENERALLY LAID IN A LAYER OF AT LEAST 5CM (2IN) THICK DURING LATE AUTUMN TO LATE WINTER.

Mulches emulate natural landscapes, where soil is rarely found without some kind of organic or inorganic covering, such as leaf mould in a forest, or scree on a mountainside. In the garden, mulching is beneficial in many different ways. It enhances the quality of the soil and promotes plant growth by introducing extra nutrients, while encouraging advantageous organisms and deterring those that can damage plants, such as slugs and snails. It helps the soil to retain moisture and suppress weeds, saving time and resources used on watering and weeding. Finally, it can warm the ground in spring, while keeping it moist and cool in the dry months of summer, protecting plant roots from high temperatures, and, in the winter, shielding them from frost and cold.

BIODEGRADABLE MATERIAL

Organic mulches can consist of any biodegradable material, which means anything that doesn't remain in the environment indefinitely and can be broken down by fungi, bacteria, and microorganisms. Materials commonly used include garden compost, cardboard, well-rotted farmyard manure, composted bark, wood chips, seaweed, straw and used hops (but note that hops are toxic and potentially lethal to dogs and, less often, to cats).

Ideally, material described as biodegradable should not take long to break down, and should not leave anything behind that is detrimental to the environment – but some biodegradable materials, such as bioplastics, can need specialized processes in order to break down, which is not ideal for a garden setting, so their use as a mulch should be avoided. As the mulch decays into the soil, the top layers will need replacing periodically.

POTENTIAL PROBLEMS

Applied correctly, mulches are reliably useful, but if you mulch too deep, close to the stems of trees or shrubs, the stem can weaken, exposing the plant to disease.

If you are mulching to discourage weeds and retain moisture, the depth of the mulch is more important than the choice of material. A shallow layer of mulch will fail to minimize evaporation from the surface of the soil and regulate the temperature, and it will allow weeds access to sunlight, which will encourage their growth.

A garden compost that has not been effectively rotted down can introduce weeds, pests, and diseases. With wood chips, there is a potential risk of honey fungus exposure if the chips are infected. If the fungus is already present in the garden, using a clean commercial mulch won't increase risk to other plants. However, if you chip your own wood, ensure you choose only material that is free of honey fungus, as even small bits of contaminated wood can infect plants. Bark chips are thought to be lower risk than wood-chip mulch.

126

An organic mulch, such as composted bark, leaf mould, or garden compost, is a great way to protect soil from erosion, lock in moisture, suppress weeds, and add nutrients.

Drought-resilient perennials, grasses, and shrubs are flourishing here in a recycled aggregate mulch, creating a Mediterranean feel to the garden. Many of these plants grow in stony and rocky landscapes, so the mulch mimics their natural environment and helps to protect the plants from winter wet, which is very important for their long-term health.

MINERAL MULCH

NON-BIODEGRADABLE MATERIALS CAN ALSO BE USED AS EFFECTIVE MULCHES. SLATE, SHINGLE, PEBBLES, GRAVEL, AND STONE CHIPPINGS ARE ALL EXAMPLES OF NON-BIODEGRADABLE MULCH. IN THE RESILIENT GARDEN DESIGN, THE GRAVEL GARDEN USES RECYCLED AGGREGATE AS A MINERAL MULCH.

Just like biodegradable mulches, non-biodegradable mulches discourage weeds by masking the sunlight needed for their seeds to germinate, and retain moisture by providing a barrier, thus minimizing water evaporation from the soil. However, they do not enhance the structure or fertility of the soil.

The colour of the mulch can make a difference: dark mulches, such as slate, will absorb heat and help to keep the soil warm, whereas light-coloured gravel will keep roots cool in an area of intense sun exposure by reflecting the heat of the sun's rays. A depth of 10cm (4in) will protect the soil and suppress weeds – although on very stony soils this depth could be reduced.

Plastic is not used as a mulch, since adding plastics to the soil can be very harmful; they may leach toxic chemicals into the soil as they break down. They can also take more than a thousand years to degrade.

GRAVEL GARDENS
Mineral mulches can also be used to create a specific aesthetic, for example in a gravel garden where the look of a particular natural landscape is wanted. A range of sizes of aggregate creates a more natural effect. These generally contain planted communities at less dense spacings than traditional herbaceous borders, often using species from Mediterranean or other dry regions. A deep mulch of gravel covers the soil, and the gravel can be walked on, providing access around the plants too.

SHEET MULCHES
Some mulches come in the form of sheets of woven fabric, often laid on fresh beds and borders, with plants positioned through incisions in the fabric. They can be made more aesthetically pleasing with a layer of decorative material, such as gravel or bark. To avoid drainage issues and surface run-off, and to make sure rain and irrigation water access the roots, use a permeable sheet material. Temporary sheet mulches, such as biodegradable cardboard, are also useful to control invasive weeds before a garden is planted.

WHEN TO MULCH?
The best times to apply mulches are from mid- to late spring, while herbaceous plants are inactive and before annual weeds have started to sprout, and again in autumn, as the plants are dying back. Fresh plantings can be mulched at any time, because discouraging weeds and retaining moisture will help the new plants to become established.

Mineral mulches can also be used to create a specific aesthetic, for example in a Mediterranean gravel garden where the look and feel of a particular natural landscape is wanted. A range of sizes of aggregate creates a more natural effect.

ORGANIC GARDENING

Sarah's garden is a testament to organic principles:
it is beautiful, full of texture and colour, and there is
not a whiff of chemical pesticide or fertilizer anywhere.

SARAH MEAD is head gardener at the Yeo Valley Organic Garden in Somerset, which is one of the few organically certified ornamental gardens in the UK. Built up by Sarah over the past 25 years, the Yeo Valley garden shows the positive impact of organic gardening and how working with nature benefits wildlife and biodiversity.

"

MANY PEOPLE THINK THAT "ORGANIC" ONLY REFERS TO GROWING FRUIT AND VEG, BUT WHAT DOES IT MEAN TO BE SOIL ASSOCIATION CERTIFIED ORGANIC?

The farm in which the garden sits has been certified organic for more than 25 years, so it was important to us to gain the SA Certification for the entire 2.6 hectare (6½ acre) garden. Here at YOG we aim to prove that organic horticulture can go hand in hand not just with fruit and veg growing but also with a design-led garden that includes flower borders as well as meadows and areas of prairie-style planting.

WHY IS COMPOSTING SO IMPORTANT AT THE YEO VALLEY ORGANIC GARDEN?

The compost area of the garden is the "engine room" and we love to show it off. We work mostly on a closed circuit and consider the condition of the soil to be of paramount importance. If the soil is in good heart, we find that the rest of the garden follows. Soil health is the backbone of organic horticulture and agriculture.

WHAT KEY PRINCIPLES CAN GARDENERS TAKE FROM A GARDEN LIKE YOURS?

Plenty! Gardening organically is not an all or nothing club – we are super-keen that people get involved in any way they feel able to. It could be partaking in 'No Mow May'; it could be actively feeding your birds over the winter; it could be allowing nature's predators to discover your blackfly. The size of your plot or the scale of your commitment doesn't matter – what matters is taking the first step.

Water butts can be aesthetically pleasing and don't need to be plastic! This one is made from natural weathering steel and has a planter on the top, adding more green to the garden.

RAINWATER HARVESTING

MAKING THE MOST OF RAINWATER NOT ONLY BENEFITS PLANTS BY GIVING THEM FRESH, NATURAL WATER, BUT IT EASES THE PRESSURE ON SEWAGE SYSTEMS AND HARD PERMEABLE SURFACES, REDUCING THE RISK OF FLOODING.

Swales – or rain gardens – are shallow, vegetated channels or pools that capture and store water, reducing the pressure on mains sewers by slowing the flow and keeping water in the landscape. (See pages 176–79 for the best plants for a swale.)

Water butts are a traditional way to collect and store water, but they can offer other functions; some have integrated features, such as planters.

There are many ways to harvest and store rainwater and slow the movement of water though a garden landscape. Sustainable drainage systems (SuDS) are essentially landscape features that act as above-ground catchment areas or drains, slowing water that moves into mains sewers, reducing pressure on the network. The SuDS features in the resilient garden are detailed on the following pages.

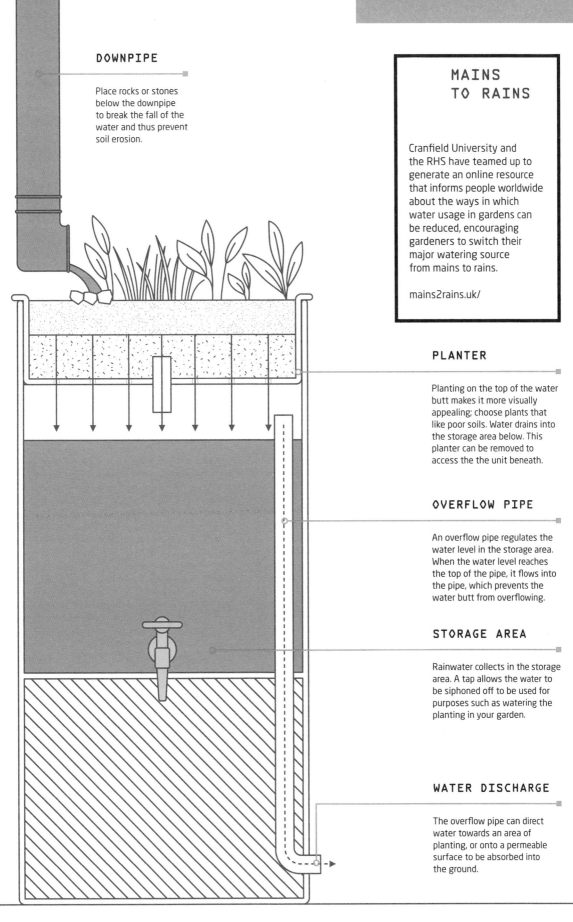

DOWNPIPE

Place rocks or stones below the downpipe to break the fall of the water and thus prevent soil erosion.

MAINS TO RAINS

Cranfield University and the RHS have teamed up to generate an online resource that informs people worldwide about the ways in which water usage in gardens can be reduced, encouraging gardeners to switch their major watering source from mains to rains.

mains2rains.uk/

PLANTER

Planting on the top of the water butt makes it more visually appealing; choose plants that like poor soils. Water drains into the storage area below. This planter can be removed to access the the unit beneath.

OVERFLOW PIPE

An overflow pipe regulates the water level in the storage area. When the water level reaches the top of the pipe, it flows into the pipe, which prevents the water butt from overflowing.

STORAGE AREA

Rainwater collects in the storage area. A tap allows the water to be siphoned off to be used for purposes such as watering the planting in your garden.

WATER DISCHARGE

The overflow pipe can direct water towards an area of planting, or onto a permeable surface to be absorbed into the ground.

133

PASSIVE IRRIGATION

A BELOW-GROUND RAINWATER HARVESTING AND PASSIVE IRRIGATION SYSTEM CAN BE IMPLEMENTED UNDER A GRAVEL GARDEN, DRIVEWAY, OR GREEN ROOF.

A cellular crate system collects and stores rainwater and passively releases it into the soil through a wicking system. This can be connected to gutter downpipes to collect rainwater falling on roof surfaces.

PLANTING

Excess rainwater falling onto the planting will find its way to the reservoir for use at a later date.

OVERFLOW PIPE

An overflow pipe stops the system from flooding. This is generally connected to the mains sewers.

PAVING

Rainwater falls on to the paving, then runs off and drains through channels between slabs and adjacent permeable surfaces, down into the reservoir system below.

SOIL

The soil moisture is regulated by the wicking system. When it is dry, more moisture is wicked up into the soil.

IRRIGATION RESERVOIR

Water is stored in a reservoir to be used in dry conditions: when the soil becomes dry the stored water is utilized.

WICKING MATERIAL

The wicking medium draws moisture up and into dry soil through capillary action - the liquid flows without the assistance of (or even in opposition to) external forces, such as gravity.

135

SUDS PLANTER

IN THE REAR GARDEN THE WATER IS COLLECTED FROM THE ROOF, WHERE IT RUNS INTO A PLANTER THAT OVERFLOWS INTO A WILDLIFE POND.

DOWNPIPE

The downpipe should fall straight onto the planted area. Place rocks or stones below the downpipe to break the fall of the water and thus prevent soil erosion.

The water level in the pond will vary depending on the rainfall each season. The pond could be topped up with mains water in dry weather, but the most sustainable option would be to fill it from water butts, limiting mains water use. During periods of heavy rainfall, excess water will be diverted into the mains sewers, but its passage will be slowed significantly by this water-saving system.

REGULATION

An overflow pipe linked to the swale stops the planter from becoming waterlogged.

SOIL AND PLANTING

The soil is deep enough to sustain a range of plants. The plants here will need to tolerate periods of dry as well as an excess of moisture (see pages 176–79 for a list of plants).

DRAINAGE PIPE

A perforated pipe near the base of the planter collects water slowly and allows it to drain out of the planter and into the pond.

LINER

Decorative aggregates and gravel cover a rubber liner. The liner keeps the water in the garden in the form of a pond.

136

As well as preventing excess pressure on mains sewer systems, keeping water within the garden landscape brings other benefits: water adds atmosphere, sound, movement, and reflection. It bring numerous benefits for wildlife too.

POND

The lined area creates a wildlife pond, the depth of which can be varied to suit different types of marginal and aquatic plants, and the differing needs of visiting wildlife.

OVERFLOW

An overflow pipe connects to the mains sewers, stopping the pond from flooding during periods of excess rainfall.

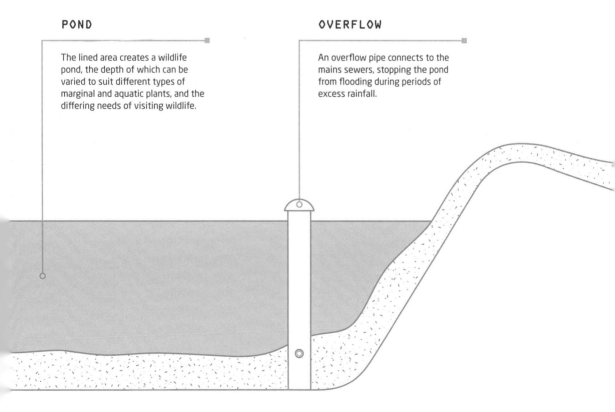

A mixed evergreen hedge windbreak makes
an attractive backdrop and a home for
wildlife as well as protecting the garden.
This dense hedge can also help to reduce
local air pollution.

PROTECTIVE BOUNDARIES

IN THE RESILIENT FRONT GARDEN, A PLANTING OF MIXED EVERGREEN HEDGING SPECIES FULFILS THE FUNCTIONS OF PROTECTING THE SPACE FROM WIND, IMPROVING AIR QUALITY BY CAPTURING POLLUTANTS FROM THE ROAD, AND PROVIDING FOOD AND SHELTER FOR WILDLIFE.

You can create a windbreak in your garden using either evergreen or deciduous plants, but make sure they are wind-resilient species for the most successful result (see pages 170–173).

WHERE TO POSITION YOUR WINDBREAK

Windbreaks should face the prevailing winds. The topography of the land will affect the wind direction; wind can gust over a hill, so a hilly site might need protection from multiple directions. Look out for wind tunnels, too.

PLANTING AND MAINTAINING LIVING WINDBREAKS

Deciduous shrubs and trees are best planted from autumn until early spring, while evergreens should ideally be planted in spring.
- Buy small, young plants, which usually establish better in their new site than mature specimens.
- Plant shrubs and trees close together, with 30–90cm (1–3ft) between most plants within the row. If you have sufficient space, you can also plant double rows with plants staggered
- If there are wild rabbits or deer in your area, put tree guards in place to protect the trunks from damage.
- Keep your new plantings well mulched, watered and weed-free until they are established. Clip trees and hedges annually to keep them dense.

- While the young plants establish, a temporary screen can be installed, such as a post and porous mesh system. A more sustainable and visibly pleasing option would be a hazel hurdle or willow/bamboo screen, which will biodegrade as the hedge establishes around it.

POLLUTION CAPTURE

Plants can also assist in capturing particulate pollution. Evergreen species are best for this, as they retain their leaves year-round, providing a longer period of protection. Other qualities to look for are rough, hairy leaves, and dense foliage. It should be noted that planting is only considered the third line of defence against air pollution: reducing emissions and moving further from the source of emissions are both considered more effective. However, if you live near a busy road, these first two options may not be possible, so planting to protect against pollution is a sensible course of action (see pages 174–75 for an interview with Dr Tijana Blanusa).

Choosing a mix of hedging species can provide other benefits too; for example, plants that fruit and flower support different animals, insects, and invertebrates. A mixed hedge will do more to support biodiversity than a single-species one.

BIODIVERSE HABITATS

THINKING ABOUT GARDENS AS SPACES WE SHARE WITH NATURE IS IMPORTANT WHEN IT COMES TO IMPROVING BIODIVERSITY AND PROTECTING LOCAL SPECIES. SEVERAL HABITATS ARE INCLUDED IN THE RESILIENT GARDEN: NATURAL WATER, ROCKS AND BOULDERS, TREES, AND EVEN THE COMPOST HEAP.

Playing with the topography of a site can add interest to a garden, as well as new habitats. The land in the existing site was flat and dull, whereas the resilient garden design has contours and different land levels. The boggy area has been turned into a swale, or rain garden, where water collects in a depression, which adds a habitat for water-loving creatures (see pages 144–45). Hugel mounds create raised beds with rich soils, providing habitats for numerous organisms (see pages 146–47).

Hidden and protected spaces in the landscape encourage biodiversity by increasing the surface area of the garden. They also help to achieve a natural effect while creating a richer and more biodiverse landscape.

Trees, especially native species, benefit wildlife, too: fruit, leaves, and flowers provide food, while the branches and canopy offer shelter for birds, animals, and insects.

Even the recycled gravel pathways can be habitat: insects and other small creatures are able to find homes in the gaps between the aggregate materials. Using a range of sizes creates habitats for a variety of species. Gaps in brick and stone walls also offer opportunities for insect life.

DEAD HEDGES

Dead hedges are stacks of brushwood and cuttings that provide a place to store woody waste as it slowly breaks down. This is also a good way of using anything that is too woody to go on the compost heap. Arranging them as deliberate structures in the garden can provide windbreaks and habitats for wildlife, as well as some fun – they can be made to look like a giant bird's nest, for example.

[Left] A habitat panel (see pp.142–43) has been installed on the side of the garden office, making use of the otherwise dead space, and providing shelter for bees, beetles, spiders, and other invertebrates.
[Below] A stack of tree branch offcuts makes up a dead hedge, laid in a decorative way and notched between recycled steel beams.

HOW TO CREATE A WILDLIFE HABITAT PANEL

The resilient garden includes three habitat wildlife panels: on the side of the bin store, on the boundary fences in the rear garden, and affixed to the side of the garden office. These are an effective way of inviting local species into your garden, and are easy to make utilizing waste materials.

Be creative in your choices and incorporate any organic waste materials from the garden, then see which creatures come to visit. However, be careful about including kitchen or food waste, as this may attract vermin such as rats.

Here are some ideas of materials to include, depending on what you want to attract:

- Dead wood and bark for beetles, centipedes, spiders, and woodlice.
- Small holes for solitary bees, made from bamboo, reeds, and drilled logs.
- Larger holes with stones and tiles, providing cool, damp conditions for frogs and toads. Site the holes deep and low down within the structure so that they provide a frost-free home during winter.
- A variety of dry leaves, sticks, or straw for ladybirds (predator to aphids) and beetles.
- Corrugated cardboard for lacewings, whose larvae eat aphids.
- Dry leaves and leaf mulch (held in place with chicken wire) to mimic a natural forest floor.

STEP 1: CHOOSE A SUITABLE SITE

The visitors to your site will depend upon the location of your habitat panels. Solitary bees, for example, prefer a sunny location, whereas frogs and toads like cool, damp conditions that are also favoured by potentially less desirable slugs and snails. However, frogs and toads eat them, so they provide an important food source. A hedgehog box could be incorporated into the base of the panel.

STEP 2: CHOOSE A HARD BASE

For the basic structure you will need a strong, stable framework. This could be made from steel, timber, or an old wooden pallet. In the resilient garden, the habitat panels on the boundary fences, the garden office, and the bin store are timber-framed, with a wire mesh cover to hold in the plant material. It's best not to use plastic for this, as it is not biodegradable.

STEP 3: ADD YOUR MATERIAL

The idea is to provide a very porous habitat with gaps, crevices, tunnels, and nooks and crannies of different sizes for wildlife to explore and make use of.

WILDLIFE PONDS

PONDS ARE ONE OF SEVERAL AREAS THAT ENCOURAGE WILDLIFE INTO THE GARDEN, INCLUDING PREDATORS THAT WILL ACT AS NATURAL CONTROL FOR LESS DESIRABLE VISITORS THAT MAY HARM OR DECIMATE PLANTS.

One of the benefits of including a natural pond in the garden is that the change in topography gives you an opportunity to plant aquatic and marginal plants, providing habitats for both aquatic and amphibious species. You can also use a pond to collect rainwater (see pages 136–37).

ENCOURAGING PREDATORS

Predators in the garden not only boost biodiversity and help to plug gaps in the local ecosystem, they are also an environmentally friendly way of dealing with creatures such as slugs, snails, aphids, and caterpillars.

Adding a swale or wildlife pond will attract amphibians such as newts, frogs, and toads, which predate on slugs and snails. You can also place bird feeders in trees: birds eat slugs, snails, and caterpillars, especially during spring when they are feeding their young. Habitat panels encourage useful insects and invertebrates: ladybirds eat aphids, so are a beneficial insect to attract.

SLUGS AND SNAILS

Slugs and snails are no longer classed as serious pests in the UK by the Royal Horticultural Society. This is part of a shift in thinking about how we perceive the wildlife in our gardens, including less popular species which still play a role in the garden ecosystem. To lessen the damage they do:
- Pick slugs and snails off your plants and move them to the compost heap, where they will help to turn waste into compost.
- Site sacrificial plants near your favourite plants so they eat those instead.
- Slugs love vulnerable young seedlings, so transfer plants into the garden only once they are mature. Add cloches for protection - these can be made from recycled items such as jars or plastic bottles.

Spot the frog! Providing shelter in water through aquatic and marginal planting will encourage beneficial predators, such as toads and frogs, to inhabit your garden.

HUGELKULTUR MOUNDS

HUGELKULTUR IS AN ANCIENT TECHNIQUE IN WHICH DECAYING WOOD AND OTHER ORGANIC MATTER IS PILED UP AND THEN COVERED WITH SOIL AND COMPOST, CREATING A MOUND. AS THE WOOD AT THE CORE OF THE MOUND BREAKS DOWN, IT EMANATES HEAT, WARMING THE SOIL, AND PROVIDING NUTRIENTS AND MOISTURE FOR THE PLANTS.

BUILDING A HUGELKULTUR MOUND

Start by clearing your selected area, removing turf or vegetation. Then follow the steps below to build your mound.

ADD SMALLER, LIGHTER WOOD MATERIALS

Smaller rotting logs, branches, twigs, and so forth help to form the structure of the bed.

FILL GAPS WITH COMPOSTED BARK MULCH OR WOOD CHIPS

The chipped woody matter adds essential nutrients more quickly than the larger logs. It also absorbs moisture better.

ADD DECAYING WOOD

Wood that has fallen or been cut down at least two to three years earlier is best.

DIG UP EXISTING TURF

In the resilient garden, some of the turf of the old lawn was reused to create this hugelkultur mound Keeping some soil on the turf adds weight to compress the timber part of the bed.

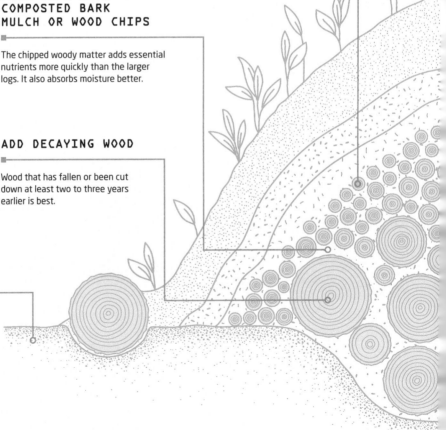

ADD NITROGEN-RICH MATTER

It's vital to include a layer of nitrogen-rich organic matter, so add the turf upside down to stop grass growing up through the soil. The weight of the turf compacts the materials, aiding decay. Rotting hay, leaf mould, or grass clippings can used as an alternative.

A hugel mound covered in vegetation; the topography of the structure also adds interest to the garden, transforming what was a flat lawn into a dynamic contoured landscape rich in biodiversity.

ADD TOPSOIL AND RICH COMPOST

The deeper the soil, the more choices you will have about what you can plant.

ADD PLANTS

See pages 180–97 for edimental and forest garden planting ideas. Note: Plants that like very dry, infertile soil conditions, such as Mediterranean herbs, will not be suitable here.

ADD MULCH

This is to protect the soil, suppress weeds, and lock in moisture. Use organic, biodegradable material (see pages 126–27).

147

RECLAIMED MATERIALS

THE LIGHT-TOUCH INTERVENTION ETHOS APPLIES NOT JUST TO PLANTING AND MAINTENANCE, BUT EXTENDS TO HARD LANDSCAPING IN A GARDEN TOO. USING RECLAIMED MATERIALS CAN BRING CHARACTER AND TEXTURE TO THE AREAS OF THE GARDEN WE USE THE MOST.

HARD MATERIALS

As our gardens must cater for human use, we need to add practical hard landscaping to suit our desired function, whether that's moving easily through the space, cooking, dining, or relaxing. Applying the light-touch ethos here, materials that weather and age well avoid the need for regular maintenance. Low-impact, minimal, and permeable paving solutions allow water to pass through and be absorbed into the landscape rather than running over it and into mains drains.

Reclaimed materials should be used and championed wherever possible, and they don't need to look shabby. Reclaimed timber, for example, can be full of character and texture. It has been used for the boardwalk in the resilient garden, which floats over the space.

Other materials have also been reused in the resilient garden: the recycled aggregate gravel has been used for pathways, on the biodiverse roof of the office, and as a gravel mulch in the front garden – celebrating and enhancing material otherwise destined for landfill. The terrazzo paving was made from rubble, then polished to reveal the intricate details and textures. With creative thinking and careful processing, waste can be beautiful too.

As our gardens must cater for human use, we need to add practical hard landscaping to suit our desired function, whether that's moving easily through the space, cooking, dining, or relaxing.

WABI-SABI

Wabi-sabi is an ideology ubiquitous across Japanese art practices and traditional aesthetics. It is centred on the practice of embracing that which is imperfect and ephemeral and can be used to describe the "imperfect, impermanent, and incomplete" beauty to be found in the natural world. Characteristics of wabi-sabi aesthetics include simplicity, asymmetry, intimacy, roughness, modesty, austerity, irregularity, coarseness, and the appreciation of both natural objects and the forces of nature.

In the resilient garden, materials such as recycled rubble terrazzo, rusty steel, and reclaimed timber contain many of the qualities admired in wabi-sabi ideology, the imperfection, weathering, and ageing adding beauty. The wild feeling of the planting, with a lack of overly controlled form, also celebrates the uncontrollable natural world. Nature does not conform to human ideals of perfection and this is celebrated in the design.

[Top] A timber boardwalk "floats" through the garden, its raised structure allowing plants and wildlife to move beneath.
[Right] Leaving channels and gaps in paved surfaces allows for better drainage and opportunities to plant the gaps. Here creeping thyme will tolerate some foot traffic and releases scent when stepped on.

01

USING RESOURCES

In the resilient garden, the dead wood in the existing garden is seen as a resource, not as waste material to be removed. This wood is used in several ways: in the hugelkultur mound, as a bench, to grow mushrooms, and as wildlife habitats.

Dead wood is important, as it provides food and habitats for many species of woodland animals, invertebrates, plants, and fungi. Keeping dead wood within a landscape or garden, rather than perceiving it to be untidy and removing it, increases habitat diversity and provides niches that are warmer, damper, and more stable than many surrounding habitats.

SAPROPHYTIC FUNGI

Of the many thousands of fungi species across the world, only a small number afflict plants or animals with disease. These are called pathogenic fungi. Most species of fungi are saprophytic, meaning they gain nourishment by absorbing dead organic matter, which is an essential step in the natural process of breaking it down; they are harmless, and often beneficial to their environment.

[01] The heart wood of the dead ash tree has been used as sculptural block seating. Over time these blocks will decay and return to the landscape, but before that happens, they will provide a function. [02] Some of the timber has been sawn to create a dining table and bench set with the bark left on, creating a textural and "raw" or "live" edge. [03] Bits of brush, twigs, and waste chunks of timber are perfect for creating habitat panels. Here they have been added to the side of the bin store, boosting its ecological function.

02

03

ASH DIEBACK

A chronic fungal disease, ash dieback has caused widespread damage to ash tree populations across Europe for 20 years. It is set to kill approximately 80 per cent of the ash trees in the UK, and has wiped out 90 percent of the ash trees in Denmark. This will have a devastating impact, irrevocably altering the landscape and jeopardizing the insect, animal, and bird species reliant on the ash tree, as well as having a huge economic effect, costing millions in the managing and felling of dead trees.

Quick facts
• Common disease name: Ash dieback, *Chalara*
• Scientific pathogen name: *Hymenoscyphus fraxineus*, formerly known as *Chalara fraxinea*
• Origin: East Asia, introduced to UK
• Species affected: Ash (*Fraxinus* species), especially the UK's native ash species (*F. excelsior*)
• Areas affected: Across the UK, Asia, and continental Europe

MUSHROOM LOGS

GROWING MUSHROOMS IS ONE OF THE BEST WAYS TO USE DEAD WOOD, AND IT IS EASIER THAN IT SOUNDS, ALTHOUGH IT DOES REQUIRE PATIENCE. MANY SUPPLIERS OFFER DIY KITS WITH EVERYTHING YOU NEED FOR THIS PROCESS.

HOW TO GROW A SHIITAKE MUSHROOM LOG

Shiitake (*Lentinula edodes*) is a wood-rotting fungus that grows on hardwood logs – beech, oak, and birch are particularly suitable. This mushroom is a good choice as it is strong, quick to colonize logs and to outcompete other fungi, and you can reliably induce logs to fruit as and when you want them. You can purchase wooden dowels or plugs inoculated with shiitake mushroom spawn.

STEP 1

First, select a log that has been felled from a healthy tree, approximately 1m (3¼ft) long and 10–20cm (4–8in) in diameter, and free of infection by other fungi to avoid competition.

The log should produce a minimum of one flush per year for several years, dependent on the size and density of the log and the environmental conditions. Very hard woods such as oak (*Quercus* species) can produce mushrooms for up to ten years, while softer woods, for example willow (*Salix* species), may only produce for five years.

STEP 2

Store the log for two weeks so that the natural fungi defences break down. Place it off the ground, sheltered from drying winds and direct sunlight to avoid it drying out too much.

STEP 3

Drill holes in the log to match the size of your mushroom plugs - usually 1cm (½in) wide and 4cm (1½in) deep. Make holes every 10–15cm (4–6in) along the length of the log. Soaking the log overnight beforehand may make drilling easier. Rotate the log and drill another series of holes in an offset diamond pattern. Aim for 50 offset holes around the log.

STEP 4

To inoculate the logs, insert the mushroom plugs into the holes with a mallet or hammer. A snug fit helps the mycelium (root system) move from the plug to the wood.

STEP 5

It is good practice to seal the holes with a layer of wax, which seals in moisture and stops competing fungi entering the log. Daub on the wax with a brush, to the thickness of a fingernail. Soy wax is a good choice as it has a low melting point: wax that is too hot will kill the mycelium.

STEP 6

The next step is incubation. Mushroom spawn will work its way through the log and digest the nutrients, preparing for fruiting. Incubation takes at least one spring/summer season, between 6 and 36 months. It is affected by many factors including wood type and size and the species of mushroom.

STEP 7

If you have inoculated multiple logs that are less than 1m (3¼ft) long, you can stack them using the common method of crib stacking. Raise them off the ground on blocks or a pallet and stack them in a criss-cross formation that creates an open structure for air flow, keeping the logs away from contamination by other fungi.

STEP 8

As the fungus colonizes the log, white mycelium should appear. The mycelium works its way up and down the vessels in the wood. When it turns a chocolate-brown colour and the logs develop an earthy smell, they are ready to fruit.

STEP 9

The mushrooms then need to be activated, or "shocked". This mimics the log falling from a tree. The best time to shock the log is spring or autumn; summer is too hot and winter too cold, so the mycelium are dormant. Bang the log on hard ground, or knock it at each end with a lump hammer.

STEP 10

Submerge the log in cold water for 1-2 days, ideally in a natural pond or water butt - avoid chemically treated water. This may not be necessary if there has been heavy rainfall.

STEP 11

After the log is removed from the water, mushroom primordia will begin to form. If conditions are reliably moist, these will quickly develop into mushroom fruiting bodies (which are very desirable to slugs and snails, so take care where you leave the logs).

STEP 12

The fruits (mushrooms) can double in size daily. In warm weather there is a risk they will dry out, so keep them out of direct sunlight and mist the fruit with a hand mister or hose on a mist setting.

After fruiting, try shocking the log again, as this can often induce an extra flush of growth.

SOUNDSCAPE

The sound of rustling
leaves, moving water,
and swaying grasses can
be relaxing, and dampens
loud and stress-inducing
city noises such as
traffic, sirens, trains,
and aeroplanes.

WILDLIFE

Wildlife is being encouraged
into the garden; seeing
wildlife lifts the spirits
and reminds us that we share
the planet with other forms
of life.

CONNECTING WITH NATURE

THE RESILIENT GARDEN HAS BEEN DESIGNED SO THAT ITS INHABITANTS WILL DEEPEN THEIR CONNECTION WITH NATURE, WHICH IS VITAL TO HUMAN WELLBEING. IN AN INCREASINGLY HECTIC WORLD, PARKS, GARDENS, AND NATURAL LANDSCAPES ARE USED AS PLACES OF RESPITE - AN ESCAPE FROM THE STRESSES AND PRESSURES OF DAILY EXISTENCE.

TREES

Trees cool and protect the space from the hot sun by casting dappled shade.

FOOD FOREST

Immersive, interactive, and sensory, it is planted with forageable species.

SOFT LANDSCAPING

Plants cover the soil and vertical surfaces, such as fences, outbuildings, and walls, softening the landscape.

THE VIEW

The plants are close to both the house and the outbuilding, meaning they are visible from indoors, enhancing the connection between the inside and outside spaces.

The BBC podcast Forest 404, which explores what it would mean to have a world without nature, discovered in a collaborative study that sounds in nature may have a positive impact on our mental health. Some 7,500 participants were played sounds from different landscapes, from English coastlines and woodlands to Papua New Guinea's tropical rainforests. The study found that stress and mental fatigue were alleviated by the sounds of birdsong. Participants described therapeutic benefits after listening to sounds such as rainfall or breaking waves. When these natural sounds were omitted, participants reported a decrease in the beneficial psychological effects, and their desire to preserve the planet's ecosystems decreased.

Alex Smalley, the principal researcher from the University of Exeter, said, "If we hope to harness nature's health benefits in the future, we need to ensure everyone has opportunities to foster positive experiences with the natural world today."

CHAPTER FIVE

RESILIENT PLANT GUIDE

FRONT GARDEN

Gravel garden: plants
that are resistant
to drought and wind.
Planted pathways:
permeable channels
for water to drain.
Hedges and trees:
a means of trapping
pollution particulates
and cooling the space.

GUIDE TO RESILIENT PLANTS

THE DESIGN OF THE RESILIENT GARDEN ENCOMPASSES SEVERAL AREAS,
EACH WITH DIFFERENT CHARACTERISTICS THAT DEMONSTRATE HOW
PLANTS CAN IMPROVE THE HUMAN EXPERIENCE OF A SPACE BY ADDING
ATMOSPHERE AND CHARACTER, AS WELL AS PRACTICAL BENEFITS.

Apart from their aesthetic appeal, planting schemes
can benefit the environment by functioning as
ecological, self-sustaining communities that provide
food and shelter for wildlife, increase biodiversity,
clean the air, and lock carbon into the soil. This
chapter lists plants that are likely to survive and
thrive in challenging conditions. The plants included
in the resilient garden design in Chapter 4 are
listed here, along with other similar plants that
have characteristics that make them resilient
performers in a garden setting. For an explanation
of the hardiness ratings, see page 247.

REAR GARDEN

Swale planting: species that can tolerate fluctuating wet and dry conditions. Forest garden: ornamental and edible plants that co-exist ecologically in a layered scheme, including ground-cover, climbers, shrubs, and trees. Plants for a green roof: species that require little or no active watering for living roof systems.

PLANTING ICONS

 Drought-resilient
Plants may have deep root systems, and fleshy/waxy, narrow, or grey, hairy leaves.

 Wind-resilient
Plants may fine or waxy leaves, flexible stems, or branches that wont break easily in high winds.

 Plants for pollinators
May have open flowers that offer easy access, or provide a high quantity of nectar or pollen.

 Edimental
Plants with ornamental qualities and edible parts, for example flowers or fruit.

 Pollution-reducing
Plants may be dense and evergreen, with hairy or rough leaves good at trapping particulates.

 Resilience to waterlogging
Species that will tolerate periods of waterlogged soil.

159

GRAVEL GARDEN

THE GRAVELLED AREA IN THE FRONT GARDEN INCLUDES DROUGHT- AND WIND-RESISTANT PLANTING WITH LOW, CREEPING PLANTS EXTENDING INTO THE DRIVEWAY. THE MIX ALSO HAS HIGH VISUAL AND SENSORY APPEAL, WITH PLENTY OF COLOUR, SCENT, AND TEXTURE.

01 *Hesperaloe parviflora*

A yucca-like perennial, forming clumps of arching, linear, leathery leaves. In summer, flower spikes up to 1.5m (5ft) long bear tubular to bell-shaped pink flowers. It can take extreme cold and tolerates drought.

Common name Small-flowered hesperaloe **Foliage** Evergreen **Height** 1–1.5m (3¼–5ft) **Spread** 5–10cm (2–4in) **Exposure** Full sun, sheltered **Soil** Well-drained loam, sand (acid/neutral) **Hardiness** H4

02 *Euphorbia rigida*

An erect, then spreading, evergreen perennial. The blue-green leaves are fleshy, and arranged spirally. Bright yellow flowers appear in small clusters at the tips of the shoots in late spring and early summer.

Common name Spurge **Foliage** Evergreen **Height** 10–50cm (4–20in) **Spread** 10–50cm (4–20in) **Exposure** Full sun or partial shade, exposed or sheltered **Soil** Well-drained/moist but well-drained chalk, clay, loam, sand (acid/alkaline/neutral) **Hardiness** H6

03 *Salvia greggii*

A bushy dwarf shrub, branching from the base and evergreen if not cut back by frosts, with small, aromatic, mid- to deep green leaves. Red, purple, pink, yellow, or violet flowers appear from late summer to autumn. A highly fragrant border for pathways.

Common name Autumn sage **Foliage** Evergreen **Height** 50–100cm (20–39in) **Spread** 50–100cm (20–39in) **Exposure** Full sun, sheltered **Soil** Well-drained/ moist but well-drained chalk, loam, sand (acid/alkaline/neutral) **Hardiness** H4

04 *Thymus serpyllum* 'Elfin'

An evergreen subshrub, 'Elfin' forms a dense mound of trailing stems with small, aromatic, grey-green leaves and small, lilac-pink flowers in summer. It releases scent when brushed against or stepped on, so it is great between gaps in paving. The aromatic leaves are used in cooking.

Common name Thyme 'Elfin' **Foliage** Evergreen **Height** 10cm (4in) **Spread** 10–50cm (4–20in) **Exposure** Full sun, exposed or sheltered **Soil** Well-drained chalk, loam, sand (alkaline/neutral) **Hardiness** H5

05 *Stachys byzantina*

A carpeting, evergreen perennial, with thick, soft, oblong elliptic leaves that are densely white-woolly. The flowers are purplish or pink, sometimes striped, borne in whorls in an interrupted spike in summer. The leaves can be deep-fried, known colloquially as "poor man's fish".

Common name Lamb's ear **Foliage** Evergreen
Height 10–50cm (4–20in) **Spread** 50–100cm
(20–39in) **Exposure** Full sun, exposed
Soil Well-drained chalk, loam, sand (acid/alkaline/neutral) **Hardiness** H7

06 *Stipa tenuissima*

A deciduous grass, forming a compact upright tuft of thread-like leaves, with narrow, arching, feathery flowering panicles in summer.

Common name Mexican feather grass
Foliage Deciduous **Height** 50–100cm (20–39in)
Spread 10–50cm (4–20in) **Exposure** Full sun,
exposed or sheltered **Soil** Well-drained/moist
but well-drained chalk, clay, loam, sand
Hardiness H4

07 *Pinus mugo* 'Mops'

'Mops' is a slow-growing evergreen conifer that makes a medium-sized shrub of bushy, rounded habit, with slender, paired, dark green needles. Its dense evergreen foliage is good at capturing particulate pollution.

Common name Dwarf mountain pine 'Mops'
Foliage Evergreen **Height** 50–100cm (20–39in)
Spread 50–100cm (20–39in) **Exposure** Full sun,
exposed or sheltered **Soil** Well-drained chalk,
clay, loam, sand (acid/alkaline/neutral)
Hardiness H7

08 *Salvia rosmarinus*

This bushy shrub has linear, dark green leaves that are used to flavour food. Its pale violet and white flowers bloom mainly in spring and summer.

Common name Rosemary **Foliage** Evergreen **Height** 1.5–2.5m (5–8ft) **Spread** 1.5–2.5m (5–8ft) **Exposure** Full sun, exposed or sheltered **Soil** Well-drained/moist but well-drained chalk, clay, loam, sand (acid/alkaline/neutral) **Hardiness** H4

09 *Lavandula stoechas*

An aromatic dwarf shrub, with narrow, grey-green leaves and short-stalked, dense heads of tiny, deep purple flowers surmounted by a tuft of purple bracts.

Common name French lavender **Foliage** Evergreen **Height** 50–100cm (20–39in) **Spread** 50–100cm (20–39in) **Exposure** Full sun, sheltered **Soil** Well-drained chalk, loam, sand (acid/alkaline/neutral) **Hardiness** H4

10 *Helichrysum italicum*

A small bushy evergreen subshrub with linear, silvery-grey, curry-scented leaves, and small yellow flowerheads in domed clusters. The potently scented leaves can be used to add a "curry" flavour to food.

Common name Curry plant **Foliage** Evergreen **Height** 10–50cm (4–20in) **Spread** 50–100cm (20–39in) **Exposure** Full sun, sheltered **Soil** Well-drained chalk, loam (alkaline/neutral) **Hardiness** H4

Nepeta racemosa 'Little Titch'

A compact herbaceous perennial that forms a low carpet of aromatic foliage topped with short spikes of lavender-blue flowers in spring and summer. It is perfect as an edging plant to pathways where its scent can be enjoyed.

Common name Catmint
Foliage Deciduous
Height 10–50cm (4–20in)
Spread 10–50cm (4–20in)
Exposure Full sun, exposed or sheltered **Soil** Well-drained chalk, loam, sand (acid/alkaline/neutral)
Hardiness H7

Geranium renardii

This herbaceous perennial forms clumps of lobed, wrinkled leaves. Its white or mauve flowers with violet veins bloom in summer.

Common name Renard geranium
Foliage Deciduous
Height 10–50cm (4–20in)
Spread 10–50cm (4–20in)
Exposure Full sun, partial shade, exposed or sheltered
Soil Well-drained/moist but well-drained chalk, clay, loam, sand (acid/alkaline/neutral)
Hardiness H6

Papaver dubium subsp. *lecoqii albiflorum*

This small pink annual poppy is called 'Beth's Poppy' after the renowned plantswoman Beth Chatto. It can be allowed to self-sow in a sunny, well-drained site.

Common name Beth's poppy
Foliage Deciduous **Height** 40cm (16in) **Spread** 15cm (6in)
Exposure Full sun, exposed or sheltered **Soil** Well-drained light loam or sand (acid/alkaline/neutral) **Hardiness** H7

Lavandula angustifolia 'Hidcote Blue'

This bushy dwarf shrub has narrow, silvery-grey leaves and dense spikes of deep violet aromatic flowers that bloom in summer.

Common name English lavender 'Hidcote'
Foliage Evergreen **Height** 10–50cm (4–20in)
Spread 50–100cm (20–39in) **Exposure** Full sun, sheltered **Soil type** Well-drained chalk, clay, loam, sand (acid/alkaline/neutral)
Hardiness H5

Festuca glauca

An evergreen blue grass that forms in clumps and becomes greener in winter. In late spring and summer it bears bristly blue-green flower plumes that turn golden-brown in autumn.

Common name Blue fescue
Foliage Evergreen
Height 10–50cm (4–20in)
Spread 10–50cm (4–20in)
Exposure Full sun, exposed or sheltered **Soil** Well-drained/moist but well-drained chalk, loam, sand (acid/alkaline/neutral)
Hardiness H5

Orlaya grandiflora

This branching annual has jagged leaves. In summer and autumn it has white flowers comprising a small inner flower and a ring of larger outer petals.

Common name White laceflower
Foliage Deciduous
Height 50–100cm (20–39in)
Spread 10–50cm (4–20in)
Exposure Full sun, exposed or sheltered **Soil** Well-drained chalk, loam, sand (acid/alkaline/neutral)
Hardiness H7

Salvia fruticosa

This sage has paired aromatic leaves and pink flowers. It can be grown as an annual or evergreen perennial herb or herbaceous shrub and is very drought tolerant once established.

Common name Greek sage
Foliage Evergreen
Height 60–90cm (2–3ft)
Spread 8m (26ft) or more
Exposure Full sun or partial shade, exposed or sheltered
Soil Well-drained chalk, clay, loam, sand (acid/alkaline/neutral)
Hardiness H4

Salvia nemorosa 'Ostfriesland'

This variety of Balkan sage is a compact, bushy perennial with narrow oval leaves and erect stems that bear deep violet flowers and pink bracts in summer and autumn. It is extremely popular with pollinators.

Common name Balkan clary **Foliage** Deciduous
Height 10–50cm (4–20in) **Spread** 10–50cm (4–20in) **Exposure** Full sun, exposed or sheltered **Soil type** Well-drained chalk, loam, sand (acid/alkaline/neutral) **Hardiness** H7

Eschscholzia californica

A bushy annual or biennial plant, California poppy has blue-green leaves and yellow, orange, or red flowers that bloom in summer. It will seed into hostile environments such as gaps in paving or walls.

Common name California poppy
Foliage Deciduous
Height 10–50cm (4–20in)
Spread 10–50cm (4–20in)
Exposure Full sun, exposed or sheltered **Soil** Well-drained chalk, loam, sand (acid/alkaline/neutral)
Hardiness H3

Salvia officinalis

This dwarf bushy shrub has aromatic, grey-green leaves that are used for culinary purposes, and short spikes of pale blue flowers in early summer.

Common name Common sage **Foliage** Evergreen
Height 50–100cm (20–39in)
Spread 50–100cm (20–39in)
Exposure Full sun or partial shade, sheltered **Soil** Well-drained clay, loam (acid/alkaline/neutral)
Hardiness H5

Eryngium ebracteatum

An erect herbaceous perennial with spiny grey-green leaves and wiry stems, this eryngium has red-brown flowerheads that bloom in summer and autumn.

Common name Burnet-flowered sea holly, thrift
Foliage Evergreen **Height** 1–1.5m (3¼–5ft) **Spread** 0.5–1m (1½–3¼ft) **Exposure** Full sun, exposed or sheltered
Soil Well-drained chalk, loam, sand (acid/alkaline/neutral)
Hardiness H4

Centranthus ruber

This woody herbaceous perennial or biennial bears dense clusters of fragrant pink or white flowers from late spring to autumn. It is often seen growing on drystone walls.

Common name Red valerian
Foliage Semi-evergreen **Height** 50–100cm (20–39in) **Spread** 10–50cm (4–20in)
Exposure Full sun, exposed **Soil** Well-drained chalk, loam, sand (alkaline/neutral)
Hardiness H5

Asphodeline lutea

A herbaceous perennial, asphodel has narrow leaves and fragrant, cheerful yellow flowers that bloom in late spring.

Common name Asphodel **Foliage** Evergreen **Height** 1–1.5m (3 ¼–6ft) **Spread** 10–50cm (4–20in) **Exposure** Full sun, exposed or sheltered **Soil** Well-drained chalk, loam, sand (acid/alkaline/neutral) **Hardiness** H4

Calamintha nepeta

A compact, bushy perennial, this plant has aromatic leaves and loose clusters of tiny, tubular white or lilac flowers from summer to early autumn.

Common name Lesser calamint
Foliage Semi-evergreen **Height** 50–100cm (20–39in) **Spread** 50–100cm (20–39in)
Exposure Full sun, exposed or sheltered
Soil Well-drained chalk, loam, sand (alkaline/neutral) **Hardiness** H5

Thymus vulgaris

A popular culinary herb, common thyme forms a bushy dwarf shrub with aromatic leaves. Spikes of small, whorled, white or pink flowers appear in early summer.

Common name Common thyme **Foliage** Evergreen **Height** 10–50cm (4–20in) **Spread** 10–50cm (4–20in) **Exposure** Full sun, exposed or sheltered **Soil** Well-drained chalk, loam, sand (alkaline/neutral) **Hardiness** H5

Echium vulgare

An erect, bristly biennial with long, hairy leaves and cylindrical spikes of bell-shaped electric-blue flowers that appear in early summer - a magnet for pollinators.

Common name Viper's bugloss
Foliage Deciduous
Height 50–100cm (20–39in)
Spread 10–50cm (4–20in)
Exposure Full sun, exposed or sheltered **Soil** Well-drained chalk, loam, sand (acid/alkaline/neutral)
Hardiness H7

Erigeron karvinskianus

This herbaceous perennial forms mats with delicate leaves and white daisy flowers in summer that turn pink. It self-seeds profusely.

Common name Mexican fleabane
Foliage Semi-evergreen
Height 10–50cm (4–20in)
Spread 50–100cm (20–39in) **Exposure** Full sun, exposed **Soil** Well-drained chalk, clay, loam, sand (acid/alkaline/neutral) **Hardiness** H5

Thymus pseudolanuginosus

This edible herb is a fragrant, creeping subshrub that forms mats of small leaves, fringed with minute hairs, and produces purple flowers in summer.

Common name Wild thyme
Foliage Evergreen **Height** 10cm (4in) **Spread** 10–50cm (4–20in)
Exposure Full sun, exposed or sheltered **Soil** Well-drained chalk, loam, sand (alkaline/neutral)
Hardiness H5

Hordeum jubatum

A tufted annual or perennial grass producing long, silky bristles with tips that turn red in summer. It is very tactile and textural.

Common name Foxtail barley
Foliage Deciduous
Height 50–100cm (20–39in)
Spread 10–50cm (4–20in)
Exposure Full sun, exposed or sheltered **Soil** Well-drained chalk, clay, loam, sand (acid/alkaline/neutral) **Hardiness** H6

HEDGES AND TREES

THESE PLANTS HAVE BEEN CHOSEN MAINLY TO REDUCE POLLUTION AND TRAFFIC NOISE, BUT ALSO TO PROVIDE A VISUAL SCREEN, SHELTER AND FOOD FOR WILDLIFE, AND AREAS OF SHADE IN A GARDEN.

01 *Pinus sylvestris*

A very wind-resistant evergreen tree, with orange-brown branches and upper trunk and a picturesque outline with age. The twisted grey-green needles are borne in pairs.

Common name Scots pine **Foliage** Evergreen **Height** 12m (59ft) or more **Spread** 8m (26ft) or more **Exposure** Full sun, exposed or sheltered **Soil** Well-drained chalk, clay, loam, sand (acid/alkaline/neutral) **Hardiness** H7

02 *Pinus sylvestris* 'Watereri'

A small, slow-growing form of Scots pine, often multistemmed, with flaky brown bark and pairs of blue-green needles, 'Watereri' bears cones throughout the year.

Common name Scots pine 'Watereri' **Foliage** Evergreen **Height** 2.5–4m (8–13ft) **Spread** 4–8m (13–26ft) **Exposure** Full sun, exposed or sheltered **Soil** Well-drained chalk, clay, loam, sand (acid/alkaline/neutral) **Hardiness** H7

03 *Callistemon viminalis* 'Captain Cook'

This dense, round shrub has narrow leaves and bright red, bottle brush-shaped flowers that bloom from early summer to autumn. The dense evergreen foliage is good for screening and providing some protection against air pollutants.

Common name Bottlebrush 'Captain Cook' **Foliage** Evergreen
Height 1.5–2.5m (5–8ft)
Spread 1.5–2.5m (5–8ft)
Exposure Full sun, sheltered
Soil Moist but well-drained clay, loam, sand (acid/neutral)
Hardiness H3

04 *Cotoneaster franchetii*

A tall shrub with arching branches and glossy leaves that trap particulates, this cotoneaster bears clusters of white flowers tinged with pink in early summer, followed by orange fruits in autumn and winter.

Common name Franchet's cotoneaster **Foliage** Evergreen
Height 2.5–4m (8–13ft)
Spread 2.5–4m (8–13ft)
Exposure Full sun or partial shade, exposed or sheltered
Soil Well-drained/moist but well-drained chalk, clay, loam, sand (acid/alkaline/neutral)
Hardiness H6

Sorbus aria

This medium-sized, upright tree has oval, dark green leaves and clusters of white flowers in spring that are followed by red berries in early autumn.

Common name Common whitebeam
Foliage Deciduous **Height** 8–12m (26–39ft)
Spread 4–8m (13–26ft) **Exposure** Full sun or partial shade, exposed or sheltered
Soil Well-drained/moist but well-drained chalk, clay, loam, sand (acid/alkaline/neutral) **Hardiness** H6

Taxus baccata

Yew forms a medium-sized bushy tree with narrow, dark green leaves but can be pruned to form a very dense hedge. The spring flowers are followed by fleshy red fruits in autumn on female plants.

Common name Common yew
Foliage Evergreen
Height 12m (39ft) or more
Spread 8m (26ft) or more
Exposure Full shade to full sun, exposed or sheltered
Soil Well-drained chalk, clay, loam, sand (acid/alkaline/neutral)
Hardiness H7

Phillyrea angustifolia

A compact shrub with narrow, dark green leaves, mock privet has small clusters of fragrant white flowers in late spring and early summer, followed by blue fruits in autumn.

Common name Narrow-leaved mock privet
Foliage Evergreen **Height** 2.5–4m (8–13ft) **Spread** 1.5–2.5m (5–8ft)
Exposure Full sun, partial shade, exposed or sheltered
Soil Well-drained sand, loam (acid/alkaline/neutral)
Hardiness H5

Elaeagnus angustifolia

This spreading shrub has spiky, red shoots and dark-green oval leaves. The fragrant yellow summer flowers are followed by yellow fruits in autumn.

Common name Bohemian oleaster
Foliage Deciduous **Height** 4–8m (13–26ft)
Spread 4–8m (13–26ft) **Exposure** Full sun, exposed or sheltered **Soil type** Well-drained/moist but well-drained chalk, clay, loam, sand (acid/alkaline/neutral) **Hardiness** H5

Quercus ilex

A large tree that develops a rounded crown, the holm oak has black bark, glossy, dark, oval-shaped leaves, and yellow catkins in spring, followed by autumn acorns. It can be pruned and trained into formal shapes.

Common name Holm oak
Foliage Evergreen **Height** 12m (39ft) or more **Spread** 8m (26ft) or more **Exposure** Full sun or partial shade, exposed or sheltered **Soil** Well-drained/moist but well-drained chalk, clay, loam, sand (acid/alkaline/neutral)
Hardiness H4

Genista aetnensis

A large shrub or small tree with arching green shoots and small, sparse leaves, Mount Etna broom bears bright yellow, fragrant, pea-shaped flowers in summer, followed by fruits in autumn.

Common name Mount Etna broom
Foliage Deciduous **Height** 4–8m (13–26ft)
Spread 4–8m (13–26ft) **Exposure** Full sun, exposed or sheltered **Soil** Well-drained chalk, clay, loam, sand (acid/alkaline/neutral)
Hardiness H5

Quercus suber

Known for its characterful cork bark, used to produce cork-based products, this slow-growing tree has dark, glossy leaves and long, slender acorns in autumn.

Common name Cork oak **Foliage** Evergreen
Height 12m (39ft) or more **Spread** 8m (26ft) or more **Exposure** Full sun, sheltered
Soil Well-drained loam, sand (acid/alkaline/neutral) **Hardiness** H5

ANTI-POLLUTION PLANTS

DR TIJANA BLANUSA is a principal scientist at the RHS and leads the Ecosystem Services Research Programme, identifying plant characteristics that might be used to benefit wider habitats and looking at the environmental value of gardens and urban green infrastructure.

In Parc Central de Poblenou in Barcelona, layers of dense vegetation are used to provide screening and protection from the adjacent city road.

"

CAN PLANTS REALLY HELP IN TRAPPING POLLUTION AND FILTERING THE AIR?

Plants can take up gaseous pollutants such as excess carbon dioxide and break them up, store them, or use them for their own metabolism. Leaves and stems can also act as surfaces onto which particulate pollution is deposited and thus removed from the air. The current scientific thinking is that plant barriers are only the third line of defence against pollution, after the reduction of pollution emissions and a greater distance to pollution sources – but the taller and deeper the barrier, the better.

ARE THERE PARTICULAR QUALITIES IN PLANTS TO LOOK OUT FOR?

Plants that have large, dense canopies are the most effective. Fast-growing, thirsty species tend to have a high level of gas exchange, indicating that they could be effective at the uptake of gaseous pollutants. Other qualities that increase particle capture are rough and hairy leaf surfaces.

HOW ELSE CAN PLANTS IMPROVE WELLBEING IN URBAN ENVIRONMENTS?

Plants cool the air via shade and evapotranspiration, and can also insulate buildings and reduce noise levels – all of those directly affect human wellbeing, not to mention the psychological benefits that come from being surrounded by greenery.

SOME SPECIES ARE REFERRED TO AS "SUPER PLANTS" – SHOULD WE BE LOOKING AT THEM IN A MORE BALANCED WAY?

Yes, we should. A plant may not excel at any singular service, but may offer multiple benefits by way of supporting biodiversity, reducing flooding risks, regulating a microclimate, and making urban spaces more pleasant to live in.

WHAT SHOULD THE FUTURE OF PLANTING DESIGN IN URBAN ENVIRONMENTS LOOK LIKE?

What we know currently suggests that diverse perennial planting combinations and the use of woody plants can deliver many environmental benefits. Evergreen vegetation (mixed in with deciduous) also seems a way to maximize year-round environmental benefits.

SWALE PLANTING

THE PLANTS IN THE SWALE AREA AND WILDLIFE POND CAN TOLERATE SEASONAL WET AND DRY CONDITIONS. THIS AREA HAS BEEN DESIGNED TO BE FLOODED IN PERIODS OF HEAVIER RAINFALL AND TO DRY OUT WHEN RAINFALL IS SCARCE.

01 *Acorus calamus*

A spreading, tufted herbaceous perennial with aromatic, sword-shaped leaves. The raw, partially grown flower stems and the young stalks in spring are sweet and tasty eaten in a salad, while the roots have a gingery taste. It is also known as sweet rush and sweet cinnamon.

Common name Silver-striped sweet flag **Foliage** Deciduous **Height** 50–100m (20–39in) **Spread** 10–50cm (4–20in) **Exposure** Full sun, exposed or sheltered **Soil** Poorly drained clay, loam, sand (acid/alkaline/neutral) **Hardiness** H7

02 *Iris pseudacorus*

A vigorous herbaceous perennial, the yellow iris forms colonies of bright yellow flowers with brown veining in the centre during early and midsummer. It spreads rapidly, so can need management in a small pond.

Common name Yellow iris
Foliage Deciduous
Height 1–1.5m (3¼–5ft)
Spread 0.5–1m (1½–3¼ft)
Exposure Full sun or partial shade, exposed or sheltered
Soil Poorly drained clay, loam (acid) **Hardiness** H7

03 *Lythrum salicaria*

This herbaceous perennial has upright stems, narrow, willowy leaves, and small vivid purplish-pink flowers borne in dense spikes over a long period in summer.

Common name Purple loosestrife
Foliage Deciduous
Height 1–1.5m (3¼–5ft)
Spread 10–50cm (4–20in)
Exposure Full sun, exposed or sheltered **Soil** Moist but well-drained or poorly drained clay, loam (acid/alkaline/neutral)
Hardiness H7

04 *Valeriana officinalis*

Valerian is an upright herbaceous perennial, with scented pinnate leaves and rounded clusters of small pink or white flowers in summer. It is an edible plant and the ground root is used medicinally.

Common name Common valerian
Foliage Deciduous
Height 1–1.5m (3¼–5ft)
Spread 0.5–1m (1½–3¼ft)
Exposure Full sun or partial shade, exposed or sheltered
Soil type Chalk, clay, loam, sand (acid/alkaline/neutral)
Hardiness H4

Juncus effusus

A clump-forming grass-like perennial with green to yellowish rounded stems held in arching fans, the common rush produces rounded heads of small green to brown flowers that bloom in spring and summer.

Common name Common rush **Foliage** Evergreen
Height 1–1.5m (3¹/₄–5ft)
Spread 0.5–1m (1¹/₂–3¹/₄ft)
Exposure Full sun to full shade, exposed or sheltered
Soil type Poorly drained clay, loam (acid) **Hardiness** H6

Osmunda regalis

This robust fern forms a large clump of bipinnate fronds with rusty-brown spore-bearing leaflets at the tips. During autumn, the foliage turns an attractive red-brown.

Common name Royal fern
Foliage Deciduous
Height 1.5–2.5m (5–8ft)
Spread 0.5–1m (1¹/₂–3¹/₄ft)
Exposure Full sun to full shade, exposed or sheltered
Soil type Moist but well-drained/ poorly drained chalk, clay, loam (acid/alkaline/neutral)
Hardiness H6

Butomus umbellatus

A herbaceous perennial, this plant has upright, twisted grassy leaves. In late summer, it produces rosy-pink flowers on stiff stems.

Common name Flowering rush
Foliage Deciduous **Height** 1–1.5m (3¹/₄–5ft)
Spread 10–50cm (4–20in) **Exposure** Full sun, exposed or sheltered **Soil type** Poorly drained clay, loam, sand (acid/alkaline/neutral)
Hardiness H5

Carex divulsa

This densely tufted sedge has arching, dark green or greyish-green leaves and short spikes of greenish-brown flowers that bloom in summer. It is resilient in a range of conditions from shade to full sun.

Common name Grey sedge
Foliage Evergreen
Height 50–100cm (20–39in)
Spread 50–100cm (20–39in)
Exposure Full sun to full shade, exposed or sheltered **Soil** Poorly drained/moist but well-drained/well-drained chalk, clay, loam, sand (acid/alkaline/neutral)
Hardiness H5

Angelica archangelica

A robust, upright perennial, angelica has two- to three-pinnate leaves and rounded umbels of light yellow flowers in early summer. Fresh stalks and leaves can be eaten raw in fruit salads, or used as a garnish. The stalks can also be stewed or candied.

Common name Angelica
Foliage Deciduous
Height 1.5–2.5m (5–8ft)
Spread 1–1.5m (3¹/₄–5ft)
Exposure Full sun or partial shade, exposed or sheltered
Soil Moist but well-drained/poorly drained chalk, clay, loam (acid/alkaline/neutral)
Hardiness H6

Symphytum officinale

A perennial that forms a clump of erect stems bearing elliptic leaves, comfrey produces clusters of tubular bell-shaped, purple, pink, or cream flowers in late spring and summer. It can be used to make "comfrey tea" which is an organic fertilizer.

Common name Common comfrey
Foliage Deciduous **Height** 1–1.5m (3¹/₄–5ft) **Spread** 1–1.5m (3¹/₄–5ft) **Exposure** Full sun or partial shade, exposed or sheltered **Soil type** Moist but well-drained or poorly drained chalk, clay, loam, sand (acid/alkaline/neutral) **Hardiness** H7

FOOD FOREST

WITH PLANT TYPES OF VARYING HEIGHTS, AND EDIBLE SPECIES PROVIDING FOOD YEAR-ROUND, FOREST GARDENS OFFER GREAT USE OF SPACE FOR PLOTS THAT MAY BE TOO SMALL FOR A TRADITIONAL PRODUCTIVE AREA. THEY ALSO SUPPORT A HUGE AMOUNT OF WILDLIFE, AS MANY PLANTS WILL FLOWER, FRUIT, AND PROVIDE SHELTER.

01 *Ficus carica*

A large shrub or small, spreading tree with rounded, lobed leaves, this plant bears insignificant flowers that are followed by edible fruit that ripens to shades of green and purple in autumn. The scented leaves can also be used to perfume and flavour food.

Common name Fig
Foliage Deciduous **Height** 2.5m–4m (8–13ft) **Spread** 2.5m–4m (8–13ft) **Exposure** Full sun, sheltered **Soil** Well-drained/moist but well-drained chalk, loam, sand (alkaline/neutral) **Hardiness** H4

02 *Malus sylvestris*

This small, rounded tree has ovate leaves and, in late spring, pink-flushed white blossom. This is followed by yellowish-green, sometimes red-flushed apples that can be used to make crab-apple jelly.

Common name Crab apple
Foliage Deciduous **Height** 8–12m (26–39ft) **Spread** 4–8m (13–26ft) **Spread** 4–8m (13–26ft) **Exposure** Full sun or partial shade, exposed or sheltered **Soil** Moist but well-drained chalk, clay, loam, sand (acid/alkaline/neutral) **Hardiness** H6

03 *Prunus avium*

This medium-sized deciduous tree bears clusters of pure white flowers 2.5cm (1in) wide in late spring. They are followed by small, shiny red-purple cherries that are popular with birds. For larger, sweeter fruits, opt for a cultivar such as 'Stella'.

Common name Wild cherry
Foliage Deciduous **Height** 12m (39ft) or more **Spread** 8m (26ft) or more **Exposure** Full sun, exposed or sheltered **Soil** Well-drained/ moist but well-drained chalk, clay, loam, sand (acid/alkaline/neutral) **Hardiness** H6

04 *Sorbus aucuparia*

An upright deciduous tree, the rowan has pinnate leaves that turn yellow in autumn, and clusters of white flowers in late spring, followed by orange-red berries in early autumn. They are acidic and best used to make jams and preserves.

Common name Rowan
Foliage Deciduous **Height** 12m (39ft) or more **Spread** 4–8m (13–26ft) **Exposure** Full sun or partial shade, exposed or sheltered **Soil** Well-drained loam, sand (acid/neutral) **Hardiness** H6

05 *Cornus kousa*

This is a small, bushy tree with oval leaves that turn reddish-purple in autumn. The small white flowers appear in summer. They are followed by deep pink, edible fruits that resemble strawberries.

Common name Kousa
Foliage Deciduous **Height** 4–8m (13–26ft) **Spread** 4–8m (13–26ft) **Exposure** Full sun or partial shade, exposed or sheltered **Soil** Well-drained/moist but well-drained chalk, loam, sand (acid/alkaline/neutral) **Hardiness** H6

06 *Monarda* 'Cambridge Scarlet'

This herbaceous perennial grows in a clump to 90cm (36in) in height, with aromatic, edible leaves and whorls of deep scarlet, two-lipped flowers that make an edible garnish for salads.

Common name Bergamot 'Cambridge Scarlet'
Foliage Deciduous
Height 50–100cm (20–39in)
Spread 10–50cm (4–20in)
Exposure Full sun or partial shade, exposed or sheltered **Soil** Moist but well-drained chalk, clay, loam, sand (acid/alkaline/neutral)
Hardiness H4

07 *Hemerocallis* 'Stafford'

A deciduous perennial that bears narrow-petalled deep red, fleshy flowers with yellow midribs and a yellow throat, appearing daily in midsummer. They are edible and delicious in salads.

Common name Daylily 'Stafford'
Foliage Deciduous
Height 50–100cm (20–39in)
Spread 10–50cm (4–20in)
Exposure Full sun, exposed or sheltered **Soil** Moist but well-drained chalk, clay, loam (acid/alkaline/neutral)
Hardiness H6

08 *Hippophae rhamnoides*

A large, deciduous shrub with narrow, silvery leaves and thorny shoots, sea buckthorn bears very small yellow flowers in spring. On female plants, they are followed by small, bright orange berries in summer. They are edible and high in vitamin C.

Common name Sea buckthorn
Foliage Deciduous
Height 4–8m (13–26ft) **Spread** 4–8m (13–26ft) **Exposure** Full sun, exposed/sheltered **Soil type** Well-drained/moist but well-drained loam, sand (alkaline/neutral) **Hardiness** H7

09 *Rubus idaeus*

This deciduous shrub bears tall biennial stems, some with prickles. The white flowers are followed by red, edible fruits (raspberries).

Common name Raspberry
Foliage Deciduous **Height** 1.5–2.5m (5–8ft) **Spread** 0.5–1m (1½–3¼ft) **Exposure** Full sun to full shade, exposed or sheltered **Soil** Well-drained/moist but well-drained loam, sand (acid/neutral) **Hardiness** H6

10 *Helianthus annuus*

A fast-growing annual with large, oval to heart-shaped, hairy leaves. The flowers, up to 30cm (12in) across, have yellow petals with brownish centres. They attract bees, and the seeds that follow are food for birds.

Common name Common sunflower
Foliage Deciduous **Height** 2.5–4m (8–13ft) **Spread** 0.5–1m (1½–3¼ft) **Exposure** Sheltered, full sun **Soil** Moist but well-drained chalk, clay, loam, sand (alkaline/neutral) **Hardiness** H4

11 *Centaurea cyanus*

Best known for the deep blue flowerheads that bloom in late spring and summer, cornflower is an upright annual with slightly lobed leaves. The flowers are edible, with a sweet/spicy clove-like flavour.

Common name Cornflower
Foliage Deciduous **Height** 0.5–1m (1½–3¼ft) **Spread** 10–50cm (4–20in) **Exposure** Full sun, exposed **Soil** Well-drained loam, sand (acid/alkaline/neutral) **Hardiness** H6

12 *Ribes nigrum*

A deciduous self-fertile shrub producing bunches of dark purple edible berries, rich in vitamin C, in midsummer.

Common name Blackcurrant
Foliage Deciduous **Height** 1–1.5m (3¼–5ft) **Spread** 1–1.5m (3¼–5ft) **Exposure** Full sun or partial shade, sheltered **Soil** Well-drained clay, loam, sand (acid/alkaline/neutral) **Hardiness** H6

13 *Alchemilla mollis*

This herbaceous perennial forms a clump of hairy, rounded, light green leaves. In summer, small, bright yellow flowers are borne in large sprays above the foliage. The young leaves are edible both raw and cooked; dried leaves are also used as a tea.

Common name Lady's mantle
Foliage Deciduous
Height 50–100cm (20–39in)
Spread 50–100cm (20–39in)
Exposure Full sun to full shade, exposed or sheltered **Soil** Moist but well-drained chalk, clay, loam, sand (acid/alkaline/neutral)
Hardiness H6

14 *Trifolium pratense*

Often used as a green manure crop because it fixes nitrogen in the soil, this perennial plant has trifoliate leaves and clusters of pinkish-red flowers from mid-spring to early autumn; both are edible. It is a great source of nectar, especially for bees.

Common name Red clover
Foliage Deciduous **Height** 10–50cm (4–20in) **Spread** 40cm (16in)
Exposure Full sun, exposed or sheltered **Soil type** Well-drained/moist but well-drained clay, loam (acid) **Hardiness** H7

15 *Fragaria vesca*

This spreading perennial forms rosettes of three-palmate, bright green leaves with toothed leaflets. In late spring it bears white flowers that are followed by red fruit (wild strawberries) in summer.

Common name Alpine strawberry
Foliage Semi-evergreen
Height 10–50cm (4–20in)
Spread 50–100cm (20–39in)
Exposure Full sun, sheltered
Soil type Moist but well-drained clay, loam, sand (acid/alkaline/neutral) **Hardiness** H6

16 *Taraxacum officinale*

A herbaceous perennial with upright stems and dark green foliage. The yellow flowerheads develop into silvery tufted seedheads that disperse in the wind. It is often considered to be a weed, but all parts are used in herbal medicine or as foods.

Common name Dandelion
Foliage Evergreen
Height 10–50cm (4–20in)
Spread 10–50cm (4–20in)
Exposure Full sun or partial shade, exposed or sheltered
Soil type Well-drained/moist but well-drained chalk, clay, loam, sand (acid/alkaline/neutral)
Hardiness H7

17 *Matteuccia struthiopteris*

A deciduous, stoloniferous fern that forms colonies of erect rosettes, this plant has lance-shaped, bright green, bipinnatifid sterile fronds that surround shorter, brownish, fertile fronds. Young unfurled fronds are edible (but note that not all ferns are edible, so check identification before consuming).

Common name Shuttlecock fern
Foliage Deciduous **Height** 1–1.5m (3¼–5ft) **Spread** 1.5–2.5m (5–8ft) **Exposure** Full shade or partial shade, sheltered
Soil type Moist but well-drained clay, loam, sand (acid/neutral) **Hardiness** H5

18 *Lonicera periclymenum*

This vigorous, twining climber has creamy-white tubular flowers 5cm (2in) long, flushed reddish-purple, that open in mid- and late summer and are very fragrant. Glossy red berries follow. Sweet nectar can be sucked from the base of plucked flowers, hence the common name.

Common name Common honeysuckle
Foliage Deciduous **Height** 4–8m (13–26ft)
Spread 2.5–4m (8–13ft) **Exposure** Full sun or partial shade, exposed or sheltered
Soil type Moist but well-drained chalk, clay, loam, sand (acid/alkaline/neutral)
Hardiness H6

19 *Hedera helix*

A self-clinging evergreen climber, this ivy develops non-clinging branches when mature. Small, nectar-rich yellow flowers in autumn are followed by black berries in winter.

Common name Common ivy **Foliage** Evergreen
Height 8–12m (26–39ft) **Spread** 2.5–4m
(8–13ft) **Exposure** Full sun to full shade, exposed or sheltered **Soil type** Well-drained/moist but well-drained chalk, clay, loam, sand (acid/alkaline/neutral) **Hardiness** H5

20 *Vitis vinifera*

This woody plant climbs by tendrils. The leaves are three- or five-lobed, and coarsely toothed. Tiny, greenish flowers bloom in summer and grapes follow in autumn. The many named cultivars are selected for edible fruits or their ornamental qualities.

Common name Grape vine **Foliage** Deciduous **Height** 12m (39ft) or more **Spread** 2.5–4m (8–13ft) **Exposure** Full sun, sheltered **Soil** Well-drained chalk, loam, sand (alkaline/neutral) **Hardiness** H5

21 *Pyracantha rogersiana*

A large, spiny, evergreen shrub, this has glossy oblong leaves. Its small, creamy spring flowers are followed by orange-red berries loved by birds.

Common name Asian firethorn **Foliage** Evergreen **Height** 2.5–4m (8–13ft) **Spread** 2.5–4m (8–13ft) **Exposure** Full sun or partial shade, exposed or sheltered **Soil** Well-drained chalk, clay, loam, sand (acid/alkaline/neutral) **Hardiness** H5

Borago officinalis

This is a large, branched annual with coarsely hairy, ovate leaves. Its clusters of bright blue flowers bloom throughout summer. It can be used to make tea, and the flowers and young leaves taste like cucumber. It is also an excellent source of nectar and pollen.

Common name Borage
Foliage Deciduous
Height 50–100cm (20–39in)
Spread 10–50cm (4–20in)
Exposure Full sun or partial shade, exposed or sheltered
Soil type Well-drained chalk, clay, loam, sand (acid/alkaline/neutral)
Hardiness H5

Actinidia arguta 'Issai'

This compact kiwi cultivar produces small, smooth fruit in late summer to early autumn. Self-fertilizing, it does not need a companion in order to bear the fruit, which can be eaten "skin on".

Common name Hardy kiwi 'Issai'
Foliage Deciduous **Height** 2.5–4m (8–13ft) **Spread** 2.5–4m (8–13ft)
Exposure Full sun, sheltered
Soil Moist but well-drained clay, loam, sand (acid/alkaline)
Hardiness H5

Passiflora caerulea

This evergreen climber with twining tendrils has dark green leaves with 5–7 finger-like lobes. The summer flowers are white, blue, and purple, and are followed by ovoid orange fruits, which are edible but not as delicious as the edible variety (*Passiflora edulis*), which is not very cold-tolerant.

Common name Blue passionflower
Foliage Semi-evergreen
Height up to 8m (26ft)
Spread up to 4m (12ft)
Exposure Full sun or partial shade, sheltered **Soil type** Moist but well-drained chalk, loam, sand
Hardiness H4

Daucus carota

A tap-rooted biennial with solid, ridged stems. In summer, wild carrot bears umbels of white flowers, tinged with pink, and with a dark red central floret. The young flowers, leaves, and roots are edible - but ensure correct identification before consuming as it looks similar to poisonous hemlock (*Conium maculatum*).

Common name Wild carrot
Foliage Deciduous
Height 50–100cm (20–39in)
Spread 10–50cm (4–20in)
Exposure Full sun, exposed or sheltered **Soil type** Well-drained chalk, loam, sand (alkaline/neutral) **Hardiness** H7

Jasminum officinale

A twining or scrambling evergreen shrub, this jasmine has glossy pinnate leaves and clusters of very fragrant white flowers in summer, appearing sporadically at other times. The flowers are used to flavour tea.

Common name Arabian jasmine
Foliage Evergreen
Height 2.5m–4m (8–13ft)
Spread 0.5–1m (11/2–31/4ft)
Exposure Partial shade, sheltered
Soil Well-drained/moist but well-drained chalk, clay, loam, sand (acid/alkaline/neutral)
Hardiness H5

Anethum graveolens

A culinary herb with thread-like dark green leaves that have a strong, distinctive taste, dill produces umbels of small yellow flowers in summer.

Common name Dill
Foliage Deciduous
Height 50–100cm (20–39in)
Spread 10–50cm (4–20in)
Exposure Full sun, sheltered
Soil Chalk, loam, sand (acid/alkaline/neutral)
Hardiness H4

Vicia sativa

A downy, scrambling annual with cerise flowers in a pea shape, borne singly or in pairs from spring to late summer. The seedpods are edible, resembling those of peas and beans.

Common name Common vetch
Foliage Deciduous
Height 0.5–1m (11/2–31/4ft)
Spread 1.5m (5ft)
Exposure Full sun, exposed or sheltered **Soil** Well-drained chalk, loam, sand (alkaline/neutral)
Hardiness H7

Allium schoenoprasum

A bulbous perennial that forms a clump of erect, cylindrical leaves. The pale purple flowers bloom in summer. Both leaves and flowers are edible.

Common name Chives
Foliage Deciduous
Height 10–50cm (4–20in)
Spread 10–30cm (4–12in)
Exposure Full sun or partial shade, exposed or sheltered
Soil Well-drained/moist but well-drained chalk, clay, loam, sand (acid/alkaline/neutral)
Hardiness H6

Phaseolus coccineus 'Tenderstar'

A twining climber with green leaves, this plant bears scarlet and pale pink flowers that develop into short, tender, runner beans. It is often grown as a summer annual.

Common name Runner bean 'Tenderstar' **Foliage** Deciduous
Height 2.5–4m (8–13ft)
Spread 1–1.5m (3¹/₄–5ft)
Exposure Full sun, sheltered
Soil Well-drained chalk, loam, sand (acid/alkaline/neutral)
Hardiness H2

Achillea millefolium

This spreading stoloniferous perennial plant has narrow, finely dissected leaves. In summer, it produces small, cream or pink flat flowerheads. Both flowers and foliage add an aromatic flavour to salads and as garnishes.

Common name Common yarrow
Foliage Deciduous
Height 10–50cm (4–20in)
Spread 10–50cm (4–20in)
Exposure Full sun, exposed or sheltered **Soil** Well-drained/moist but well-drained chalk, clay, loam, sand (acid/alkaline/neutral)
Hardiness H7

Filipendula ulmaria

Meadowsweet is a vigorous perennial with divided leaves and creamy-white flowers in dense terminal clusters on erect leafy stems in summer. All parts of the plant can be added to soups and stews for aromatic flavour.

Common name Meadowsweet **Foliage** Deciduous **Height** 50–100cm (20–39in) **Spread** 50–100cm (20–39in) **Exposure** Full sun or partial shade, exposed or sheltered **Soil** Moist but well-drained/poorly drained clay, loam (acid/alkaline/neutral) **Hardiness** H6

Foeniculum vulgare

This robust, upright, aromatic biennial or short-lived perennial has pinnate leaves and flat umbels of small yellow flowers in summer. The edible leaves, flowers, and seeds add an aniseed flavour to food.

Common name Common fennel **Foliage** Deciduous **Height** 1.5–2.5m (5–8ft) **Spread** 10–50cm (4–20in) **Exposure** Full sun or partial shade, sheltered **Soil** Moist but well-drained chalk, clay, loam, sand (acid/alkaline/neutral) **Hardiness** H5

Myrrhis odorata

An erect, aniseed-scented perennial, sweet cicely has bright green pinnate leaves and white flowers in umbels that bloom in summer, followed by spindle-shaped fruits in summer and autumn.

Common name Sweet cicely **Foliage** Deciduous **Height** 1–1.5m (3¼–5ft) **Spread** 0.5–1m (1½–3¼ft) **Exposure** Partial shade, sheltered **Soil** Moist but well-drained loam (acid/alkaline/neutral) **Hardiness** H5

Allium ursinum

This vigorous, bulbous perennial spreads widely, with paired, elliptic leaves and erect stems bearing umbels of starry white flowers in late spring. The leaves and flowers are edible, with a garlic taste.

Common name Ramsons **Foliage** Deciduous **Height** 10–50cm (4–20in) **Spread** 10–50cm (4–20in) **Exposure** Full sun, sheltered **Soil** Well-drained/moist but well-drained chalk, loam, sand (acid/alkaline/neutral) **Hardiness** H7

Mentha requienii

A vigorous, mat-forming perennial, this plant has slender creeping and rooting stems that form extensive colonies. The bright green leaves are peppermint-scented and in summer, tubular lilac flowers are borne in short spikes. Many varieties are available with different scents.

Common name Corsican mint
Foliage Deciduous **Height** Up to 10cm (4in) **Spread** Indefinite **Exposure** Full shade or partial shade, exposed or sheltered **Soil** Poorly drained/moist but well-drained clay, loam (acid/alkaline/neutral) **Hardiness** H7

Galium odoratum

This stoloniferous, spreading perennial forms rosettes of three-palmate, bright green leaves with toothed leaflets. In late spring it bears cymes of white flowers that are followed by red fruit in summer. The leaves are used to add a vanilla or almond flavour to drinks.

Common name Sweet woodruff
Foliage Deciduous **Height** 10–50cm (4–20in) **Spread** 1–1.5m (3¹/₄–5ft) **Exposure** Partial shade, sheltered **Soil** Moist but well-drained chalk, clay, loam, sand (acid/alkaline/neutral) **Hardiness** H7

Aronia × prunifolia

A natural hybrid between *A. arbutifolia* and *A. melanocarpa*, this shrub has a multistemmed habit. Its white flowers in late spring are followed by purple-black berries and matt, dark green leaves that turn reddish-purple colours in autumn. The edible round black fruits have a slightly tart flavour.

Common name Purple chokeberry
Foliage Deciduous
Height 2.5–4m (8–13ft)
Spread 1.5–2.5m (5–8ft)
Exposure Full sun or partial shade, exposed or sheltered **Soil** Moist but well-drained clay, loam, sand (acid/neutral) **Hardiness** H7

Ajuga reptans

A spreading perennial, bugle forms a wide mat of dark green leaves with spikes of dark blue flowers in late spring and early summer. The young shoots can be eaten in salads or sautéed.

Common name Bugle
Foliage Evergreen
Height 10–15cm (4–20in)
Spread 50–100cm (20–39in)
Exposure Partial shade, sheltered **Soil** Moist but well-drained/poorly drained chalk, clay, loam, sand (acid/alkaline/neutral) **Hardiness** H7

Prunus spinosa

A small, thorny tree with dark green, ovate leaves, blackthorn produces small white flowers in early spring, followed by ovoid, bloomy black fruits in autumn used to flavour sloe gin.

Common name Blackthorn
Foliage Deciduous
Height 2.5–4m (8–13ft)
Spread 2.5–4m (8–13ft)
Exposure Full sun, exposed or sheltered **Soil** Moist but well–drained chalk, clay, loam, sand (acid/alkaline/neutral)
Hardiness H7

Rosa canina

The dog rose is a vigorous, arching shrub with mid-green foliage and pale pink or white flowers, either solitary or in small clusters, in early summer. They are followed by ovoid red fruits (rose hips) in autumn that can be used to make jams and syrups.

Common name Dog rose **Foliage** Deciduous
Height 2.5–4m (8–13ft) **Spread** 1.5–2.5m (5–8ft)
Exposure Full sun, exposed or sheltered
Soil Moist but well-drained chalk, clay, loam, sand (acid/alkaline/neutral) **Hardiness** H7

Zanthoxylum simulans

This bushy, spiny, deciduous shrub or small tree has leaves up to 8cm (3in) long. In early summer, it bears flat-topped sprays of small, yellow-green flowers, followed by open clusters of small red fruits that split open in autumn, revealing black seeds. The leaves, fruit, and bark are all aromatic, while the reddish-pink seedcases are edible and can be used as a pepper substitute.

Common name Sichuan pepper
Foliage Deciduous
Height 2.5–4m (8–13ft)
Spread 2.5–4m (8–13ft)
Exposure Full sun, sheltered
Soil type Well-drained chalk, loam, sand (acid/alkaline/neutral)
Hardiness H6

Glycyrrhiza glabra

This vigorous herbaceous perennial has mid-green leaves up to 20cm (8in) long and pale blue to violet flowers, either solitary or in small clusters, in early summer. They are followed by coppery-red seedpods in autumn. Liquorice root is commonly used as a flavouring for sweets and herbal teas.

Common name Liquorice
Foliage Deciduous
Height 1–1.5m (3¹/₄–5ft)
Spread 0.5–1m (1¹/₂–3¹/₄ft)
Exposure Full sun, sheltered
Soil type Moist but well–drained chalk, clay, loam, sand (acid/alkaline/neutral
Hardiness H5

Cydonia oblonga

Quince is a dense large shrub or small tree with oval, mid-green leaves. The pale pink to white late spring flowers are followed by edible, golden-yellow, pear-shaped fruit in autumn.

Common name Quince **Foliage** Deciduous
Height 2.5m–4m (8–13ft) **Spread** 2.5m–4m
(8–13ft) **Exposure** Full sun, sheltered
Soil Moist but well-drained clay, loam (acid/
alkaline/neutral) **Hardiness** H5

Mespilus germanica

This small tree or large shrub has oblong leaves turning yellow-brown in autumn. White flowers in late spring are followed by brown fruit in autumn, used to make medlar jelly.

Common name Common medlar
Foliage Deciduous **Height** 4–8m (13–26ft)
Spread 4–8m (13–26ft) **Exposure** Full sun
or partial shade, exposed or sheltered
Soil Well-drained/moist but well-drained chalk,
clay, loam, sand (acid/alkaline/neutral)
Hardiness H6

Corylus avellana

This large, spreading deciduous shrub or small tree has yellow male catkins in early spring followed by edible nuts in autumn, when the rounded leaves turn yellow before falling.

Common name Hazel **Foliage** Deciduous
Height 4–8m (13–26ft) **Spread** 4–8m (13–26ft)
Exposure Full sun or partial shade, exposed
or sheltered **Soil** Well-drained/moist but
well-drained chalk, loam, sand (alkaline/
neutral) **Hardiness** H6

Crataegus monogyna

A small, rounded deciduous tree, this has glossy, lobed leaves and flat sprays of cream flowers in spring, followed in autumn by dark red berries. Its nickname of "bread and cheese" refers to the fresh growth of leaves (the bread) and the spring buds (the cheese), both of which are edible.

Common name Common hawthorn
Foliage Deciduous **Height** 4–8m (13–26ft)
Spread 4–8m (13–26ft) **Exposure** Full sun or
partial shade, exposed or sheltered
Soil Well-drained/moist but well-drained chalk,
clay, loam, sand (acid/alkaline/neutral)
Hardiness H7

Vaccinium myrtillus

This deciduous, suckering, usually prostrate shrub has dense, bright green stems and ovate, glossy leaves, often flushed red in autumn. The pink flowers in late spring to early summer are followed by blue-black, edible berries in autumn.

Common name Common bilberry
Foliage Deciduous **Height** 10–50cm
(4–20in) **Spread** 50–100cm (20–39in)
Exposure Full sun or partial shade,
exposed or sheltered
Soil Well-drained/moist but
well-drained loam, sand (acid)
Hardiness H6

DESIGNING A FOOD FOREST

MARTIN CRAWFORD has spent more than 30 years in organic agriculture and horticulture and is the founder of the Agroforestry Research Trust. His Forest Garden Project incorporates diverse trees, shrubs, and ground cover, all contributing to a self-sustaining ecosystem with edible and medicinal produce.

Martin's forest garden in Devon is dense and complex, with a rich tapestry of productive plants designed to emulate a natural forest.

"

DESIGNING A FOREST GARDEN CAN BE OVERWHELMING. DO YOU HAVE ANY TIPS FOR GETTING STARTED?

Good forest garden design aims to maximize diversity, often with 200 or more species, but this could be far less in small spaces. This level of complexity can appear overwhelming, but generally, designing from the top down works well: plant the canopy (tree) layer first; next the shrub layer; and finally the ground layer. This process is often spread over 3–10 years, which means that shade starts to develop, so shade-loving plants can be introduced in the understorey planting.

HAVE YOU SEEN ANY CLIMATE-INDUCED CHANGES INFLUENCING WHAT YOU CAN GROW SINCE YOU HAVE BEEN EXPERIMENTING WITH FOREST GARDENS IN DEVON?

Medlar fruits ripen on trees now, and persimmons ripen in Devon increasingly frequently; some formerly herbaceous plants are becoming evergreen. Some of the changes are negative, such as Devon varieties of apples doing increasingly poorly.

One of our projects is a subtropical "forest garden greenhouse" using a novel ground-heat storage system for winter heating; it has a climate 5°C (9°F) warmer than outside (moving Devon to SW Portugal). In here we're experimenting with crops, some of which will become more viable outside as our climate warms.

YOUR FOREST GARDENS HAVE A STAGGERING AMOUNT OF BIODIVERSITY IN THE PLANTING. HAVE YOU COMPARED THEM WITH NATIVE WOODLAND?

Two studies have compared the invertebrate diversity of the Dartington forest garden with native woodland. In one, a comparison with a reforested site showed that the forest garden hosts not only a more diverse but also a more even and abundant community of invertebrates than the reforested site.

In a comparison with another native woodland site, the forest garden was seen to support a more robust and varied population of invertebrates. These results show that diversity can be at least as important to wildlife as native species.

GREEN ROOF PLANTING

01

THE PLANTINGS USED FOR A GREEN ROOF ARE OFTEN PRE-GROWN IN A MAT OR TRAY. THERE ARE A NUMBER OF PRODUCTS AVAILABLE OFF THE SHELF, MANY OF WHICH CONTAIN A MIX OF SEDUM SPECIES, OR YOU CAN USE CONTAINERIZED OR BARE-ROOT INDIVIDUAL PLANTS.

The depth of the soil on a green roof is important, as it dictates the type of plants that will succeed. The plants suggested here are based on a shallow substrate depth of 4–6cm (1½–2½in). This depth is referred to as an extensive green roof (see page 108). If your roof structure can take a greater substrate depth, then the choice of plants increases dramatically. If, for example, you have 10cm (4in) of soil, many planted pathway species that are drought-resilient could be sustained. If you have deeper soil still, such as 20cm (8in), then many of the drought-resilient gravel garden plants would also be sustainable on the green roof. At this depth, the roof is referred to as semi-extensive. A depth of 30–50cm (12–20in) would enable a huge range of perennials and shrubs to be grown, but at these depths, the green roof weight gets very heavy. Trees can generally be grown in soil depths of 80–130cm (2½–4½ft).

SEDUM

Sedum species are ubiquitous in green roof plantings as they are well suited to a hot, exposed, and arid site; these are the conditions in which they grow naturally. Their fleshy, succulent leaves are designed to store water and have a thick, waxy surface with the ability to close its pores rather than lose water through respiration.

01 *Chamaemelum nobile*

This mat-forming perennial has finely divided, aromatic leaves and white daisy flowers with yellow centres, 1.5cm (½in) across. The dried flower heads of the plant can be used to make a relaxing herbal tea.

Common name Common chamomile
Foliage Deciduous
Height 10–50cm (4–20in)
Spread 10–50cm (4–20in)
Exposure Full sun or partial shade, exposed or sheltered
Soil Well-drained chalk, loam, sand (acid/alkaline/neutral)
Hardiness H7

02 *Phedimus spurius*

A vigorous, mat-forming, semi-evergreen perennial, this plant has fleshy, toothed leaves that are held on spreading, rooting stems. In late summer, star-shaped, pink or white flowers are borne in clusters.

Common name Caucasian stonecrop **Foliage** Semi-evergreen **Height** 10cm (4in)
Spread 10–50cm (4–20in)
Exposure Full sun, sheltered
Soil Well-drained/moist but well-drained chalk, loam, sand (alkaline/neutral)
Hardiness H5

03 *Sedum reflexum*

A fast-growing, mat-forming perennial, this sedum has succulent, pointed, cylindrical leaves. In summer, stems up to 15cm (6in) tall bear clusters of star-shaped yellow flowers which are pendent in bud but turn upward as they open.

Common name Cock's comb stonecrop **Foliage** Evergreen
Height 10–50cm (4–20in)
Spread 10–50cm (4–20in)
Exposure Full sun, sheltered
Soil Well-drained chalk, loam, sand (alkaline/neutral)
Hardiness H5

Sedum acre

This mat-forming, hairless, succulent perennial has small, ovoid, fleshy leaves close to the stems. Yellow, star-shaped flowers bloom in spring and summer.

Common name Biting stonecrop
Foliage Evergreen
Height 10cm (4in)
Spread 10cm (4in)
Exposure Full sun, exposed or sheltered **Soil** Well-drained or moist but well-drained chalk, loam, sand (acid/alkaline/neutral)
Hardiness H7

Sempervivum montanum

A vigorous, mat-forming, evergreen succulent with rosettes of sharp-pointed, fleshy, finely hairy leaves. Short, leafy stems bear reddish-purple flowers in summer.

Common name Mountain houseleek
Foliage Evergreen **Height** 10cm (4in)
Spread 30cm (12in) **Exposure** Full sun, exposed or sheltered **Soil** Well-drained loam, sand (acid/alkaline/neutral) **Hardiness** H4

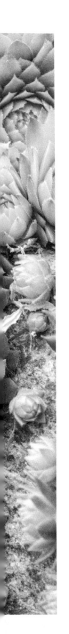

Sedum kamtschaticum

This low, clump-forming, semi-evergreen perennial has bright green leaves, accompanied in late summer by golden-yellow flowers with finely pointed petals.

Common name Orange stonecrop
Foliage Semi-evergreen **Height** 10cm (4in)
Spread 10–50cm (4–20in) **Exposure** Full sun, exposed or sheltered **Soil** Well-drained chalk, loam, sand (alkaline/neutral) **Hardiness** H5

Sedum kamtschaticum var. *floriferum* 'Weihenstephaner Gold'

This variety forms a low, spreading clump of spoon-shaped leaves tinged with bronze. In late summer, it bears starry pale yellow flowers that take on a tinge of pink.

Common name Orange stonecrop 'Weihenstephaner Gold'
Foliage Semi-evergreen
Height 10cm (4in) **Spread** 10–50cm (4–20in)) **Exposure** Full sun or partial shade, exposed
Soil type Well-drained chalk, loam, sand (alkaline/neutral)
Hardiness H5

Sedum album 'Coral Carpet'

This evergreen, mat-forming perennial has small, succulent, rounded green leaves that are flushed with red. Clusters of starry white flowers bloom in early summer.

Common name Coral carpet
Foliage Evergreen
Height 10cm (4in)
Spread 10cm (4in)
Exposure Full sun, sheltered
Soil type Well-drained loam, sand (acid/alkaline/neutral)
Hardiness H7

Sempervivum arachnoideum

This evergreen perennial forms a mat of fleshy rosettes of green or reddish leaves with cobwebby white hairs at the tips. It bears starry pink flowers in summer.

Common name Cobweb houseleek
Foliage Evergreen **Height** 10cm (4in) **Spread** 10–50cm (4–20in)
Exposure Full sun, exposed or sheltered **Soil type** Loam, sand (acid/alkaline/neutral)
Hardiness H7

Sempervivum tectorum

A vigorous mat-forming perennial, this plant has clusters of fleshy rosettes up to 10cm (4in) across, the blue-green leaves suffused with reddish-purple. Purplish-pink flowers with narrow pointed petals are borne on stems up to 20cm (8in) tall.

Common name Common houseleek
Foliage Evergreen **Height** 10cm (4in)
Spread 10–50cm (4–20in) **Exposure** Full sun, exposed or sheltered **Soil type** Well-drained loam, sand (acid/alkaline/neutral)
Hardiness H7

CHAPTER SIX

SUSTAINABLE MATERIALS

For this project by Peter and Anneliese Latz, a steelworks has been transformed into a landscape park. A unique design approach led to the buildings being recycled rather than torn down. Blast furnaces are used as follies, concrete tanks as walled gardens, and water tanks as water gardens. Rather than importing new soils, if an industrial process left an unusual soil mixture, plants that could tolerate the substrate were chosen.

SUSTAINABLE MATERIALS

HARD MATERIALS ARE IMPORTANT TO ALLOW US TO MOVE
THROUGH A LANDSCAPE, AS WELL AS TO PROVIDE A STABLE
SURFACE FOR ELEMENTS SUCH AS DINING TABLES AND SEATING.
THIS CHAPTER EXPLORES WHERE COMMON BUILDING MATERIALS
COME FROM AND HOW SUSTAINABLE THEY ARE.

As urban sprawl increases across the globe, we need to view our gardens as part of the wider landscape. From the outset, we need to consider the carbon footprint of the hard landscaping we plan to install. How much carbon would it cost to remove it? Is it biodegradable, or does it contain plastic, concrete, or other materials that will take hundreds or thousands of years to break down? How far will the materials travel from supplier to the garden, and how many suppliers are they coming from? Sourcing locally or from fewer suppliers could drastically reduce the carbon footprint of a hard-landscaping scheme.

CONSIDER MAINTENANCE

Certain materials require a lot of maintenance, such as a painted wall or fence; unless you accept the aesthetic of the weathered paint, you will need to repaint periodically to keep it looking fresh. In contrast, materials such as natural stone or weathering steel (which develops a layer of rust that protects the steel beneath) need little or no maintenance, and they harmonize with their environment as they age, improving their aesthetic.

WASTE MATERIALS

The construction industry produces huge amounts of waste, but waste materials have their own aesthetic and can be made beautiful. Reclaimed timber, for example, has a patina of age, character, and texture that cannot be imitated. The same is true of natural reclaimed stone rather than an imitation product such as precast cement. The age, character, and unique aesthetic of every slab gives each piece an inherent beauty.

DURABLE VS SUSTAINABLE

Durability is often seen as an important factor in the choice of materials: concrete, stone, and other heavy materials will have a long lifespan if installed correctly. However, if this is in a sensitive landscape, or in a dwelling that won't be occupied long-term by the current residents, the lifespan is irrelevant. It is common to see gardens that were built to last 100 years being replaced because fashions or requirements have changed. So, durability is only sustainable if the long-term installation of the scheme is ensured. Otherwise, a more sustainable choice would be low-impact, biodegradable materials that are easy to remove or recycle, such as timber.

EMBODIED CARBON

PUT SIMPLY, EMBODIED CARBON IS THE CARBON FOOTPRINT OF A LANDSCAPING OR BUILDING PROJECT. IT REFERS TO THE CARBON DIOXIDE (CO_2) EMISSIONS ASSOCIATED WITH THE MATERIALS AND CONSTRUCTION PROCESSES THROUGHOUT THE LIFECYCLE OF A PROJECT.

Embodied carbon refers to the CO_2 that is produced by maintaining and eventually demolishing the project, transporting the waste, and recycling it. It can be measured in three ways: from cradle to (factory) gate, from cradle to site (of use), or from cradle to grave (end of life).

HOW TO REDUCE THE EMBODIED CARBON OF YOUR PROJECT

- Limit the use of high-carbon materials such as cement, metal, and plastic. Wood is becoming increasingly popular as a building material due to its lower embodied carbon levels and, if produced sustainably, carbon storage potential.
- Limit new materials: construction processes have a high carbon footprint. Reclaiming, renovating, reusing, or repurposing existing materials can greatly reduce a project's embodied carbon levels.
- Use recycled materials where possible, especially those with high levels of embodied carbon such as metal and plastic. This saves on the amount of carbon being emitted to produce new materials.
- Source materials locally instead of shipping from overseas to reduce emissions associated with transportation. Research where the materials you want to use come from and aim to source from as close as possible to the site.
- Consider complexity: if your project is easy and quick to construct it is likely that less carbon will be emitted from the construction process.

THE COMPLEXITY OF CARBON DATA

Embodied carbon data is constantly evolving as manufacturing processes develop and are updated; the information on the graph opposite is from the University of Bath Inventory of Carbon and Energy (ICE) Database V3, 2019. Also, manufacturing processes vary globally and embodied carbon levels associated with materials will fluctuate from one region to another. The calculations are complex, too. For smaller residential projects this level of data calculation may be impractical, but an understanding of emissions involved in the production of materials can still inform sustainable material choices.

LIFECYCLE

This flow chart shows approximate distribution of emissions in the lifecycle of a material: 50 per cent of the embodied carbon is produced in manufacturing the product; 5 per cent in the construction; 43 per cent in the lifecycle; and 2 per cent at the end of its life.

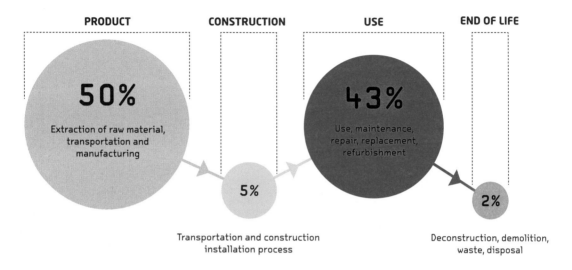

PRODUCT

50%

Extraction of raw material, transportation and manufacturing

CONSTRUCTION

5%

Transportation and construction installation process

USE

43%

Use, maintenance, repair, replacement, refurbishment

END OF LIFE

2%

Deconstruction, demolition, waste, disposal

EMBODIED CARBON

This graph shows embodied carbon from source to manufacturing for a number of common landscaping materials. The graph illustrates the amount of carbon used to produce each material, but doesn't account for carbon emissions in shipping or installation on site, as these will vary greatly depending on where and how they are being installed. The carbon stored in timber means it can have a negative value, essentially reducing the embodied carbon of a project. However, carbon storage can only be claimed for sustainably sourced timber.

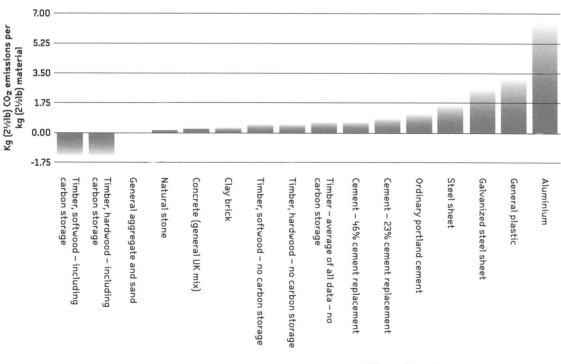

Kg (2½lb) CO_2 emissions per kg (2½lb) material

- 7.00
- 5.25
- 3.50
- 1.75
- 0.00
- -1.75

Timber, softwood – including carbon storage
Timber, hardwood – including carbon storage
General aggregate and sand
Natural stone
Concrete (general UK mix)
Clay brick
Timber, softwood – no carbon storage
Timber, hardwood – no carbon storage
Timber – average of all data – no carbon storage
Cement – 46% cement replacement
Cement – 23% cement replacement
Ordinary portland cement
Steel sheet
Galvanized steel sheet
General plastic
Aluminium

HARDWOOD AND SOFTWOOD

Generally, hardwood comes from slower growing deciduous trees that shed their leaves every year: the slow rate of growth causes the timber to be denser and harder. Softwood is derived from faster-growing coniferous trees, which usually remain evergreen; the faster growth rate means the timber is less dense. Hardwoods have a longer lifespan as their density means they are more resilient to weathering.

However, both softwoods and hardwoods can be treated to extend lifespan. Treatments often require regular application so need to be factored into the maintenance regime. Also, access needs to be considered: a stained fence covered in climbing plants will be difficult to re-stain unless all of the plants are removed. Leaving timber to weather naturally is often the most sustainable and low-maintenance option.

WEATHERED WOOD

Timber changes colour due to lignin being degraded by the UV light present in natural sunlight. The degraded lignin is then washed out of the wood by rainfall and ambient moisture in the air. The remaining fibres on the wood surface are more resistant to leaching and UV degradation, and contain high levels of cellulose, which is white/grey, giving weathered timber its silvery colour.

RECLAIMED TIMBER

High-quality reclaimed timber is available from reclamation yards. It may need processing, such as sanding, but as it is a recycled product, the carbon footprint is lower – particularly compared to virgin tropical hardwood timber, which is often removed from a sensitive habitat and shipped long distances. If reclaimed timber is difficult to source, sustainable softwood timber products also exist as good low-carbon alternatives.

TIMBER

TIMBER IS WOOD PREPARED FOR BUILDING, LANDSCAPING, OR CARPENTRY, WITH DIFFERING CHARACTERISTICS, SUCH AS GRAIN, DENSITY, COLOUR, AND HARDNESS. MANY SPECIES OF TREE ARE SUITABLE FOR USE AS TIMBER, BUT THEY MAY ALSO BE UNDER THREAT FROM ILLEGAL LOGGING, CAUSING DEFORESTATION IN HIGHLY SENSITIVE ENVIRONMENTS.

[Top] The trees native to the Konkan western coastline forest in Maharastra, India, are prey to illegal deforestation. Logging operations need careful and considered management to ensure that resources are not depleted faster than they are regrown.

[Left] A path through lush vegetation in Costa Rica, Central America, where conservation efforts are in place to protect local species.

TEAK

Tectona grandis
When teak trees are grown in sustainably managed forests, the carbon sequestration and the potential for diverse land use means using teak can be sustainable – but illegal logging diminishes habitats.

Slow-growing hardwood

Origin South and Southeast Asia. Myanmar's teak forest makes up almost half the world's naturally growing teak.

Shipping From Asia, shipping distances for use in Europe and the US are considerable.

Lifespan Hard and durable; resistant to termite, fungus, and weathering; it has a long lifespan and the potential to be recycled for bioenergy.

YELLOW BALAU

Shorea laevis
Yellow balau can have a fairly low carbon footprint when the waste is used to make byproducts, offsetting emissions produced during processing. But it is considered vulnerable: it is logged for timber and deforested for agriculture.

Tropical hardwood

Origin Native to Myanmar, Thailand, Sumatra, Peninsular Malaysia, and Borneo.

Shipping Long travel distances between tropical regions and Europe and the US.

Lifespan Durable and resistant to rot. The wood can be reused or burned as bioenergy.

20–25 YEARS TO MATURITY

20–30 YEARS TO MATURITY

40–50 YEARS TO MATURITY

20–30 YEARS TO MATURITY

45–55 YEARS TO MATURITY

TYPES OF TIMBER

THE TYPES OF TIMBER COMPARED HERE ARE COMMONLY USED FOR LANDSCAPING AND GARDENING PROJECTS. THERE ARE SEVERAL THINGS TO BEAR IN MIND WHEN MAKING SUSTAINABLE CHOICES.

WESTERN RED CEDAR

Thuja plicata
Western red cedar is considered fast-growing, and the durable wood is good for construction.

Fast-growing softwood

Origin Western North America; naturalized in the UK and assimilated into other temperate zones, such as Western Europe, Australia, and New Zealand.

Shipping Carbon impact is low when sourced from sustainable local forests.

Lifespan Possesses a natural preservative making it resistant to fungal attack. Cedar cladding can last for 40–60 years.

SIBERIAN LARCH

Larix sibirica
Siberian larch is being replanted faster than it is being harvested, making this a very sustainable choice. Its resistance to rot when in contact with the ground makes it suitable for fence posts.

Softwood

Origin Northern hemisphere; the European larch (*Larix decidua*) is native to the mountains of Central Europe.

Shipping Carbon impact is low when sourced from sustainable local forests.

Lifespan Moderately durable and resistant to rot; does not require preservatives to sustain its longevity.

100–120 YEARS TO MATURITY

EUROPEAN OAK

Quercus robur
Manufacturing oak can be sustainable, as a lot of the energy required can be produced from burning wood waste. Oak is a common tree species and often grown for harvesting. If forests are well managed then this can be a sustainable choice.

Slow-growing hardwood

Origin Northern hemisphere.

Shipping Carbon impact is low when sourced from sustainable local forests.

Lifespan Durable, long-lasting, and can be reused and recycled.

IROKO

Milicia excelsa
Illegal logging has jeopardized iroko in many areas. It is classified as "at risk" due to a reduction of more than 20 per cent over the past 75 years, caused by a dwindling of its natural span and exploitation.

Tropical hardwood

Origin Native to the west coast of Africa.

Shipping For use in Europe and the US, the carbon impact of shipping should be considered for a resilient garden.

Lifespan Iroko is very durable and is resistant to rot and insect assault.

GARDEN DURABILITY

Several factors will affect how long timber lasts in your garden, such as atmospheric moisture, installation quality, and local insects. This graph ranks the durability of popular types of timber when installed above ground. 1: 25 years or more, 2: 15–25 years, 3: 10–15 years.

Teak	1
Yellow balau	2
Western red cedar	3
Iroko	2
European oak	2
Siberian larch	3

CARBON STORING CAPACITY

The natural forest environments these species grow in have huge capacity to store carbon, and need sensitive management to keep the carbon out of the atmosphere. This graph represents carbon stored per hectare of the natural environments these species are found in.

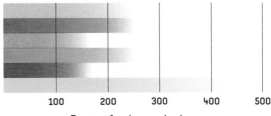

100   200   300   400   500
Tonnes of carbon per hectare

COMMON USES

Each type of timber can be used in multiple ways in the garden. Hardwood types tend to last longer.

Fencing				●	●	●	○
Furniture		●			●	●	
Cladding				●	●	●	○
Decking			●	●	●		○

NATURAL STONE

NATURAL STONE AND OTHER MINERAL-BASED PRODUCTS ARE OFTEN USED IN GARDEN LANDSCAPING, POPULAR FOR THEIR APPEARANCE AND LONGEVITY. AS STONE IS HEAVY, THE CARBON FOOTPRINT IS HIGH WHEN IT IS SHIPPED OVER LONG DISTANCES.

Natural stone indicates organic rock quarried directly from the Earth. It is durable, and can stand up to varying weather conditions and fluctuating temperatures. This makes it an environmentally green choice in terms of longevity, and it can be crushed up and used as aggregate when it is no longer in good condition. However, where it comes from is pertinent in terms of proximity to the site, as long-distance transport of a high-weight product can command a high carbon footprint.

ROCK TYPES

Igneous rocks form when magma or lava (molten rock) from beneath the Earth's crust cools and then solidifies. They often have visible large crystals and are extremely hard.
Examples: basalt, gabbro, granite.

Metamorphic rocks originate when igneous, sedimentary, or existing metamorphic rocks are changed via environmental factors such as heat or pressure.
Examples: marble, quartzite, slate.

Sedimentary rocks form on or near the surface of the Earth. They result from rock erosion that produces sedimentary material such as sand and mud, which is then compressed into new layers of rock.
Examples: chalk, limestone, sandstone.

[Left] Heavy-duty machinery is used to extract and cut natural stone, which can be damaging to the environment. However, stone is a natural material and requires little additional processing, so embodied carbon in its manufacture is relatively low in comparison with some heavily processed materials.

[Below] Quarrying for stone can scar the natural landscape and damage habitat, but disused quarries can become biodiversity hotspots, the diverse topography providing habitat for plants and invertebrates.

TYPES OF STONE

HERE ARE SOME OF THE MANY TYPES OF NATURAL
STONE AND STONE-BASED PRODUCTS, SUCH AS
PORCELAIN, THAT CAN BE USED FOR PATHS,
WALKWAYS, SEATING AREAS, RETAINING WALLS,
WATER FEATURES, CLADDING, AND SCULPTURES.

BRAZILIAN SLATE

Slate extracted from Brazil is regarded as a
high-quality natural stone. It only requires
low-intensity production after extraction, but
shipping it long distances can be carbon intensive.

Origin 95 per cent of Brazilian slate is a
metamorphic rock extracted from the Minas
Gerais region, about 450 km (280 miles) north
of Rio de Janeiro.

Lifespan Natural slate can withstand
fluctuating conditions such as temperature
and moisture. Strong and hardwearing, it can
endure for centuries, hence its use for roofing
tiles. It can be recycled into chippings.

YORKSTONE

This sandstone is extracted from quarries in Yorkshire, UK, using heavy machinery. It requires little processing after extraction and no toxic chemicals are used in production. It has a relatively low carbon footprint.

Origin Sedimentary rock quarries in Yorkshire, UK.

Lifespan Yorkstone was used historically in the UK for paving in market towns with a lot of human traffic and horses and carts. A popular choice for its strength and durability, it is very resistant to damage and can serve a useable lifespan of more than 100 years.

PORCELAIN

Porcelain tiles are made by mixing natural clay with feldspar (a group of rock-forming aluminium tectosilicate minerals), quartz, water, and pigment, then baking it in a kiln at very high temperatures. The tiles can be produced with recycled elements, but the manufacturing process is more intensive than that for natural stone, resulting in a higher carbon footprint.

Origin Porcelain tiles are processed on an industrial scale in many countries globally.

Lifespan Baking at high temperatures makes porcelain tiles very hardwearing and they can sustain a lot of human traffic. They are viewed as very long-lasting, but the thickness and quality of the tiles can vary from different suppliers, so be wary of low-cost options.

CHINESE GRANITE

Like all natural stone, granite is extracted with heavy machinery and requires little processing. Granite from China tends to be cheaper than European granite, but can have ethical drawbacks, with some supply chains being linked to slavery and child labour.

Origin An igneous rock quarried in China.

Lifespan Granite is incredibly hard-wearing and long-lasting when it is correctly installed, with a potential lifespan of more than 100 years.

INDIAN SANDSTONE

Indian sandstone is usually extracted from the ground by placing explosives at fault lines. Ethical credentials vary; look for importers who are signed up to the Ethical Trade Initiative.

Origin A sedimentary rock quarried in India.

Lifespan Indian sandstone is softer and less durable than harder and denser types of stone, and is therefore generally cheaper. When it is correctly installed, Indian sandstone paving has a lifespan of about 30–50 years or more, so it is still considered a durable material.

GRAVEL

GRAVEL REFERS TO A MIX OF COARSE ROCK OR MINERAL FRAGMENTS: ANYTHING LARGER THAN 4 MM (0.2 IN) AND UP TO ABOUT 76 MM (3 IN).

01

Gravel is used for many purposes, including sub-base and drainage, driveways and decorative mulches. Laid on a permeable subbase, it allows water to permeate to the ground below.

Aggregates for gravel are sourced from quarries or strip-mined from the seabed at many locations worldwide. Examples are pea shingle, granite, and limestone. Many countries around the world have sources of aggregate for gravel but these take a lot

03

[01] Beth Chatto's famous gravel garden in Essex, a dry part of the UK. The gravel is used as a mulch to improve the drought resilience of the planting scheme. [02] Harbour dredging near Venice, Italy, where material is ripped from the sea bed, which can damage the marine environment. [03] Prospect Cottage was the home of British filmmaker Derek Jarman, located on a shingle beach. The harsh environment supports only the most rugged plants.

220

of resources to extract, which can cause damage to the environment; when materials for gravel are dredged from the sea bed this can disturb marine life and destroy habitats. Recycled aggregate is usually a repurposed waste product such as washed and graded demolition rubble, crushed concrete or ceramics, or reclaimed stone.

When gravel is transported from afar its weight can command a large carbon footprint, but locally sourced gravel is an option in many countries. Recycled aggregate is often handled close to the construction site and can be found locally to many sites. Reusing material also circumvents the demand for landfill disposal, along with all the associated transport and environmental repercussions.

With appropriate installation and maintenance, a gravel driveway can last for more than 100 years, with the benefit that it is easy to top it up with more material if needed.

RECYCLED GRAVEL

In 2020, recycled and secondary sources of aggregates accounted for 28 per cent (61.8 million tonnes/69.2 US tons) of total aggregates supply in the UK, a leading position internationally in the use of these materials.

Secondaries
7 million tonnes
(7.7 million US tons)

Recycled
55 million tonnes (60 million US tons)

Primary aggregates
159 million tonnes (175 million US tons)

China is the biggest manufacturer of cement; it is estimated to have produced 2.5 billion metric tonnes (2.8 billion US tons) in 2021, approximately half of the world's cement. Concrete is the most used building material in the world, and second only to water as a resource used globally.

CEMENT

Cement is used to bind materials together in the form of mortar, which is composed from a mixture of a fine aggregate (typically sand), cement, and water. It is used as a bedding later for paving, or to bond bricks together in a wall.

CONCRETE

An amalgamation of aggregate fused together with cement, usually activated by water, concrete hardens as it cures. As concrete is very durable and able to stand up to extreme weather, it is used to make furniture, sculptural elements, and paving. It is thought that concrete uses nearly 10 per cent of global industrial water consumption and accounts for 4–8 per cent of carbon dioxide emissions globally – coal, oil, and gas are the only substances emitting higher levels of greenhouse gas. The production of clinker (nodules of limestone and clay heated to high temperatures in a kiln) is the most energy-exhaustive stage of manufacturing cement, and this is thought to account for 50 per cent of concrete's carbon dioxide emissions.

CEMENT AND CONCRETE

CEMENT IS USED TO BIND MATERIALS TOGETHER AS IT SETS. IN CONSTRUCTION, IT IS USUALLY INORGANIC MATTER WITH A LIME OR CALCIUM SILICATE BASE. WHEN COMBINED WITH WATER, SAND, AND AGGREGATES, CEMENT PRODUCES CONCRETE.

Concrete buildings are expected to last for at least 100 years if sufficiently maintained. In areas with increased exposure to wear and tear, such as pavements, concrete is anticipated to have a lifespan of about 50 years.

CEMENT PRODUCTION

Cement production emits a lot of carbon dioxide. This graphic shows that producing a tonne of conventional cement in Australia emits about 0.82 tonnes of carbon dioxide.

GROWING EMISSIONS

This graph shows global carbon dioxide emissions from rising cement production over the past century. There isn't an easy way of reducing the emissions from cement production, but a move towards alternative products will help to reduce global emissions.

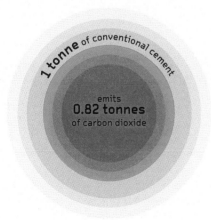

1 tonne of conventional cement

emits
0.82 tonnes
of carbon dioxide

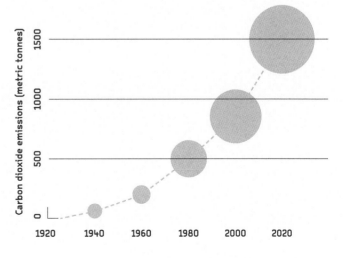

Carbon dioxide emissions (metric tonnes)

1500
1000
500
0

1920   1940   1960   1980   2000   2020

CONCRETE ALTERNATIVES

CONCRETE IS USED WIDELY IN GARDEN LANDSCAPING, FROM FOUNDATIONS TO SURFACE PAVING, BUT THERE ARE SOME ALTERNATIVES THAT CAN DO THE SAME JOB WITH A REDUCED CARBON FOOTPRINT.

GREEN CONCRETE

One of the best ways to move towards an eco-friendly construction material rather than using traditional concrete is to fully or partly replace energy-intensive cement with recycled or waste materials. Fly ash (waste from burning coal), silica fume (a superfine dust, a byproduct of silicon and ferrosilicon alloy production), and wood ash are some examples. By making use of the byproducts and waste from various manufacturing sectors, concrete needs less energy to produce and also eases the pressure on natural resources. Not only does it cause lower carbon dioxide emissions, it is also thought of as being less costly and can be even more durable than conventional concrete. Reducing water consumption by reusing wash water is among the many tactics employed to accomplish more sustainable concrete production.

Green concrete is defined as concrete that uses waste materials as at least one element of its material composition, and/or the manufacturing process isn't environmentally damaging, and/or it has a sustainable life cycle, for example long durability. It can have a low carbon footprint if based on reused water and locally sourced waste materials and aggregates. Considered extremely durable, it has a high tensile strength and is resistant to corrosion. A slower rate of shrinkage can mean it is more long-lasting than traditional concrete.

RAMMED EARTH

Rammed earth is an ancient building technique, with evidence of its use dating back to the Neolithic period. Materials such as dampened subsoil, clay, and aggregates are compressed in layers between a temporary timber structure known as formwork that is removed once the rammed earth has dried out. Robust, naturally insulating, and environmentally friendly, it also provides a striking, earthy aesthetic.

The materials can be found on or close to site, so transport emissions are low. Rammed earth has a carbon footprint around 40 times lower than concrete. It is also entirely recyclable and non-toxic.

TERRAZZO

A composite material, terrazzo is traditionally made from waste marble chippings set into cement or, for internal use, resin. It is either formed and poured by hand or precast into large blocks that are then sawn to size. Terrazzo can be set in a green cement binder and a range of waste materials used in place of marble – for example wood chips, rubble, or even scrap metal or plastic. The waste materials take on a new aesthetic when polished smooth, with the individual elements providing a mosaic texture. Waste material, particularly construction waste, is abundant across the globe, so using it creatively is a sustainable practice to avoid it going to landfill.

COB

Cob comprises straw, sand, earth, and clay combined with water. Lime is also sometimes a component. It can be moulded into versatile forms, and the technique results in a long-lasting and sturdy structure. Cob-work has been used for centuries, with some ancient structures surviving to this day. It has become a popular sustainable choice for construction.

[01] A desire to create a locally sourced and sustainable paving material led me to collaborate with Diespeker & Co in London to produce a terrazzo-like material using rubble and waste materials – the name Rubblazzo reflects the mixture of rubble and terrazzo. When set in green concrete and polished back, the rubble takes on a new aesthetic, with the individual elements – crushed concrete, brick, ceramic, or glass – providing a mosaic texture.

02

NATURAL RESOURCES

By making use of the byproducts and waste from various manufacturing sectors, green concrete uses less energy to produce than conventional concrete and also eases the pressure on natural resources.

03

[02] Rammed earth walls were a stunning feature on Sarah Price's 2018 show garden at the RHS Chelsea Flower Show.
[03] Cob has been used for centuries in construction and is highly sustainable, especially when made with materials from the site. It sits beautifully here alongside local stone.

Using 10 cu m (350 cu ft) of green concrete saves 2.8 tonnes (3 US tons) of carbon dioxide – the equivalent of planting 14 trees.

PLASTIC

PLASTICS ARE A BROAD RANGE OF MATERIALS THAT ARE SYNTHETIC OR SEMI-SYNTHETIC, USING POLYMERS AS A CHIEF COMPONENT. WHILE MANY CAN BE RECYCLED, MOST TAKE THOUSANDS OF YEARS TO BREAK DOWN.

Plastic is versatile, lightweight, generally low-cost, and widely used in most gardens. Compost and tools come wrapped in it, plants are sold in plastic pots, and it is used for hoses, weed barriers, spray bottles – the list of products is extensive. While some plastics are recyclable, and there is a range of recycled plastic products available – including decking, furniture, and pots – where possible, try to use alternative materials in the garden that are less environmentally damaging.

Ocean plastic waste is a common sight across the globe, from busy city beaches to remote islands. Here, a boy in Manila, in the Philippines, collects plastic waste for recycling on the beach.

RECYCLING PLASTIC

The recycling logo on plastics shows numbers that are resin identification codes, which helps recycling plants to sort materials. The numbers 1-7 inform workers what kind of plastic it is, and how it should be processed.

PETE OR PET

Used for most clear plastic bottles.

Full name Polyethylene terephthalate

Origin Crude oil and natural gas are used to extract the raw materials to make PET plastic.

Lifespan PET bottles can be reused, including as cloches to cover seedlings. While PET is not biodegradable, it can be recycled.

HDPE

Used for everyday items such as milk, shampoo, and detergent bottles, drainpipes, gutters and garden furniture.

Full name High density polyethylene

Origin HDPE is made from petroleum.

Lifespan It can be repurposed in the garden, such as a carrier for water or to hold feed for birds. It is not biodegradable but is recyclable.

PVC

A rigid, light plastic, PVC is used widely for house and garden functions such as pipes, door and window frames, or greenhouses.

Full name Polyvinyl chloride

Origin PVC is made with chlorine and hydrocarbons.

Lifespan If exposed to high temperatures persistently, PVC will exude harmful chemicals. It requires a specialized recycling process.

PLASTIC WASTE

Unless global changes are made to plastic production and disposal, plastic waste entering the aquatic ecosystem could nearly triple from 9-14 million tonnes (10-15 million US tons) in 2016 to 23-37 million tonnes (25-41 million US tons) per year by 2040.

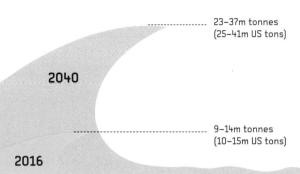

23–37m tonnes
(25–41m US tons)

9–14m tonnes
(10–15m US tons)

2040

2016

RECYCLED PLASTIC

In 1950, 1.5 million tonnes (1.7 million US tons) of plastic were produced, and all of this went into landfill. By 2020, the amount had increased to a huge 367 million tonnes (400 million US tons). Only 9 per cent of plastic was recycled; 22 per cent of plastic ended up in the natural environment, on land or in water.

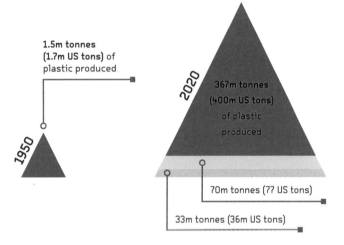

1.5m tonnes
(1.7m US tons) of
plastic produced

1950

2020

367m tonnes
(400m US tons)
of plastic
produced

70m tonnes (77 US tons)

33m tonnes (36m US tons)

● Landfill / terrestrial or aquatic environments

◌ Recycled

◌ Incinerated

DPE

flexible, lightweight plastic, is is used in plastic bags, rdboard cup linings, food orage bags, and squeezable ttles.

ll name Low-density lyethylene

igin LDPE is a thermoplastic ade from the monomer hylene.

fespan It can be reused t is difficult to recycle. As cup lining it can take 2–20 ars to break down.

PP

Used in crisp packets and also to make rigid containers such as plant pots, potting trays, and microwaveable meal trays.

Full name Polypropylene, also known as polypropene

Origin PP, is a thermoplastic polymer.

Lifespan This plastic can be reused multiple times and is generally able to be recycled, but not if it is black as this is not recognized by automated sorting machines.

PS

Found in packaging, takeaway food boxes, and foam cups.

Full name Polystyrene

Origin Polystyrene is made from the monomer styrene, which is derived from oil, as in the case of most plastics.

Lifespan As polystyrene has been found to be toxic and possibly carcinogenic, it should not be used in the garden. It is not widely recyclable, requiring a specialized process.

OTHER

This category of plastics indicates different resin mixes and also other specialized types of plastic packaging. Many plastics under this umbrella are toxic and should be avoided in the garden or anywhere plants are grown. They cannot usually be recycled.

PLASTIC ALTERNATIVES

UNFORTUNATELY, IT'S STILL ALMOST IMPOSSIBLE TO BE PLASTIC-FREE IN THE GARDEN AND IN THE HORTICULTURE INDUSTRY, BUT ALTERNATIVE MATERIALS ARE ARRIVING ON THE MARKET AND THERE ARE WAYS THAT WE CAN REDUCE PLASTIC IN THE GARDEN.

PLASTIC-FREE HORTICULTURE?

Everything from bagged compost and gravel to tools, plant pots, and general sundries contains types of plastic. For the Yeo Valley Organic Show Garden, we tried to limit this by using biodegradable rice husk pots – the traditional and widely used black plastic pots are not recyclable as they contain pigments that make them undetectable to the machinery used to sort plastics. However, they can be reused many times, and a number of nurseries will accept them for reuse. It is also becoming more common to use coloured plastic pots so they can be recognized and recycled by sorting machinery.

Other steps towards avoiding waste plastic can be taken, such as getting soils, aggregates, or gravel delivered loose rather than bagged, depending on local conditions and access. Bare-root plants are also becoming more widely used, though these need to be planted out quickly to avoid them drying out and perishing. Tackling plastic use in the horticulture industry will take joined-up thinking; examples include allotment gardeners clubbing together to purchase bulk loads of materials, and consumers pressurizing suppliers who use excessive or unnecessary plastics in packaging, demanding that they provide viable alternatives.

HOW TO AVOID PLASTIC IN THE GARDEN

- Buy loose materials where possible.
- Buy plants bare root, or in pots that are biodegradable.
- Make compost at home.
- Use natural and biodegradable materials such as hazel, willow, bamboo, and natural fibre twine for garden structures.
- Most garden products or tools have a plastic-free alternative, so look at the available range before purchasing.
- Research suppliers and check on their commitments to reducing plastic use and choosing compostable plastics.

228

These pots are made from rice husks – a waste material in rice production. They provide an alternative to the commonly used black plastic pots, which are not recyclable. Made from plant fibre, bound together using a mixed natural and synthetic compound, they have a smooth finish similar to that of plastic. They are practical, hardwearing, and reusable and, once composted, they will biodegrade after approximately five years.

BIOPLASTICS

These plastics are produced from renewable organic origins, such as vegetable fats and oils, plants, corn starch, straw, woodchips, sawdust, and food waste.

Bioplastics can make use of agricultural byproducts, using less fossil fuels than conventional plastics in the manufacturing process and having the capability to biodegrade. Useful formulas are still being refined, but bioplastics are being used more frequently for items such as disposable cutlery, straws, bowls, and packaging.

Some bioplastics are compostable and are even claimed to be suitable for putting in a home food waste bin, but they still take time to break down, and often require particular conditions, such as heat. Research is still being done into the sort of residual matter they leave behind after they break down, which, as they are a fairly new material, is still relatively unknown.

BIOPLASTIC PRODUCTION

Out of the millions of tonnes of plastic produced annually, bioplastics make up just 1 per cent, but demand for them is growing, and capacity for producing them is set to rise. Global bioplastic production is forecast to reach 7.59 million tonnes (7.72 million US tons) in 2026.

- Biodegradable
- Bio-based/non-biodegradeable
- Total amount

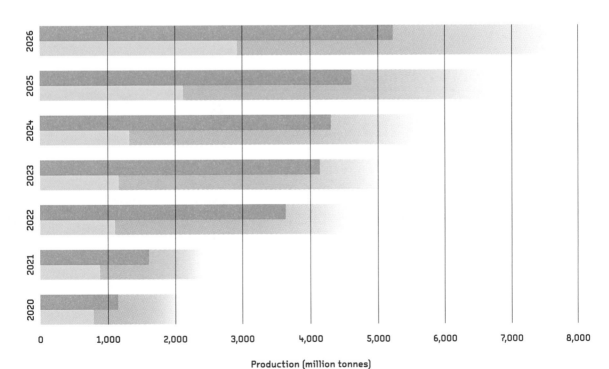

Production (million tonnes)

229

01

[01] In this garden, I used hard industrial steel in multiple finishes to offset the soft planting. It is an incredibly versatile, strong, and beautiful material, able to be formed and perforated. [02] Steel has long been used for water features, as it is naturally impermeable. The liquid reflectiveness of the water provides a beautiful counterpoint to the rigid hardness of the steel.
[03] On the roof terrace of the Lemon Tree Trust garden at Chelsea Flower Show in 2018, patterns for zinc planters were laser cut from sheet thin material, and then folded by hand on site. No screws or fixings were needed and the idea was that the plans could be sent anywhere in the world and produced low cost, to create long lasting, light weight and durable planters.

02

METAL

METAL IS A SOLID MATERIAL WITH VARYING LEVELS OF LUSTRE THAT CAN BE ALTERED BY POLISHING. IT IS CHARACTERIZED AS EITHER MALLEABLE (CAN BE HAMMERED INTO THIN SHEETS) OR DUCTILE (CAN BE DRAWN OUT INTO THIN WIRES).

METAL IN LANDSCAPING

Versatile and durable, metal can be incorporated into a range of styles and schemes. Rusting and weathering can change its appearance over time, allowing it to settle naturally into its surroundings. It is naturally robust and can be used for large structures such as staircases, pergolas, or laser cut screens, but is equally good for smaller details like bird feeders or containers. It is generally a heavy, dense material, so its environmental impact is increased by shipping, and manufacture is carbon intensive.

03

MILD STEEL

In its raw state, iron is soft and therefore not feasible for use as a construction material. The main technique for strengthening iron and transforming it into steel is the incorporation of small levels of carbon. Globally, steel production is one of the most energy-exhaustive and carbon-abundant industries - in 2020 it was responsible for around 7 per cent of the world's carbon dioxide emissions. Currently, China produces more steel than the rest of the world put together, making it the global leader by a long way.

Origin Alloy of iron and carbon.

Lifespan Depending on the thickness of the steel and the environmental conditions, mild steel can last for decades.

TYPES OF METAL

SEVERAL METALS ARE SUITABLE FOR USE IN THE GARDEN, BOTH TO FULFIL PRACTICAL FUNCTIONS AND TO PROVIDE VISUAL EFFECTS.

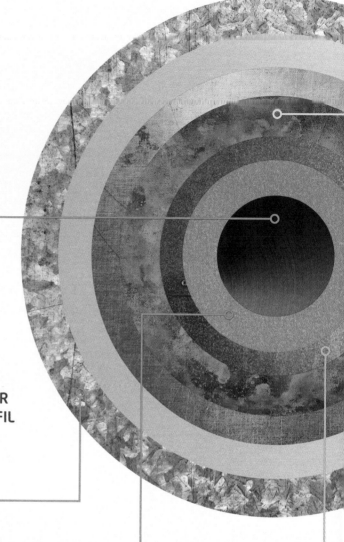

GALVANIZED STEEL

Galvanization is a process where steel is dipped into a vat of molten zinc, creating a protective coating and preventing rust. Zinc can make steel stronger and prolong its life, but high levels of zinc can be harmful to the environment and can pollute water when not properly sanitized during manufacturing.

Origin Steel, zinc

Lifespan Galvanization can deliver 50+ years of protection against rust and corrosion, without any maintenance. At the end of its life, galvanized steel can be recycled.

WEATHERING STEEL

The process of manufacturing weathering steel starts with combining iron, copper, chromium, and nickel, with further alloying components such as phosphorus, silicon, and manganese. These facilitate the development of a layer of rust on the surface of the metal that improves resistance to weathering and corrosion.

Origin Weathering steel is an alloy of iron, copper, chromium and nickel.

Lifespan The lifespan is generally longer the thicker it is, but the protective rust layer means the metal can last for many decades before needing to be replaced.

ZINC

Zinc is extracted by concentrating and heating the ore, then processing it into a usable metal by heating with carbon or using electrolysis.

Origin Zinc is extracted from the earth, with the main sources being zinc sulphide ore and zinc silicate (calamine) ore. The prime mining areas are in China, Australia, and Peru.

Lifespan Zinc reacts with oxygen and carbon dioxide to develop a protective patina, making zinc very durable, and it can last for up to 100 years. At the end of its life, zinc retrieved from modern products can be recycled without deteriorating.

COPPER

Copper is generally extracted from oxide ores and sulphide ores, which require different processes to produce usable copper sheets. Hydrometallurgy uses water-based solutions to extract and purify copper from oxide ores.

Origin Copper is found in sedimentary and igneous rocks in the form of minerals and ore. El Teniente in Chile is the largest copper mine globally.

Lifespan Copper can last for more than 100 years outside. Waste copper can be re-smelted and recycled, which uses less energy than mining for fresh ore. Copper is a finite resource and about a third used globally is recycled.

BRONZE

Bronze is an alloy of copper and tin, formed by melting both materials together. Tin is mined from the Earth's crust and is a fairly scarce resource - around half of tin produced today is from Southeast Asia. To extract tin, the mineral cassiterite is heated with carbon in a furnace at very high temperatures.

Origin An alloy of copper and tin.

Lifespan Ancient artefacts are testament to the enduring durability of bronze. While it is recycled, information on energy saved is lacking as bronze is costly, and therefore used less often in construction.

ALUMINIUM

Alumina or aluminium oxide is drawn out of bauxite using heat and caustic soda. Bauxite occurs relatively close to the Earth's surface and so is fairly easy to extract. Pure aluminium is produced using electrolytic reduction, which requires huge amounts of electricity, making it an expensive and carbon-heavy process.

Origin Aluminium is one of the most plentiful metals occurring naturally. Around 90 per cent of the world's bauxite is located in tropical and subtropical regions, and around 73 per cent occurs in five countries – Guinea, Brazil, Jamaica, Australia, and India.

Lifespan Aluminium can last for up to 100 years outside and can be repeatedly recycled without compromising its qualities.

RECYCLING METAL

Almost all metals can be recycled, and this chart shows the percentage of recycled metals consumed in the US in 2007. While bronze is widely recycled, it is less commonly used, so accurate data is not available.

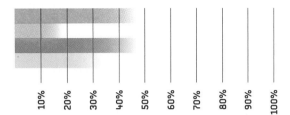

10% 20% 30% 40% 50% 60% 70% 80% 90% 100%

Percentage of metals recycled, US 2017

ENERGY SAVED

Amount of energy saved by recycling compared to extracting the metal from raw. As above, the data is not available for bronze as it is less commonly used.

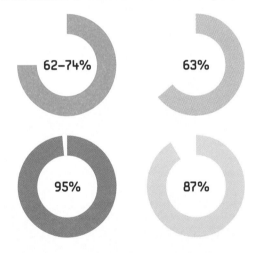

62–74%   63%

95%   87%

COMMON USES

The metals featured here can all be used within our gardens. Steel and aluminium are the most versatile.

Sculptures/Features	●	●	●	●	●
Planters	●	●	●		
Furniture	●		●		
Edging	●		●		
Cladding	●	●	●	●	●

COMPOST

USUALLY COMPOSED OF RECYCLED ORGANIC MATTER, SUCH AS PLANT AND FOOD WASTE, COMPOST IS USED AS A SOIL IMPROVER AND FERTILIZER. COMPOSTS ARE FULL OF NUTRIENTS TO ENCOURAGE HEALTHY PLANT GROWTH AND ADVANTAGEOUS ORGANISMS, SUCH AS EARTHWORMS AND FUNGAL MYCELIUM.

01

Valued at USD 5592.3 million in 2020, and forecast to reach USD 7516.5 million by the end of 2027, the global compost market is huge and continues to grow. Although compost is used to cultivate and sustain plant life, the production of it is not always without controversy or environmental impact.

THE ROLE OF PEAT

Peat is used as a component of many commercially sold composts, as a soil improver and for potting up seedlings. It has long been a popular material for compost as it can provide ideal conditions for establishing young plants, being free-draining but also remaining moist.

However, it has been apparent for a long time that the extraction of peat from the land is damaging to the environment. Consisting of partly decayed vegetation and other organic material, peat is formed over many generations. For peat to develop, the vegetation must be buried in waterlogged soils with little or no access to oxygen, which stops the organic material from decomposing completely. Peat is found specifically in natural

peatlands, including moors, bogs, and fens. These peatlands occur globally; the largest area of peatland in the world is the tropical Cuvette Centrale peatland in the central Congo basin, covering an area of 145,500 sq km (56,178 sq miles), more than the area of England.

Peatlands are the most effective carbon sinks (an area that absorbs more carbon than is released) in the world; a natural balance is sustained because peatland plants absorb the carbon dioxide naturally exuding from the peat. When peat is extracted for commercial use, not only are large amounts of carbon dioxide released, the local flora and fauna are destroyed. In the UK, peat is to be banned from use in home gardening.

03

[01] At this peat extraction site, the landscape is bare and devoid of life. The use of peat is damaging to the environment and therefore a problematic material in the garden. [02] In order to collect peat, the upper surface of the peatland is removed, destroying unique and threatened flora and fauna while also liberating huge amounts of carbon dioxide into the atmosphere. [03] Viru Bog at Lahemaa National Park, Estonia, is protected and thriving. To preserve the vegetation and peat-rich soil, visitors must stay on the boardwalks.

PEAT-FREE ALTERNATIVES

ALTERNATIVES TO PEAT COMPOST ARE AVAILABLE, AND ENCOMPASS BLENDS OF DECAYED ORGANIC MATTER SUCH AS BARK, COCONUT FIBRE, AND WOOD CHIPS. THEY CAN BE COMBINED WITH INORGANIC MATERIAL INCLUDING GRIT, SHARP SAND, ROCK WOOL, AND PERLITE.

Most of the alternatives to peat are easily sourced and some are even available without any cost. Making use of them in the garden avoids some going to landfill, too.

SHEEP'S WOOL WASTE

Wool improves water retention and provides a slow release of nitrogen into the soil as well as acting as a weed-suppressant and regulating temperature. It is considered a sustainable, eco-friendly alternative to using peat. Available from garden centres and online, it can be incorporated in the soil or used as a mulch on the surface.

BRACKEN

Fresh green bracken fronds can be put on a compost heap, where they will enhance the nutrients in the compost as they rot down. Avoid the roots as they can germinate and create new plants. In the autumn, dead bracken can be broken down to make mulch in the same way as leaf mould (see below).

WOOD FIBRE

Used as a mulch, woody matter such as sawdust or composted bark can improve the soil's ability to retain moisture. It is most sustainable, and cheapest, when acquired as a locally sourced untreated wood byproduct.

PINE NEEDLES

Abundant and easily obtained, these are best used as a mulch on top of the soil, where they can bond together as a permeable mat that is not easily blown away. While they can change the texture of the soil, they do not retain water or hugely affect nutrient levels.

COMPOSTED MANURE

Manure is one of the most effective alternatives to peat, as it improves the important microbes in the soil, aids plant growth, and increases moisture

01

02

03

04

[1] Sheep's wool waste
[2] Bracken
[3] Wood fibre
[4] Pine needles

236

retention. Fresh manure is very acidic and contains high levels of nitrogen, which can have a negative impact on plants, so it should be composted down before application. Bagged composted manure is widely available.

LEAF MOULD

As leaf mould is created when dead leaves are left to rot down, it is an inexpensive, renewable, and locally available resource. All that is required is for leaves to be piled up and turned over periodically in order to speed up the decomposition process. When added to the soil, leaf mould can aid moisture retention and supply nutrients.

BIOCHAR

This soil improver is produced through pyrolysis (heating to very high temperatures without oxygen). Like charcoal, it can be made from organic substances, generally wood. When organic material breaks down, the inherent carbon is released into the atmosphere. Biochar decomposes very slowly, over hundreds of years, so organic material converted into biochar essentially sequesters the inherent carbon, preventing it from being released. It is extremely moisture-retentive, and good at retaining nutrients, so is an ideal soil improver. Available online, it can be incorporated into compost mixes or used on directly on the soil as a mulch.

COIR (COCONUT FIBRE)

Composed of the fibres found between the flesh layer and the shell of coconuts, coir is used for many products such as doormats and brushes, but leftover short fibres act as a peat alternative. As it can hold up to 10 times its weight in water, it is extremely efficient at retaining moisture. The harvesting and shipping means it is not the ideal peat replacement, but as it is a by-product of coconuts already grown for eating, it is a more sustainable option than peat.

RICE HULLS

Hulls are the outer layer of rice grains, removed before the rice is packaged for eating. They are usually thrown away, but can be used as a valuable soil improver as they help to incorporate air in the soil and retain water. They add nutrients to the soil as they rot down, improving conditions for a full growing season. Available online, they can also be found in some garden supplies stores.

[5] Composted manure
[6] Leaf mould
[7] Biochar
[8] Coir
[9] Rice hulls

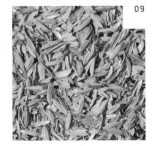

INNOVATIVE MATERIALS

LOOKING INTO THE FUTURE, THERE ARE MANY NEW AND EXCITING MATERIALS BEING ENGINEERED FOR USE IN LANDSCAPES, BUILDINGS, AND GARDENS. SOME AVOID WASTE BEING SENT TO LANDFILL AND BREATHE NEW LIFE INTO OTHERWISE DISCARDED MATTER, WHILE OTHERS ENGINEER NATURE FOR HUMAN BENEFIT.

INNOVATIVE PAVING

Manufacturers are finding ways of combining environmental solutions and functional surfaces. For example, AquiPor Technologies has created a permeable concrete that filters out harmful pollutants as stormwater flows through it, combatting urban flooding from increased rainfall; Pavegen has developed paving that generates electricity using kinetic energy from footsteps as it is walked on.

RECYCLED MATERIALS

Incorporating waste and recycled materials into new sustainable products serves a dual purpose. In the Netherlands, Stone Cycling collects and processes debris from construction and demolition, turning waste material into new bricks. Recycled plastics are also being used to create products such as decking, sheet materials, and garden furniture.

ENGINEERED TIMBER PRODUCTS

Modern processes have been formulated to improve the lifespan and properties of natural wood, ranging from thermally treating to pickling. Accoya wood is mature softwood species such as pine treated with acetic acid to give it the properties of a hardwood, creating a rot-resistant material that can be recycled just like natural timber. Tricoya uses the same process to treat MDF. Transparent wood composites are new wood materials which have up to 90 per cent transparency and are much more biodegradable than glass and plastic.

MANURE

Animal manure is a familiar garden staple, found globally in abundance. Merdacotta has given it a new lease of life, using cow dung, clay, straw, and farm waste to produce flower pots and tiles that have a terracotta-like finish but are lighter and more resistant to fluctuating climates. The Mestic project discovered a process to extract cellulose from dung and use it to make biomaterial products such as paper, textiles, and bioplastics.

FUNGAL MATERIAL

Mycelium, the fast-growing, underground network of fungi, is being used in innovative design. New York design practice The Living worked on the Hy-Fi project, a temporary mycelium brick tower at the Museum of Modern Art. Formed in moulds in less than a week, the bricks were composted once the structure was dismantled. Italian design firm Carlo Ratti Associati created the Circular Garden, a series of arches formed by injecting fungal spores into organic material, while Officina Corpuscoli, a multidisciplinary design studio, supports multiple projects dedicated to evolving mycelium-based technology.

02

03

[01] The organic brick structure known as 'Hy-Fi' was designed by David Benjamin of New York architects The Living. It is built from organic, biodegradable bricks consisting of cultures of fungus and farm waste grown to fit a brick-shaped mould.

[02] Stone Cycling aim to prove that it's possible to build high-quality, aesthetic materials from waste. Their WasteBasedBricks are made from waste materials and are extensively tested to ensure success. [03] In Sarah Eberle's 2022 Chelsea Garden, a waterfall inspired by natural rock strata cascaded into a pool. It was constructed of Tricoya, made to look like stone. More durable than standard timber materials, Tricoya can be used for wider applications, including those that require a higher degree of moisture resistance, such as this water feature.

GLOSSARY

AIR POLLUTION
Harmful chemicals or particles in the air, often derived from vehicular traffic or industry

BIODEGRADABLE
Describes substances that decay naturally without causing harm to the environment.

BIODIVERSITY
Also known as biological diversity or species richness, the variety of life found in a particular place or on Earth generally. A common measure of this is the count of species in a specified area.

BIODIVERSITY CRISIS
The rapid loss of species and degradation of ecosystems caused by human actions that have a negative impact upon them.

BIOMATERIAL
A substance that is derived from, or produced by, biological organisms such as plants and animals, and can be used as a material for making things or as fuel.

BIOME
A large area of land and the particular combination of climate, plants, and animals that are found in it.

BIOSECURITY
Measures to prevent the introduction and/or spread of harmful organisms to animals and plants.

CARBON CAPTURE
A way of collecting the carbon dioxide (CO_2) emissions produced from industrial processes or the burning of fossil fuels so that it is not released into the air.

CARBON DIOXIDE EQUIVALENT (CO2E)
The number of metric tonnes of CO_2 emissions with the same global warming potential as one metric tonne of another greenhouse gas.

CARBON FOOTPRINT
A measure of the total greenhouse gas emissions caused directly and indirectly by a person, organization, event, or product.

CARBON NEUTRAL
Causing no net release of carbon dioxide into the atmosphere, especially as a result of carbon offsetting.

CARBON OFFSET
A reduction in emissions of carbon dioxide or other greenhouse gases, or an increase in carbon storage, used to compensate for emissions that occur elsewhere. Offsets are measured in tonnes of carbon dioxide equivalent (CO_2e). One tonne of carbon offset represents the reduction of one tonne of carbon dioxide or its equivalent in other greenhouse gases.

CARBON SEQUESTRATION
The capture and secure storage of carbon that would otherwise be emitted to the atmosphere. It is also referred to as "carbon draw-down".

CIRCULAR PLASTIC
The process of keeping existing plastic in use for as long as possible by recovering and regenerating it to make new products, thus extracting the maximum value from it.

CLIMATE CRISIS
The highly dangerous, irreversible changes to the global climate resulting from global warming, causing problems such as environmental degradation, natural disasters, weather extremes, food and water insecurity, and economic disruption.

CLIMATE POSITIVE
A commitment to go beyond net zero (see below) by investing in nature-based solutions that will make a net beneficial impact on the climate.

CLIMATE RESILIENCE
The ability to prepare for and respond to hazardous events, disturbances, or trends that are related to climate. Improving climate resilience requires assessing how climate change will engender new, or alter current, climate-related risks, and taking steps to lessen these risks through adaptation and mitigation.

CULTIVATED PLANT DIVERSITY
A mixture of native and cultivated plants grown in gardens or landscapes.

ECOLOGICAL GARDENING
Gardening with a natural balance for wildlife and human wellbeing, including herbicide- and pesticide-free management.

FOREST GARDEN
A designed agronomic system using trees, shrubs, and perennial plants in a way that echoes the structure of a natural forest.

FOSSIL FUELS

Fuels such as coal and natural gas formed from organic matter laid down millions of years ago that fossilized, creating an underground carbon store. When these fuels are burned, CO_2 is released.

GREENHOUSE EFFECT

An increase in the amount of carbon dioxide and other gases in the atmosphere (mixture of gases around the Earth) that causes a warming of the surface of the Earth.

GREENHOUSE GAS (GHG) EMISSIONS

Gases discharged into the Earth's atmosphere as a result of human activity that are accelerating global warming, especially carbon dioxide resulting from the burning of fossil fuels.

GREY WATER

Previously used domestic water that contains no faecal matter and can be stored and reused, for example for watering.

HEAT SINK

A substance or an object that absorbs heat.

NATURE-BASED SOLUTIONS

Actions to protect, sustainably manage, and restore natural or modified ecosystems to benefit both human wellbeing and biodiversity.

NET EMISSIONS REDUCTION

Reducing annual greenhouse gas emissions with projects that prevent or reduce emissions.

NET POSITIVE

Putting back more into society, the environment, and the global economy than is taken out.

NET ZERO

Of a country, city, etc., removing as many emissions of gases that cause global warming as it produces.

PASSIVE IRRIGATION SYSTEM

A system by which the runoff from rain is directed to landscapes, either at the surface (where the water filters down through the soil) or through subsurface systems that recharge soil moisture at a depth where plant roots can access it.

PEAT

An accumulation of partially decayed organic matter, peat is unique to natural areas called peatlands, bogs, mires, moors, or muskegs.

PLANETARY BOUNDARIES

Introduced in 2009, the Planetary Boundaries concept aimed to define the environmental limits within which humanity can safely operate and has influenced the development of global sustainability policy.

RAINWATER HARVESTING

In a rainwater harvesting system, water is collected and stored in a tank and then pumped to direct the water where it is needed in the home.

RENEWABLE ENERGY

Energy produced by natural and self-replenishing resources, such as sunlight, wind, rain, waves, tides, geothermal heat, and bioenergy derived by burning organic material.

REWILDING

The process of protecting an environment and returning it to its original state by letting natural processes shape the landscape and bringing back wild animals that used to live there.

SUBSTRATE

The surface on which a plant lives; the soil is the substrate of most plants.

SUSTAINABILITY

The integration of environmental health, social equity, and economic vitality to create thriving, diverse, and resilient communities for the present and future.

SWALE

A low-lying or depressed and often wet and vegetated stretch of land. Artificial swales are often infiltration channels, designed to manage water runoff, filter pollutants, and increase rainwater infiltration.

UN COP SUMMIT

The United Nations Climate Change Conference of the Parties (COP) attended by representatives from different countries.

WATER-NEUTRAL

Where total water use is equal to, or less than, total natural water supply. This involves using less water and capturing, reusing, and recycling water.

ZERO WASTE

At least 99 per cent of generated waste is diverted away from landfill, which means that all waste produced is reused, recycled, composted, or sent to energy recovery.

ENDNOTES

Chapter 1

10 Richmond Park is a site of both national and international importance for wildlife conservation: The Royal Parks, 2019. frp.org.uk/wp-content/uploads/2019/01/RICHMOND-PARK-DESIGNATIONS-NNR-SSSI-SAC-and-Listed-Buildings.pdf

11 A scene typical of Richmond Park, which contains an estimated 1,300 veteran oak trees: Friends of Richmond Park, 2018. frp.org.uk/ancient-oaks-in-the-park

11 There are an estimated 3 billion yellow meadow ants residing in Richmond Park: The Royal Parks. royalparks.org.uk/media-centre/press-releases/eye-popping-stats-show-billions-of-ants-re-designing-one-of-europes-most-important-parks

Chapter 2

26 In February 2022, the Royal Society in London published a report that looked at the first flowering times of plants, using more than 400,000 studies and starting as far back as 1753: "Plants in the UK Flower a Month Earlier Under Recent Warming", Ulf Büntgen, Alma Piermattei, Paul J. Krusic, Jan Esper, Tim Sparks, and Alan Crivellaro, 2022. royalsocietypublishing.org/doi/10.1098/rspb.2021.2456

26 Solastalgia is a word coined by Glenn Albrecht: "'Solastalgia' : a new concept in health and identity", Glenn Albrecht, 2016. bridges.monash.edu/articles/journal_contribution/_Solastalgia_a_new_concept_in_health_and_identity/4311905

28 If every UK gardener planted a medium-sized tree, these trees would store carbon the equivalent of driving 11.4 million times around the planet: RHS, 2021. rhs.org.uk/about-the-rhs/sustainability/sustainability-strategy-document

29 The American Psychology Association (APA) describes eco-anxiety: "Mental Health and our Changing Climate: Impacts, Implications, And Guidance", Susan Clayton Whitmore-Williams, Christie Manning, Kirra Krygsman, Meighen Speiser, 2017. apa.org/news/press/releases/2017/03/mental-health-climate.pdf

30 There are more than 30 million people involved in gardening in the UK alone: RHS. rhs.org.uk/get-involved/wild-about-gardens

31 The total area of gardens in the UK is estimated at approximately 433,000 hectares (1,670 square miles): Wildlife Gardening Forum. wlgf.org/The%20garden%20Resource.pdf

38 A report that was issued in 2021 by the Intergovernmental Panel on Climate Change (IPCC) attested to the fact that we are in a state of climate catastrophe: "Climate Change 2021: The Physical Science Basis", IPCC, 2021. ipcc.ch/report/ar6/wg1/

38 Global climate change map: "Understanding Climate Change from a Global Analysis of City Analogues", Jean-Francois Bastin, Emily Clark, Thomas Elliott, Simon Hart et al, 2019. doi.org/10.1371/journal.pone.0217592

41 It is estimated that if we continue to emit these gases at the present rate, there could be a temperature rise of 2.5–5°C (4.5–9°F) by the end of the century. With a turn towards sustainable energy, this could drop to a rise of 0.25–1.75°C (0.4–3.1°F): "Climate Change 2021: The Physical Science Basis", IPCC, 2021. ipcc.ch/report/ar6/wg1/

41 In 2019, the Oxford Dictionary word of the year was "climate emergency": Oxford University Press, 2022. languages.oup.com/word-of-the-year/2019/

42 An interactive map is available that details the future climates of 530 cities across the world and links them to those that have their anticipated 2050 climate in the present day: OpenStreetMap, Bastin et al, 2019. hooge104.shinyapps.io/future_cities_app

42 The IPCC's third report instalment states that without immediate and deep reductions of emissions across all sectors, limiting global warming to 1.5°C (2.7°F) is beyond reach: "Climate Change 2022: Impacts, Adaptation and Vulnerability", IPCC, 2022. www.ipcc.ch/report/sixth-assessment-report-working-group-ii

42 "The decisions we make now can secure a liveable future," said IPCC Chair Hoesung Lee: IPCC, 2022. ipcc.ch/2022/04/04/ipcc-ar6-wgiii-pressrelease

43 At the climate change conference COP21 in Paris in 2015, an international treaty was signed with the goal of limiting global warming to below 2°C (3.6°F): United Nations Climate Change. unfccc.int/process-and-meetings/the-paris-agreement/the-paris-agreement#

43 COP26 in Glasgow in 2021 failed to reassert the goals for 2030: UN News, 2021. news.un.org/en/story/2021/11/1105792

45 "Healthy ecosystems are more resilient to climate change and provide life-critical services" said IPCC Working Group II co-chair professor Hans-Otto Pörtner: IPCC, 2022. ipcc.ch/2022/02/28/pr-wgii-ar6/

48 Psychoanalyst Erich Fromm introduced the word "biophilia" in his book *The Anatomy of*

Human Destructiveness. He described it as the "passionate love of life and of all that is alive... whether in a person, a plant, an idea, or a social group". Fromm, Erich, *The Anatomy of Human Destructiveness* (Holt, Rinehart and Winston, 1973)

51 Every 1kg (2¼lb) of site-made compost typically saves 100g (3½oz) of carbon dioxide emissions: RHS, 2021.
rhs.org.uk/about-the-rhs/sustainability/sustainability-strategy-document

53 Green roof systems can be incorporated into any structures to increase biodiversity and sequester carbon: "Carbon Sequestration Potential of Extensive Green Roofs", Kristin L. Getter, D. Bradley Rowe, G. Philip Robertson, Bert M. Cregg, and Jeffrey A. Andresen, 2009.
pubs.acs.org/doi/abs/10.1021/es901539x

53 Cut flowers and foliage can save up to 7.9kg (17 ½lb) carbon per bunch compared with buying imported or commercially produced bunches: RHS, 2021.
rhs.org.uk/about-the-rhs/sustainability/sustainability-strategy-document

54 Sir Robert Watson, chair of the Intergovernmental Science-Policy Platform on Biodiversity and Ecosystem Services, states "We are eroding the very foundations of our economies, livelihoods, food security, health, and quality of life worldwide": United Nations, 2019.
un.org/sustainabledevelopment/blog/2019/05/nature-decline-unprecedented-report/

55 Professor Dave Goulson states: "Insects make up about two-thirds of all life on Earth [but] there has been some kind of horrific decline": *The Guardian*, 2018.
theguardian.com/environment/2018/jun/17/where-have-insects-gone-climate-change-population-decline

59 An example of a bacterial disease that has damaging effects on a wide range of plants is *Xylella fastidiosa*: Megan Bickle, 2019.
planthealthportal.defra.gov.uk/assets/uploads/EvidenceStatement-XylellaFastidiosa.pdf

Chapter 3
64 The urban heat island effect can cause temperatures in cities to rise by 5°C (9°F): World Meteorological Organization, 2020.
community.wmo.int/activity-areas/urban/urban-heat-island

66 In the UK, the RHS offers a soil analysis service: RHS, 2022.
rhs.org.uk/membership/rhs-gardening-advice/soil-analysis-service

68 Identifying soil types: RHS, 2022.
rhs.org.uk/soil-composts-mulches/soil-types

70 Testing the acidity/alkalinity of your soil: RHS, 2022.
rhs.org.uk/soil-composts-mulches/ph-and-testing-soil

79 By 2050, 5 billion people could be affected by water shortages: "The United Nations World Water Development Report 2018: Nature-Based Solutions For Water", UNESCO World Water Assessment Programme, 2018.
unesdoc.unesco.org/ark:/48223/pf0000261424

79 More than 2 billion of the world's population do not have safe drinking water available in their homes: World Health Organization, 2019.
who.int/news/item/18-06-2019-1-in-3-people-globally-do-not-have-access-to-safe-drinking-water-unicef-who

79 SuDS imitate a flow of water similar to that of a non-developed site, expelling water into the surrounding environment in a regulated way: Local Government Association, 2022.
local.gov.uk/topics/severe-weather/flooding/sustainable-drainage-systems

79 In the UK in 2020, there were more than 400,000 discharges of untreated sewage into rivers and almost 5,500 discharges into UK coastal bathing waters: Surfers Against Sewage, 2022.
sas.org.uk/water-quality

81 Types of sun and shade: RHS, 2022.
rhs.org.uk/garden-design/shade-gardening

82 Understanding wind and temperature: National Geographic, 2022.
education.nationalgeographic.org/resource/wind

84 Windbreaks and shelterbelts: RHS, 2022.
rhs.org.uk/plants/types/hedges/windbreaks-shelterbelts

89 "Green walls" have the capacity to reduce pollution by 30 per cent: "The Effectiveness of Green Infrastructure for Improvement of Air Quality in Urban Street Canyons," Pugh, T. A. M., A. R. MacKenzie, J. D. Whyatt, and C. N. Hewitt, 2012.
birmingham.ac.uk/news/2012/researching-the-air-pollution-filtering-effects-of-green-walls-1

Chapter 4
96 Heat islands in cities: United States Environmental Protection Programme, 2022.
epa.gov/heatislands/learn-about-heat-islands

108 Installing a green roof: RHS, 2022.
rhs.org.uk/garden-features/green-roofs

114 Planting a food forest, or forest garden: Centre for Alternative Technology (CAT), 2022.
cat.org.uk/info-resources/free-information-service/growing-and-eating/forest-garden/

118 British organic gardener Charles Dowding is a pioneer of the no-dig approach: Charles Dowding, 2022.
charlesdowding.co.uk

122 The micro-organisms that transform waste material into compost work most effectively at consistent levels of temperature and moisture: RHS, 2022.
rhs.org.uk/soil-composts-mulches/composting

125 Home-made garden compost is usually ready to use in six months to two years: RHS, 2022.
rhs.org.uk/soil-composts-mulches/composting

126 The benefits of mulching: RHS, 2022.
rhs.org.uk/soil-composts-mulches/mulch

132 The value of sustainable drainage systems (SuDS): HebdenBridge.org, 2019.
hebdenbridge.org/slow-the-flow-nfm-and-suds-opportunity-mapping-in-mytholmroyd-west-yorkshire/

133 An online resource explains how water usage in gardens can be reduced: RHS and Cranfield University.
mains2rains.uk/

134 Storm water management: Water Network Research, 2020.
thewaternetwork.com/article-FfV/changing-the-nature-of-storm-watermanagement-l1A2YatvIwd4FJZAE4G3Fw

139 Creating a windbreak in your garden with wind-resilient species: RHS, 2022.
rhs.org.uk/plants/types/hedges/windbreaks-shelterbelts

139 Plants can assist in capturing particulate pollution: RHS, 2022.
rhs.org.uk/science/articles/super-cotoneaster

146 Hugelkultur mounds: Permaculture, 2022.
permaculture.co.uk/articles/the-many-benefits-of-hugelkultur/

148 Wabi-sabi is a Japanese ideology embracing that which is imperfect and ephemeral to be found in the natural world: Koren, Leonard, *Wabi-Sabi for Artists, Designers, Poets and Philosophers*, (Stone Bridge Press, 1994)

150 The growth of saprophytic fungi: RHS, 2022.
rhs.org.uk/biodiversity/saprophytic-fungi

151 Ash dieback has caused widespread damage to ash trees across Europe for 20 years: Woodland Trust, 2022.
woodlandtrust.org.uk/trees-woods-and-wildlife/tree-pests-and-diseases/key-tree-pests-and-diseases/ash-dieback/

152 Growing shiitake on hardwood logs: Urban Farm-It, 2022.
urban-farm-it.com/how-to-grow-mushrooms/

155 Sounds in nature may have a positive impact on our mental health: BBC, 2022.
bbc.co.uk/news/uk-england-devon-60840759

Chapter 6

211 Lifecycle flow chart: Adapted from Figure 5.2, 'LETI Embodied Carbon Primer: Supplementary guidance to the Climate Emergency Design Guide', Alex Johnstone et al, 2020.
leti.uk/_files/
ugd/252d09_8ceffcbcafdb43cf8a19ab9af5073b92.pdf

215 Carbon storing capacity chart: Visual Capitalist, 2022.
visualcapitalist.com/sp/visualizing-carbon-storage-in-earths-ecosystems

216 Igneous rocks form when magma or lava from beneath the Earth's crust cools and then solidifies: National Geographic, 2022.
education.nationalgeographic.org/resource/igneous-rocks

220 Recycled gravel infographic adapted from: "Global CO2 Emissions from Cement Production", Andrew, R. M., Earth Syst. Sci. Data, 10, 195–217, fig.2, doi.org/10.5194/essd-10-195-2018, 2018, CC BY 4.0.

222 China is estimated to have produced half of the world's cement in 2021: "Leading Cement Producing Countries Worldwide 2021", M. Garside, 2022.
statista.com/statistics/267364/world-cement-production-by-country/#statisticContainer

222 It is thought that concrete uses nearly 10 per cent of global industrial water consumption and accounts for 4–8 per cent of CO2 emissions globally: *The Guardian*, 2019.
theguardian.com/cities/2019/feb/25/concrete-the-most-destructive-material-on-earth

222 Production of clinker is thought to account for 50 per cent of concrete's CO2 emissions: "Making Concrete Change: Innovation in Low-carbon Cement and Concrete", Johanna Lehne and Felix Preston, 2018.
chathamhouse.org/sites/default/files/publications/2018-06-13-making-concrete-change-cement-lehne-preston-final.pdf

223 Cement production infographic: Heidrich, Craig & Hinczak, Ihor & Ryan, Bridget. (2022). SCM's potential to lower Australia's greenhouse gas emissions profile.

223 Growing emissions chart: Earth System Science Data adapted from: "Global CO2 emissions from cement production", Andrew, R. M., Earth Syst. Sci. Data, 10, 195–217, fig.2, doi.org/10.5194/essd-10-195-2018, 2018, CC BY 4.0

224 Green concrete uses less energy to produce and can be more durable than conventional concrete: "Toward Green Concrete for Better Sustainable Environment", BambangSuhendro, 2014.
sciencedirect.com/science/article/pii/S1877705814032494

224 Rammed earth has a carbon footprint around 40 times lower than concrete: Friends & Co, 2020.
friendsandco.co.uk/is-rammed-earth-the-building-material-of-the-future

225 Natural resources infographic: DB Group, 2022.
dbgholdings.com/cemfree/

227 Plastic waste infographic: UN Environment Programme, 2022.
unep.org/interactives/beat-plastic-pollution

227 Recycled plastic infographic: "Global plastic production 1950–2020", Ian Tiseo, 2022.
statista.com/statistics/282732/global-production-of-plastics-since-1950/

229 Bioplastic production chart: European Bioplastics, nova-Institute, 2021.

233 Recycling metal chart: USGS, 2022, with data courtesy of the British Metals Recycling Association.
usgs.gov/centers/national-minerals-information-center/recycling-statistics-and-information

233 Energy saved infographic: University of Cambridge, 2022.
doitpoms.ac.uk/tlplib/recycling-metals/what.php

234 Valued at US $5592.3 million in 2020, the global compost market is huge and continues to grow: Digital Journal, 2022.
digitaljournal.com/pr/compost-market-size-in-2022

234 The largest area of peatland in the world is the tropical Cuvette Centrale peatland in the central Congo basin: *The Guardian*, 2017.
theguardian.com/environment/2017/jan/11/worlds-largest-

peatland-vast-carbon-storage-capacity-found-congo

236 Peat-free alternatives: RHS, 2022.
rhs.org.uk/science/gardening-in-a-changing-world/
peat-use-in-gardens/peat-alternatives

238 AquiPor Technologies has created a
permeable concrete:
aquipor.com

238 Pavegen has developed paving that generates
electricity using kinetic energy from footsteps:
pavegen.com

238 Stone Cycling turns waste material into
new bricks:
stonecycling.com/wastebasedbricks

238 Accoya wood is mature softwood species treated
with acetic acid to give it the properties of a hardwood:
accoya.com.

238 Tricoya uses the same process to treat MDF:
tricoya.com

238 Merdacotta uses cow dung, clay, straw, and farm
waste to produce flower pots and tiles
theshitmuseum.org/prodotti/i-prodotti-da-tavola/

238 The Mestic project discovered a process to extract
cellulose from dung and use it to make biomaterial
products such as paper, textiles, and bioplastics:
inspidere.com

238 New York design practice The Living worked on
the Hy-Fi project, a temporary mycelium brick tower
at the Museum of Modern Art: The Living, 2014.
thelivingnewyork.com

238 Italian design firm Carlo Ratti Associati created
the Circular Garden, a series of arches formed by
injecting fungal spores into organic material: Carlo
Ratti Associati, 2019
carloratti.com/project/the-circular-garden

238 Officina Corpuscoli, a multidisciplinary design
studio, supports multiple projects dedicated to
evolving mycelium-based technology:
corpuscoli.com

BIBLIOGRAPHY

Books
Boswall, Marian *Sustainable Garden: Projects,
Insights and Advice for the Eco-conscious Gardener*
(Frances Lincoln, 2022)

Chatto, Beth *Beth Chatto's Gravel Garden:
Drought-Resistant Planting Through the Year*
(Francis Lincoln, 2000)

Chatto, Beth *Beth Chatto's Green Tapestry
Revisited: A Guide to a Sustainably Planted Garden*
(Berry & Co, 2021)

Chatto, Beth *Beth Chatto's Shade Garden: Shade-
Loving Plants for Year-Round Interest* (Pimpernel
Press, 2017)

Chatto, Beth *Drought-Resistant Planting:
Lessons from Beth Chatto's Gravel Garden*
(Francis Lincoln, 2016)

Chatto, Beth *The Damp Garden* (W&N, 2018)

Chatto, Beth *The Dry Garden* (W&N, 2018)

Crawford, Martin *Creating a Forest Garden: Working
with Nature to Grow Edible Crops* (Green Books, 2010)

Crawford, Martin *How to Grow Perennial Vegetables:
Low-Maintenance, Low-Impact Vegetable Gardening*
(Green Books, 2012)

Crawford, Martin *Shrubs for Gardens, Agroforestry
and Permaculture* (Permanent Publications, 2020)

Crawford, Martin *Trees for Gardens, Orchards and
Permaculture* (Permanent Publications, 2015)

Crawford, Martin and Aitken, Caroline *Food from
Your Forest Garden: How to Harvest, Cook and
Preserve Your Forest Garden Produce*
(Green Books, 2013)

Dunnett, Nigel *Naturalistic Planting Design: the
Essential Guide* (Filbert Press, 2019)

Dunnett, Nigel *Planting Green Roofs and Living
Walls* (Timber Press, 2008)

Dunnett, Nigel and Clayton, Andy *Rain Gardens*
(Timber Press, 2007)

Dunnett, Nigel, Gedge, Dusty, and Little, John
Small Green Roofs: Low-Tech Options for Homeowners
(Timber Press, 2011)

Dunnett, Nigel and Hitchmough, James (editors)
*The Dynamic Landscape: Design, Ecology and
Management of Naturalistic Urban Planting* (Taylor
& Francis, 2004)

Filippi, Olivier *Bringing the Mediterranean Into Your
Garden: How to Capture the Natural Beauty of the
Mediterranean Garrigue* (Filbert Press, 2019)

Filippi, Olivier *Planting Design for Dry Gardens:
Beautiful, Resilient Groundcovers for Terraces, Paved
Areas, Gravel and Other Alternatives to the Lawn*
(Filbert Press, 2016)

Filippi, Olivier *The Dry Gardening Handbook:
Plants and Practices for a Changing Climate*
Filbert Press, 2019

Franklin, Kate and Till, Caroline *Radical Matter:
Rethinking Materials for a Sustainable Future*
(Thames and Hudson, 2019)

Fromm, Erich *The Anatomy of Human Destructiveness*
(Pimlico 1997)

Golden, James *The View from Federal Twist: A New
Way of Thinking About Gardens, Nature and
Ourselves* (Filbert Press, 2021)

Hitchmough, James *Sowing Beauty* (Timber Press, 2017)

Hitchmough, James and Cameron, Ross
*Environmental Horticulture: Science and Management
of Green Landscapes* (CABI, 2016)

Kingsbury, Noel *Wild, The Naturalistic Garden*
(Phaidon Press, 2022)

Koren, Leonard *Wabi-Sabi: For Artists, Designers,
Poets and Philosophers* (Stone Bridge Press, 2003)

Miles, Ellen (editor) *Nature is a Human Right: Why
We're Fighting for Green in a Grey World* (DK, 2022)

Nex, Sally *RHS How to Garden the Low-carbon Way: The Steps You Can Take to Help Combat Climate Change* (DK, 2021)

Oudolf, Piet and Kingsbury, Noel *Planting: A New Perspective* (Timber Press, 2013)

Rainer, Thomas and West, Claudia *Planting in a Post-Wild World* (Timber Press, 2015)

Rees-Warren, Matt *The Ecological Gardener: How to Create Beauty and Biodiversity from the Soil Up* (Chelsea Green Publishing Co, 2021)

Tree, Isabella *Wilding: The Return of Nature to a British Farm* (Picador, 2019)

Wallington, Jack *Wild About Weeds: Garden Design with Rebel Plants* (Laurence King Publishing, 2019)

Papers

"Climate Change 2021 The Physical Science Basis", 2021.
ipcc.ch/report/ar6/wg1/downloads/report/IPCC_AR6_WGI_Full_Report.pdf

"Efficient Removal of Ultrafine Particles from Diesel Exhaust by Selected Tree Species: Implications for Roadside Planting for Improving the Quality of Urban Air", Huixia Wang, Barbara A. Maher, Imad A.M. Ahmed and Brian Davison, 2019.
pubs.acs.org/doi/pdf/10.1021/acs.est.8b06629

"Evaluating the Effectiveness of Urban Hedges as Air Pollution Barriers: Importance of Sampling Method, Species Characteristics and Site Location", Tijana Blanuša, Zeenat Jabeen Qadir, Amanpreet Kaur, James Hadley and Mark B. Gush, 2020.
mdpi.com/2076-3298/7/10/81

"Great Dixter Biodiversity Audit 2017–2019", prepared by Andy Phillips for the Great Dixter Charitable Trust, 2020.
greatdixter.co.uk/great-dixter-biodiversity-audit

"Impact of Sand Extraction from the Bottom of the Southern Baltic Sea on the Relief and Sediments of the Seabed", Szymon Uscinowicz, Wojciech Jeglinski, Grazyna Miotk-Szpiganowicz, Jarosław Nowak, Urszula Paczek, Piotr Przezdziecki, Kazimierz Szefler, Grzegorz Poreba, 2014.
sciencedirect.com/science/article/pii/S0078323414500504

"Mental Health and Our Changing Climate", Susan Clayton Whitmore-Williams, Christie Manning, Kirra Krygsman and Meighen Speiser, 2017.
apa.org/news/press/releases/2017/03/mental-health-climate.pdf

"New Approaches to Ecologically Based, Designed Urban Plant Communities in Britain: Do These Have Any Relevance in the United States?" James D. Hitchmough, 2008.
digitalcommons.lmu.edu/cgi/viewcontent.cgi?article=1019&context=cate

"Plant Disease, Plant Pest and Invasive Alien Species Prevention and Control (England) Scheme", Department for Environment, Food and Rural Affairs, 2014.
assets.publishing.service.gov.uk/government/uploads/system/uploads/attachment_data/file/387352/plant-disease-pest-nvasive-alien-species-prevention-control-state-aid.pdf

"Plants in the UK Flower a Month Earlier Under Recent Warming", Ulf Büntgen, Alma Piermattei, Paul J. Krusic, Jan Esper, Tim Sparks and Alan Crivellaro, 2022.
royalsocietypublishing.org/doi/10.1098/rspb.2021.2456

"RHS Gardening in a Changing Climate", Eleanor Webster, Ross Cameron and Alistair Culham, 2017.
rhs.org.uk/science/pdf/rhs-gardening-in-a-changing-climate-report.pdf

"Sand, Gravel, and UN Sustainable Development Goals: Conflicts, Synergies, and Pathways Forward", Mette Bendixen, Lars L. Iversen, Jim Best, Daniel M. Franks, Christopher R. Hackney, Edgardo M. Latrubesse, Lucy S. Tusting, 2021.
sciencedirect.com/science/article/abs/pii/S2590332221004097

"Solastalgia: A New Concept in Health and Identity", Glenn Albrecht, 2005.
bridges.monash.edu/articles/journal_contribution/_Solastalgia_a_new_concept_in_health_and_identity/4311905

"The Effects of Marine Sand and Gravel Extraction on the Macrobenthos at a Commercial Dredging Site (results 6 years post-dredging)", S.E. Boyd, D.S. Limpenny, H.L. Rees, K.M. Cooper, 2005.
academic.oup.com/icesjms/article/62/2/145/602082

"Toward Green Concrete for Better Sustainable Environment", Bambang Suhendro, 2014.
sciencedirect.com/science/article/pii/S1877705814032494

"Understanding Climate Change from a Global Analysis of City Analogues", Jean-Francois Bastin, Emily Clark, Thomas Elliott, Simon Hart et al, 2019.
doi.org/10.1371/journal.pone.0217592

WEBSITES

Agroforestry Research Trust, The
Agroforestry is the growing of both trees and agricultural/horticultural crops on the same piece of land – useful advice and resources.
agroforestry.co.uk

British Plastics Federation
Advice and guidance on plastic
bpf.co.uk/Sustainability/Plastics_Recycling.aspx

Charles Dowding – No Dig Gardening
No dig gardening resources and advice
charlesdowding.co.uk

Climate Matching Tool
Match future climates across the globe.
climatematch.org.uk

Current vs Future Cities
Cities of the future – visualizing climate change to inspire action.
crowtherlab.pageflow.io/cities-of-the-future-visualizing-climate-change-to-inspire-action#213121

Everyday Recycler
General recycling advice
everydayrecycler.com

Forest Monitoring Designed for Action
Global Forest Watch (GFW) is an online platform
that provides data and tools for monitoring forests.
By harnessing cutting-edge technology, GFW allows
anyone to access near real-time information about
where and how forests are changing around the world.
globalforestwatch.org

Garden Organic
The essence of organic growing is to work within
natural systems and cycles. The basic principle is
that the soil is as important as the plants it supports.
gardenorganic.org.uk/principles

Grey Water Action
Tips and advice on grey water reuse.
greywateraction.org/greywater-choosing-plants-and-
irrigating

Grow Peat-free
Advice on how to grow plants without peat.
growpeatfree.org/whats-in-peat-free

**How to stop invasive non-native plants
from spreading**
Advice and guidance from the UK Government
gov.uk/guidance/prevent-the-spread-of-harmful-invasive-
and-non-native-plants

IPCC
The Intergovernmental Panel on Climate Change
(IPCC) is the United Nations body for assessing the
science related to climate change.
https://www.ipcc.ch/

Mains 2 Rains
Mains water usage in our homes and gardens is often
highest in hot, dry periods when water availability is
lowest. However, by adopting a few simple pledges, we
can all make our gardens and outdoor spaces thrive
on the rainfall we receive by collecting it and reusing
it during dry spells.
mains2rains.uk

Plume Labs
Combatting air pollution
plumelabs.com/en

RHS Advice
A huge resource of gardening advice from the RHS
covering a wide range of topics
rhs.org.uk/advice

Biodiversity advice
rhs.org.uk/biodiversity

Disease advice
rhs.org.uk/disease

Gardening for the environment
rhs.org.uk/gardening-for-the-environment

Gardening for wildlife
rhs.org.uk/wildlife

Growing guides for popular plants
rhs.org.uk/plants/popular

Plant problem advice
rhs.org.uk/problems

Sustainability strategy
rhs.org.uk/about-the-rhs/sustainability/sustainability-
strategy-document

Soil Association, The
The Soil Association is the charity working with
everyone to transform the way we care for our
natural world.
soilassociation.org

Surfers Against Sewage
Clean water action group
sas.org.uk/water-quality

What are SuDS?
A good description of SuDS
ambiental.co.uk/what-are-suds-sustainable-drainage-
systems-guide

HARDINESS RATINGS

Rating	Temperature ranges	Category
H1a	>15°C (59°F)	Heated greenhouse – tropical
H1b	10–15°C (50–59°F)	Heated greenhouse – subtropical
H1c	5–10°C(41–50°F)	Heated greenhouse – warm temperate
H2	1–5°C (34–41°F)	Cool or frost-free greenhouse
H3	-5–1°C (23–34°F)	Unheated greenhouse/mild winter
H4	-10– -5°C (14–23°F)	Average winter
H5	-15– -10°C (5–14°F)	Cold winter
H6	-20– -15°C (-4–5°F)	Very cold winter
H7	<-20°C (-4°F)	Very hardy

[01] The first stage was to create a "white card" model. This is an untextured landscape, placing the elements and 3D massing – the shapes and forms. **[02]** For the next stage, textures were added to the model to bring the design to life, testing elements like reflectiveness of water and the desired level of weathering on the timber.

[03] At the final stage, plants were added. Structural plants were placed individually, then underplanting was "scattered" in pre-selected mixes for a randomized feel. The brief was for the plantings to feel naturalistic and wild.

MICHAEL POWELL and **SAM TAYLOR** of AVA CGI created the computer-generated resilient garden in this book from my designs, as well as the existing site before the redesign, and the virtual reality accompaniment. Michael and Sam explain their process here.

COMPUTER GENERATED IMAGERY (CGI) HAS COME A LONG WAY; SOME OF THE VISUALS YOU PRODUCED LOOK ALMOST PHOTOREALISTIC. HOW WAS THAT ACHIEVED?

The minimum set-up in the pursuit of photorealism is a combination of detailed 3D modelling, physically based rendering materials (PBR), and image-based lighting. Images and animations can then be exported using a path tracing renderer, which is currently the most accurate way of representing global illumination (the way light bounces off and through objects). However, most professionals within the CG industry would agree that photorealism lies within surface imperfections, be they cracks in paint, dust on a vase, or fingerprints on a pane of glass – imperfections are everywhere in the real world, and these subtleties can trick the eye into believing that a 3D image is real.

HOW DO YOU SOURCE THE PLANTS? SOME OF THE 3D MODELS ARE STUNNING IN THEIR DETAIL.

Modelling organic assets such as plants can be complex and time-consuming, often requiring specialist software to achieve good results. Over the years we have built up a library of professional-grade 3D plant models by either creating them ourselves or purchasing from online stores. Studying and recording flora is essential for accurate modelling and texturing; a simple leaf has many properties that require capturing for realism. This information is then fed into a PBR material in the form of dedicated images that dictate such details as colour, transparency, and reflectancy.

LIGHTING AND FRAMING ARE KEY TO SHOWING THE MODEL SUCCESSFULLY. HAVE YOU ANY TIPS ON HOW TO GET THE SHOTS RIGHT?

There are many rules of thumb about what creates a pleasing image; ultimately, we aim to lead the viewer towards a subject to explore further. The eye will always focus on the brightest part of an image first, so it is good practice to position the focal point in the most exposed area of the scene. A dappled lighting effect is also used in many of the images where light filters through the trees, creating atmosphere and interest.

Additionally, using compositional guides is an effective way to structure and balance an image. If you look closely you may identify where principles such as symmetry, the golden ratio, and the rule of thirds have been used within the book's CGIs.

Illustrations pages are in bold

253

ACKNOWLEDGMENTS

PICTURE CREDITS

The publisher would like to thank the following for their kind permission to reproduce their photographs:

(Key: a-above; b-below/bottom; c-centre; f-far; l-left; r-right; t-top)

Page 8: t **Tom Massey**, b **Britt Willoughby Dyer**; **10: Alamy Stock Photo**/Marek Stepan; **11:** b **Shutterstock**/FLPA; **12:** t **Alamy Stock Photo**/Will Perrett, b **Chris Leather** www.cornawlls.co.uk; **15:** t **Alamy Stock Photo**/P Tomlins, bl **Samuel North**, br **Tom Massey**; **16:** t **Dirk-Jan Visser**, b **Britt Willoughby Dyer**; **17:** t **Britt Willoughby Dyer**, b **Dirk-Jan Visser**; **19:** t **Britt Willoughby Dyer**, b **Alamy Stock Photo**/PA Images; **20-21: Noshe**; **24: Dreamstime**/SJors737; **25:** t **Getty Images**/Saeed Khan/AFP, b **Dreamstime**/Silkenphotography; **27: Alamy Stock Photo**/Mauritius images GmbH; **29:** t and b **Alister Thorpe**; **30-31: Alamy Stock Photo**/Duncan Cuthbertson; **32 and 33: Harvey Wang**; **35:** t **GAP Photos**/Stephen Studd-Sam Ovens, b **Britt Willoughby Dyer**, **36 Francis Augusto**; **44: Britt Willoughby Dyer**; **46: Ed Reeve**; **48-49: Nigel Dunnett**; **49:** b **Britt Willoughby Dyer**; **50:** t **Britt Willoughby Dyer**, b **Alister Thorpe**; **50-51:** b **Alister Thorpe**; **51:** br **Shutterstock**/Alison Hancock; **52:** tl **Alamy Stock Photo**/Pat Tuson, tr **Dreamstime**/Niradj, bl **Alamy Stock Photo**/Jeffrey Blackley, br **Richard Bloom**; **53: Nigel Dunnett**; **55:** t **Dreamstime**/Stevendalewhite, b **Shutterstock**/RHJ Photos; **56: GAP Photos**/Annette Lepple; **57:** tl **GAP Photos**/Maddie Thornhill, tr **GAP Photos**/Ernie Janes, c **Marianne Majerus**/RHS Garden Wisley, Designer: James Hitchmough, bl **Britt Willoughby Dyer**, br **Tim Green**; **58: Alamy Stock Photo**/RM Flavio Massari; **62: GAP Photos**/Jonathan Buckley – Demonstrated by Nick Bailey; **63:** t **Alister Thorpe**, b **Marianne Majerus**/Designer: Thomas Doxiadis; **69:** tl **Dreamstime**/Andrii Kozlytskyi, tr **Dreamstime**/Marek Uliasz, cl **Dreamstime**/Atthaphol Sileung, cr **Shutterstock**/Govindamadhava 108, b **Dreamstime**/ Larisa Rudenko; **72:** t **Alamy Stock Photo**/Appeal Photos, b **Alamy Stock Photo**/Larry Geddis; **75:** t **Sarah Price**/design: Sarah Price and Nigel Dunnett, b **Alamy Stock Photo**/eye35; **76:** t **Nigel Dunnett**, b **GAP Photos**/Michael King; **82: Alamy Stock Photo**/Rudmer Zwerver; **83:** b **Jay Davey Bespoke Willow**; **86: Clive Nichols**; **88: Dreamstime**/Bojana Zuzu; **89: Britt Willoughby Dyer**; **90:** t **Shutterstock**/Amelia Armstrong, b **Britt Willoughby Dyer**; **112: Sarah Cuttle**; **124:** tl and tr **Dreamstime**/Graham Corney, b **Dreamstime**/Shamils, **120: Rob Cardillo**; **125:** t **Dreamstime**/Darren Curzone, bc **Dreamstime**/Shawn Hempel, b **Dreamstime**/Marilyn Barbone; **130 Britt Willoughby Dyer**; **164:** tl **GAP Photos**/Nova Photo Graphik, tc **GAP Photos**/Tommy Tonsberg, tr **GAP Photos**/Jason Ingram, b **GAP Photos**/Fiona Rice; **165:** l **Dreamstime**/Maddie Thornhill, r **Dorling Kindersley**/Mark Winwood/Hampton Court Flower Show 2014; **166:** l **Dreamstime**/Whiskybottle, r **GAP Photos**/Elke Borkowski; **167:** t **Marianne Majerus**, bl **Dorling Kindersley**/Mark Winwood/RHS Wisley, br **GAP Photos**/Jason Ingram; **168:** tl **Dreamstime**/Iva Vagnerova, tr **Dreamstime**/Orest Lyzhechka, bl **GAP Photos**/Robert Mabic, br **GAP Photos**/Tim Gainey; **169:** tl **Dorling Kindersley**/Andrew Lawson, tc **Dorling Kindersley**/Mark Winwood/RHS Wisley, tr **Dorling Kindersley**/Neil Fletcher, b **Dreamstime**/Tikhonova Vera; **172:** tl **Dreamstime**/Apugach 5, tc **GAP Photos**/Sarah Cuttle, tr **GAP Photos**/Howard Rice, b **GAP Photos**/Charles Hawes; **173:** tl **Marianne Majerus**, tr and b **GAP Photos**/Torrie Chugg; **174: Shutterstock**/Vladislav Marvin, **178:** l **GAP Photos**/Andrea Jones, c **GAP Photos**/Richard Bloom, r **GAP Photos**/Howard Rice; **179:** l **Marianne Majerus**, c **GAP Photos** Dianna Jazwinski, r **GAP Photos**/Ernie Janes; **188:** l **Dorling Kindersley**/Peter Anderson, c **GAP Photos**/Nova Photo Graphik, **188 189:** **GAP Photos** Evgeniya Vlasova; **180** r **GAP Photos**/Nova Photo Graphik; **190:** t **Dorling Kindersley**/Mark Winwood/RHS Wisley, c **GAP Photos**/Heather Edwards, r **GAP Photos** Gary Smith; **191:** l **GAP Photos**/Gary Smith, r **GAP Photos**/Richard Bloom; **192:** tl **GAP Photos**/Fiona Lea, tc **GAP Photos**/Fiona McLeod, tr and b **GAP Photos**/Jonathan Buckley, **193:** tl **GAP Photos**/John Glover, tc **GAP Photos**/Mark Bolton, tr **Alamy Stock Photo**/Blickwinkel, b **GAP Photos**/Mark Turner; **194:** l **Dorling Kindersley**/Mark Winwood/RHS Wisley, r **GAP Photos**/Jonathan Buckley; **195:** l **GAP Photos**/Julie Dansereau – Loseley Park, r **GAP Photos**/Jason Ingram, **196:** tl **GAP Photos**/Jo Whitworth, bl **Dorling Kindersley**/Brian North, r **GAP Photos**/Juliette Wade; **197:** t **GAP Photos**/Jonathan Buckley, b **Dreamstime**/Igor Dolgov; **198: Tom Massey**; **202:** l **Dorling Kindersley**/RHS Tatton Park, **202-203: Dreamstime**/Milanvachan, **203:** r **GAP Photos**/Nova Photo Graphik, **204:** l **GAP Photos**/Geoff Kidd, c **GAP Photos**/Ernie Janes, **204-205: GAP Photos**/Bjorn Hansson, **205:** r **GAP Photos**/John Glover, **208: Shutterstock**/haveseen, **213:** t **Shutterstock**/Amit kg, b **Dreamstime**/Seadam, **214:** t **Dreamstime**/Wuttichok, c **Shutterstock**/Wong Gunkid, b **Dreamstime**/Bert Folsom, **215:** t **Dreamstime**/Harald Biebel, c **Dreamstime**/Krishna Maharana111, b **Dreamstime**/Gualtiero Boffi, **216-217:** b **Alamy Stock Photo**/Jaramír Chalabala, **217:** t **Dreamstime**/Andreadonetti, **218:** t and b **cedstone.co.uk**, **219:** l and c **London Stone**, r **Alamy Stock Photo**/Panther Media GmbH, **220:** t **GAP Photos**/Andrea Jones – Design Beth Chatto, b **GAP Photos**/Mark Bolton – Prospect Cottage, Derek Jarman; **222: Arcaid**; **225:** tl **GAP Photos**/Rob Whitworth – Designer Sarah Price; bl **Alamy Stock Photo**/Selecta, r Rublazzo; **226: Shutterstock**/Aldarhino; **229: Deborah Husk**; **230:** t **Alister Thorpe**, b **Britt Willoughby Dyer**; **231: Britt Willoughby Dyer**; **232 and 233: Dreamstime** and **Shutterstock**; **235:** t **Shutterstock**/ Taechit Tanantornanutra, bl **Dreamstime**/Candy 1812, br **Alamy Stock Photo**/Kevin Foy; **236:** t **Alamy Stock Photo**/Kevin Walker, cl **Alamy Stock Photo**/Dave Bevan, bl **Dreamstime**/Joel Gafford, br **Dreamstime**/Europixel; **237:** tl **Dreamstime**/Marek Uliasz, tr **Alamy Stock Photo**/RM Floral, c **Shutterstock** Worawit Sanasri, bl **Shutterstock**/Kolidzei, br **Alamy Stock Photo**/Alexandra Scotcher; **239:** tl **The Living**, Photo: Amy Barkow, tr **Stone Cycling**/Dim Baslem, br **Marianne Majerus**; **256 Wax London**.

Images on the following pages © **AVA CGI**: 2, 80, 95, 97, 98–99, 100–110, 115, 116, 123, 127, 128, 132, 137, 138, 141, 142–143, 145, 147, 149, 150–151, 152, 154, 158–159, 161, 162–163, 170–171, 176–177, 181, 182, 185, 186–187, 201, 248.

FROM TOM

Writing my first book has been a journey of discovery, forcing me to reflect and review my own practice and priorities. Having time to research, reflect, and share my findings though words, designs, and ideas has been a privilege: one that I have many people to thank for.

Firstly, my wife Anna, for unswerving support. My life has often been consumed by my profession and she has been patient and supportive even when my time for friends and family has been limited. Anna's eye for detail and gift for writing makes her the perfect sounding board.

Thanks to the DK team, whose knowledge, skill, and support made writing this book hugely rewarding. Chris, Ruth, Max, and Katie, for their belief, trust, and a shared vision. Sophie, Barbara, and Diana for keeping everything on track and pushing with creative design and editorial comments.

Thanks to the designers: Alex with initial concepts and Vicky with layouts and book design, keeping it collaborative and graphically exciting. Thanks to AVA CGI, Michael and Sam, for bringing the garden concepts to life in stunning detail. Deserving of a special mention are photographers Britt and Alister, who have captured my work so beautifully, and picture researcher Emily for all of her hard work finding and sourcing images to illustrate the text.

Thank you to the interviewees: Je, John, Martin, Olivier, Sarah, Tayshan, Tijana, and Thomas, for taking time to share your knowledge, expertise, and experience.

A big thank you to the RHS for trusting me to write this book. Access to the RHS science team has been invaluable, and a special mention goes to Tijana, who has been supportive and critical, linking to other members of the science team, ensuring the book is grounded in real RHS research and is true to the RHS aims: to enrich people's lives through plants and to make the world a greener and more beautiful place.

Finally, thank you to my mother, for connecting me with nature from a young age. I hope this book inspires others to garden and grow.

FROM THE PUBLISHER

The publisher would like to thank Tom Morse for his help with technical prepress, Michael Powell and Sam Taylor of AVA CGI, Jane Simmonds for the proofread, and Ruth Ellis for the index.

Senior Editor Sophie Blackman
Senior Designer Barbara Zuniga
Production Editor David Almond
Production Controller Rebecca Parton
Jackets and Sales Material Coordinator
Jasmin Lennie
DTP and Design Coordinator Heather Blagden
Editorial Manager Ruth O'Rourke
Design Manager Marianne Markham
Art Director Maxine Pedliham
Publishing Director Katie Cowan

Editor Diana Vowles
Designer Vicky Read
Picture Researcher Emily Hedges
Consultant Gardening Publisher Chris Young
Design Styling Concept Alex Hunting Studio
Illustrator Andrew Torrens
VR AVA CGI

ROYAL HORTICULTURAL SOCIETY
Consultant Simon Maughan
Publisher Helen Griffin

First published in Great Britain in 2023 by
Dorling Kindersley Limited
DK, One Embassy Gardens, 8 Viaduct Gardens,
London, SW11 7BW

The authorised representative in the EEA is
Dorling Kindersley Verlag GmbH. Arnulfstr. 124,
80636 Munich, Germany

A CIP catalogue record for this book
is available from the British Library.
ISBN: 978-0-2415-7583-3

Printed and bound in Slovakia

For the curious
www.dk.com

MIX
Paper | Supporting
responsible forestry
FSC™ C018179

This book was made with Forest Stewardship Council™ certified paper – one small step in DK's commitment to a sustainable future. **For more information go to** www.dk.com/our-green-pledge

255

Tom Massey is an award-winning garden designer and principal designer at Tom Massey Studio. He strives to produce sustainable gardens that support wildlife, promote biodiversity, and support the local environment.

After growing up in southwest London, Tom graduated from the London College of Garden Design at the Royal Botanic Gardens, Kew, where he is now a visiting tutor. He founded Tom Massey Studio in 2015 and designs gardens for private and commercial clients, public spaces, shows, and festivals in the UK and overseas.

Tom has designed and exhibited two gardens at the RHS Chelsea Flower Show: in 2018, he was awarded an RHS Silver-Gilt Medal for the Lemon Tree Trust Garden, and in 2021, the Yeo Valley Organic Garden received an RHS Gold Medal and the BBC People's Choice Award.

In 2020, he designed the planting scheme for the "Hothouse" installation: a collaboration with Studio Weave for the London Design Festival. In 2022, he received an award from the Society of Garden Designers for an outstanding residential garden in Twickenham, London.

Tom featured on the BBC television series *Your Garden Made Perfect*, designing gardens focused on supporting wildlife, promoting biodiversity, and experimenting with growing mediums. *RHS Resilient Garden* is his first book.